Studia Fennica
Linguistica 20

The Finnish Literature Society (SKS) was founded in 1831 and has, from the very beginning, engaged in publishing operations. It nowadays publishes literature in the fields of ethnology and folkloristics, linguistics, literary research and cultural history.

The first volume of the Studia Fennica series appeared in 1933. Since 1992, the series has been divided into three thematic subseries: Ethnologica, Folkloristica and Linguistica. Two additional subseries were formed in 2002, Historica and Litteraria. The subseries Anthropologica was formed in 2007.

In addition to its publishing activities, the Finnish Literature Society maintains research activities and infrastructures, an archive containing folklore and literary collections, a research library and promotes Finnish literature abroad.

Studia Fennica Editorial Board
Editors-in-chief
Pasi Ihalainen, Professor, University of Jyväskylä, Finland
Timo Kaartinen, University Lecturer, University of Helsinki, Finland
Taru Nordlund, Professor, University of Helsinki, Finland
Riikka Rossi, Title of Docent, University Researcher, University of Helsinki, Finland
Katriina Siivonen, Title of Docent, University Teacher, University of Turku, Finland
Lotte Tarkka, Professor, University of Helsinki, Finland

Deputy editors-in-chief
Anne Heimo, Title of Docent, University of Turku, Finland
Saija Isomaa, Professor, University of Tampere, Finland
Sari Katajala-Peltomaa, Title of Docent, Researcher, University of Tampere, Finland
Eerika Koskinen-Koivisto, Postdoctoral Researcher, Dr. Phil., University of Helsinki, Finland
Laura Visapää, Title of Docent, University Lecturer, University of Helsinki, Finland

Tuomas M. S. Lehtonen, Secretary General, Dr. Phil., Finnish Literature Society, Finland
Tero Norkola, Publishing Director, Finnish Literature Society, Finland
Virve Mertanen-Halinen, Secretary of the Board, Finnish Literature Society, Finland

oa.finlit.fi

Editorial Office
SKS
P.O. Box 259
FI-00171 Helsinki
www.finlit.fi

Linking Clauses and Actions in Social Interaction

Edited by
Ritva Laury, Marja Etelämäki, **and** Elizabeth Couper-Kuhlen

Finnish Literature Society • SKS • Helsinki • 2017

STUDIA FENNICA LINGUISTICA 20

The publication has undergone a peer review.

The open access publication of this volume has received part funding via Helsinki University Library.

© 2017 Ritva Laury, Marja Etelämäki, Elizabeth Couper-Kuhlen and SKS
License CC-BY-NC-ND 4.0. International

Cover Design: Timo Numminen
EPUB: Tero Salmén

ISBN 978-952-222-858-1 (Print)
ISBN 978-952-222-900-7 (PDF)
ISBN 978-952-222-899-4 (EPUB)

ISSN 0085-6835 (Studia Fennica)
ISSN 1235-1938 (Studia Fennica Linguistica)

DOI: http://dx.doi.org/10.21435/sflin.20

This work is licensed under a Creative Commons CC-BY-NC-ND 4.0. International License.
To view a copy of the license, please visit http://creativecommons.org/licenses/by-nc-nd/4.0/

 A free open access version of the book is available at http://dx.doi.org/10.21435/sflin.21 or by scanning this QR code with your mobile device.

BoD – Books on Demand, Norderstedt, Saksa

Contents

List of transcription and glossing symbols 7

Marja Etelämäki, Elizabeth Couper-Kuhlen, and Ritva Laury
Introduction 11

I Linking of clauses and physical actions

Maria Frick
Combining physical actions and verbal announcements as "What I'm doing" combinations in everyday conversation 27

Leelo Keevallik
Linking performances: The temporality of contrastive grammar 54

II Linking of questions and answers

Katariina Harjunpää
Mediated questions in multilingual conversation: Organizing participation through question design 75

Saija Merke
Tackling and establishing norms in classroom interaction: Student requests for clarification 103

Aino Koivisto
On-line emergence of alternative questions in Finnish with the conjunction/particle *vai* 'or' 131

III Linking of grammatical structures

Anna Vatanen
Delayed completions of unfinished turns: On the phenomenon and its boundaries 153

Elizabeth Couper-Kuhlen and Marja Etelämäki
Linking clauses for linking actions: Transforming requests and offers into joint ventures 176

Lauri Haapanen
Directly from interview to quotations? Quoting practices in written journalism 201

List of Authors 240

Abstract 243

Transcription symbols

.	falling intonation
;	slightly falling intonation
,	level intonation
?	rising intonation
↑	step up in pitch
↓	step down in pitch
[space] -	unfinished intonation unit
sp<u>ea</u>k	emphasis
ˋspeak	emphasis (in some Estonian extracts)
>speak<	faster pace than in the surrounding talk
<speak>	slower pace than in the surrounding talk
°speak°	quiet talk
SPEAK	loud talk
sp-	word cut off
sp'k	vowels omitted from pronunciation
spea:k	lengthening of a sound
#speak#	creaky voice
£speak£	smiley voice
@speak@	other change in voice quality
.h	audible inhalation
h	audible exhalation
.speak	word spoken during inhalation
he he	laughter
sp(h)eak	laughter within talk
[	beginning of overlap
]	end of overlap
* + ∧	timing of embodied demonstrations
#1	point when image is taken
=	latching of units
(.)	micropause (less than 0.2 seconds)
(0.6)	pause length in tenth of a second
(speak)	item in doubt

(-)	item not heard
(( ))	comment by transcriber (sometimes concerning gaze or embodied behavior)
- -	talk continues, data not shown
->	target line
=>	target line
boldface	focused item in the transcript
ʔ	glottal stop (IPA symbol)
*	point when still image is taken

Gaze and embodiment[1]

SPEAKER EMBODIMENT:	(DESCRIPTION)
SPEAKER GAZE:	(SEE THE SYMBOLS)
01 Speaker:	turn
RECIPIENT GAZE:	(SEE THE SYMBOLS)
RECIPIENT EMBODIMENT:	(DESCRIPTION)

gaze to recipient	_____
gaze elsewhere	--- (TARGET SPECIFIED) -------
eyes meet	X
gaze shift away from recipient	,,,
gaze shift towards recipient	...
change in gaze direction	GAZE>NAME
onset (and end) point of embodied behavior	|
point when still image is taken	#1 (in transcription line)

Symbols in the translation line

(item)	item that is not expressed in the original language but that belongs grammatically to the English equivalent
((item))	item not expressed in the original language, added for the sake of clarity
V	verb, not specified
/	alternative translations in the translation line

---

1 Adapted from Goodwin, Charles 1981: *Conversational Organization: Interaction Between Speakers and Hearers*. New York: Academic Press.

Glossing symbols

Case

ACC	accusative
ABL	ablative ('from')
ADE	adessive ('at, on')
ALL	allative ('to')
COM	comitative ('with')
ELA	elative ('out of')
GEN	genitive (possession)
ILL	illative ('into')
INE	inessive ('in')
PAR	partitive (partitiveness)
TRA	translative ('to', 'becoming')

Verbal morphemes

1SG	1st person singular ('I')
2SG	2nd person singular ('you')
3SG	3rd person singular ('she', 'he')
1PL	1st person plural ('we')
2PL	2nd person plural ('you')
3PL	3rd person plural ('they')
COND	conditional
FREQ	frequentative
GER	gerund
IMP	imperative
IMPS	impersonal
INF	infinitive
PAS	passive
PPC	past participle
PPPC	passive past participle
PST	past tense

Other abbreviations

ADJ	adjective
ADV	adverb
ART	article
CLI	clitic
CONJ	conjunction
COMP	complementizer
CMP	comparative
DEM	demonstrative
DEM1	demonstrative ('this')
DEM2	demonstrative ('that')
DEM3	demonstrative ('it', 'that over there')
LOC	location
MAN	manner

NEG	negation (particle in Estonian, verb in Finnish)
PL	plural
POSS	possessive
PREP	preposition
PREP.ART	fusion of preposition and article
PRT	particle
SG	singular
Ø	zero person

Marja Etelämäki
http://orcid.org/0000-0002-3896-7159

Elizabeth Couper-Kuhlen
http://orcid.org/0000-0003-2030-6018

Ritva Laury
http://orcid.org/0000-0003-2808-6523

Introduction

This collection of papers arises out of the Finland Distinguished Professor research project entitled *"Grammar and interaction: the linking of actions in speech and writing"*, funded by the Academy of Finland 2009-2013. From its inception the project focused on the syntax, pragmatics, and prosody of clauses and clause combinations using genuine, naturally occurring data from spoken and written interactions in Finnish, Swedish, English, and related languages. The methodology was empirical and inductive, with close micro-analysis of audiotaped, videotaped, and written materials being considered a privileged means of access to the data. To the extent possible, hypotheses were generated and validated through observable evidence provided by the participants themselves.

To mark the end of the FiDiPro project, a retreat was organized in May 2013 at which project members and other associated researchers presented a sampling of their findings on the research topic. The present volume unites a selection of the papers presented on that occasion. With its diverse yet focused contributions, this "Billnäs" volume thus provides a state-of-the-art reflection on current thinking and at the same time embodies the quintessence of FiDiPro research on the subject of linking clauses and actions in interaction. Most of the papers included here employ Conversation Analysis and Interactional Linguistics as a basic theoretical framework.

In preparation for the Billnäs retreat, the research team met in advance to discuss the underlying assumptions of the symposium theme and to anticipate potential problems in dealing with it. This led to agreement on a number of terminological fundamentals as well as to the formulation of a series of open questions, for which it was hoped the empirical research presented at the symposium might provide first answers. Accordingly, in the following sections we present (1) some fundamentals concerning the technical terms used in this volume, (2) short summaries of the papers collected here, and (3) open questions together with possible answers suggested by our findings.

Terminological fundamentals

The theme of the symposium and of this volume presents three terms in need of clarification: *clause, action, linking*. We discuss our conceptualizations of each of these in turn.

WHAT DO WE MEAN BY "CLAUSE"?
Many of the papers in this volume deal with clauses and, moreover, many of the linking elements are understood as combining clauses in traditional grammatical descriptions. Therefore we will first discuss the notion of a clause. Surprisingly, "clause" is not a universal grammatical category (see also Thompson, Forthc.; Laury, Ono & Suzuki, Forthc.). In fact, what counts as a clause can differ significantly from language to language. Traditionally, *English* grammar defines a clause as a unit constituted (minimally) by a verb and its obligatory complements together (typically) with its subject. Independent clauses, by definition finite, form simple sentences. Dependent clauses can be finite or non-finite, including infinitival and participial clauses (Quirk et al. 1985). In the *Finnish* grammatical tradition, clauses are referred to as *lause*. A *lause* is by definition finite (Hakulinen et al. 2004: 827). Non-finite verbal constructions are classified as *lauseenvastike* (roughly 'clause equivalents'). Therefore, as this comparison shows, we must exercise extreme caution in transferring what look like equivalent terms from one language to another.

Rather than relying on grammatical labels, typologists recommend using basic conceptual-semantic notions to talk about grammatical categories cross-linguistically (for enlightening discussions see, e.g., Dryer 1997; Croft 2001; Haspelmath 2010a). For example, Haspelmath (2010b: 697) defines the clause as "an expression that contains one predicate and potentially at least some of its arguments and that can be independently negated", that is, without reference to categories such as verb or subject, which many standard definitions rely on, but which may not be/are not cross-linguistically valid. We shall follow the typologists' recommendation in our general discussion of linguistic categories. For the single-language studies reported on here, the term *clause* – and *a fortiori* other grammatical labels – should be understood as defined in the grammatical tradition of the language being examined.

Are clauses relevant for interaction? There has been such a claim made in the literature (Thompson & Couper-Kuhlen 2005; Helasvuo 2001): participants have been said to orient to clause-type units and to use them as resources for social action, for instance, in turn-taking, incrementing, and action formation. Yet clearly, if the clause is not a universal, there will be restrictions on the validity of this claim. More radically, it could be argued that it is not the clause but the turn-constructional unit that is the relevant unit for interaction (Schegloff 1996). This of course would not necessarily exclude the pertinence of its morphosyntactic or conceptual-semantic make-up for interactional analysis. The chapters that follow come down on different sides of this debate; in particular, those dealing with nonverbal social actions (see below) would seem to harbor the biggest challenge to the relevance of the clause as a basic interactional unit. The challenge lies in determining whether a nonverbal action can function as an interactional unit equivalent to a clause.

WHAT DO WE MEAN BY "ACTION"?

Since we are dealing here with the linking of clauses and actions in social interaction, our understanding of action must be narrow enough to capture actions implemented with words, i.e., *verbal* speech acts (roughly, things we do with words (Austin 1962)). Indeed we start from the assumption that speaking is a vehicle for action (see, e.g., Schegloff 2007). But at the same time our understanding of action must be broad enough to capture 'wordless' or nonverbal actions.[1] Although many speech acts can be described with vernacular labels such as "question", "answer", or "proposal", "request", this is not necessarily the case with nonverbal acts (Levinson 2013). The latter may require instead peraphrastic description. Yet, regardless whether they have conventionalized labels or not, the verbal and nonverbal actions we are talking about here must be conceptualized at a similar level of *granularity* (cf. Schegloff 2000): this is especially needed if we wish to speak meaningfully of their being combined with one another. (Combining requires the linkage of like objects.) Finally, nonverbal actions – just like verbal actions implemented through turns at talk – must be thought of as *social* actions, i.e., ones that involve the other, since our inquiry concerns their deployment in interaction, which is always dialogic (Linell 2009). Purely physical actions such as, e.g., leaving the room or executing a dance step, are made interactionally relevant in the data examined here.

WHAT DO WE MEAN BY "LINKING"?

Although *linkage* may be thought of vernacularly as a kind of combining, here we wish to make a terminological distinction between the two. When two objects are *combined*, they are commonly understood to result in a 'combination', which is an object in itself. Thus, combining two clauses produces a clause combination, a larger unit composed of smaller parts (see, e.g., Matthiessen & Thompson 1988). In the same vein, when two actions are combined, the result might be said to be a single (complex) action combination. When two objects are *linked*, by contrast, one is simply put in relation to another: they do not necessarily form a larger unit together. Anaphoric pronouns, for instance, link to prior antecedents but do not form a unit with them. Linkage can occur between incomplete or only partially complete pieces, while combining conventionally takes place between two or more wholes. Finally, combining requires that two or more parts be commensurate with one another, while things that are linked can be vastly different in terms of type, size, and/or scope. Combining then can be thought of as a special type of linkage. In language evolution, combining elements can develop into linking elements, as when conjunctions come to be used as particles (Mulder & Thompson 2008; Koivisto 2011).

---

1 One anonymous reviewer suggested 'embodied' instead of 'nonverbal' but since language is always embodied when used, we prefer 'nonverbal' for reasons of clarity. Despite this label, we are not implying that these resources lack anything.

In conversation analysis, the linking of turns is typically referred to as "tying" (Sacks 1992a; 1992b). The simple contiguity of turns, i.e., their adjacency in focused interaction, is considered to be the most basic form of relating turns to each other. For Sacks, the adjacency pair is a formal means for harnessing the power of adjacency between turns at talk. Adjacent turns need no explicit tying: "for adjacently placed utterances, where a next intends to relate to a last, no other means than positioning is necessary in order to locate which utterance you're intending to deal with" (1992b: 559). Explicit "tying devices", e.g., conjunctions or repetition, when deployed within adjacency pairs, are therefore accomplishing more than the underlying relation created through adjacency (see, for instance, the 'format tying' described by M. H. Goodwin 1990).

The papers collected here

With the above understanding of *clause*, *action*, and *linking*, the papers collected in this volume will be seen to fall rather naturally into three groups:

I. LINKING OF CLAUSES AND PHYSICAL ACTIONS

This group encompasses papers that deal with linkage between clausal verbal actions and nonverbal actions, and with verbal linkage between nonverbal actions.

1. Maria Frick, Combining physical actions and verbal announcements as "What I'm doing" combinations in everyday conversation

Frick's paper examines a particular type of announcement in spoken interaction, one in which a speaker verbalizes what they are about to do next. These announcements are accompanied/followed by the speaker's executing the announced action. Therefore, they are said to form an 'action combination': clausal verbal announcement + physical action, constituting a "What I'm doing" combination. This type of action combination is an initial (i.e., non-responsive) but not an initiating action, as it does not make a response conditionally relevant. It is distinct from an informing (and is thus not epistemically driven), and also distinct from a directive (thus is not deontically driven). It is appropriate when participants are about to do something that departs from a social norm: break out of a group unilaterally, leave the room, take more than one's share of food, use a boarding-house reach to help oneself at the dinner table, etc. The paper thus makes an original contribution to the understanding of (one kind of) announcement and its use in everyday Finnish conversation, while at the same time pointing to a hitherto unexplored action combination. It demonstrates that declarative clauses are combined with simultaneous or following physical actions within the social action of treating the physical action as accountable and as a departure from social norms.

2. Leelo Keevallik, Linking performances: The temporality of contrastive grammar

Keevallik's paper investigates how dance teachers combine nonverbal behavior with linguistic means in order to build pedagogical activity in real time. The paper targets contrastive conjunctions and prepositions that are regularly used to link clausal constructions with upcoming non-verbal actions, hence linking clause and action. More specifically, it describes a practice for bringing about a combination of incorrect and correct bodily performances for pedagogical purposes, and the grammatical linking devices between them that mark the contrast. Keevallik's paper demonstrates how grammatical elements are used for organizing temporally unfolding nonverbal actions, and in that way, points to the possibility of an emergent and multimodal grammar.

II. LINKING OF QUESTIONS AND ANSWERS

The second group of papers encompasses verbal actions such as, e.g., questions and answers, and their linkage to one another, including not only linking an answer to a question but also linking a question to another question, linking an answer to another answer, and linking a question to a prior answer.

3. Katariina Harjunpää, Mediated questions in multilingual conversation: Organizing participation through question design

Harjunpää's paper examines sequences in multilingual conversation (Brazilian Portuguese-Finnish) where a question is orally translated, i.e., repeated or re-said in a different language, for the benefit of a recipient who would otherwise lack access. This situation can arise in three different sequential environments: (1) when the original question is not addressed to the ultimate recipient but lies within his/her epistemic domain, (2) when the original question is a topic proffer indirectly addressed to the ultimate recipient through third-person reference, and (3) when the original question is a topic follow-up directly addressed to the ultimate recipient. The argument is that the design of the translatory turn reflects these different participation frameworks. Harjunpää distinguishes full resayings, or first sayings – which are clausal – from partial ones, or second sayings – which can be phrasal. The former are done as independent, autonomous turns: the translator passes on the question as his/her own inquiry. The latter are designed in a way that displays their secondness: the autonomy of the speaker is diminished because the question is marked as deriving from someone else's talk. The phenomenon described in this paper is a prime example of action linking by means of adjacency and different tying devices, undertaken here to overcome a language barrier. The establishment of a different participation framework is the result of the social action of translation and its design.

4. Saija Merke, Tackling and establishing norms in classroom interaction: Student requests for clarification

In her paper, Merke shows how student requests for clarification and confirmation create learning occasions in a university-level foreign language classroom. She shows that such requests emerge when students are confronted with a violation of expectations. Linguistically, the turns are formatted as questions with negative polarity, as adversative declaratives, or as causal questions that imply contrast; all these clausal formats evoke a competing or conflicting state of affairs and thus express resistance. Also important in the analysis is the sequential embedding of the questions: requests for clarification and confirmation in first position tend to object to untoward 'behavior' by the language, while expressions of an opposing viewpoint in sequence-final position concern the epistemic identities of the participants and their access to knowledge.

5. Aino Koivisto, On-line emergence of alternative questions in Finnish with the conjunction/particle *vai* 'or'

Koivisto's paper addresses the use of Finnish *vai* 'or' as a link to build, extend, and/or readjust questions and question-formatted turns in talk-in-interaction. It begins by pointing out that the canonical distinction between conjunction-like *vai* (after interrogative clauses) and question-particle *vai* (after declarative clauses and phrases) is too simplistic. Instead, one type of *vai* can be transformed into the other in enchronic time. The examples analyzed here reveal that *vai* is used incrementally at TCU junctures (in turn-final, turn-initial, and post-possible completion positions) when questions or question-formatted turns do not receive adequate responses or are in danger of receiving dispreferred responses. *Vai* does this by projecting a second question that offers a more agree-able alternative, masked as an extension of the original question rather than as a reaction to its (incipient) failure. The study thus provides more empirical evidence that many clause combinations in conversation emerge on-line in response to interactional contingencies.

III. LINKING OF GRAMMATICAL STRUCTURES

The third group of papers encompasses grammatical structures, often clausal in size, and their linkage to one another both within one speaker's turn as well as across speakers and contexts.

6. Anna Vatanen, Delayed completions of unfinished turns: On the phenomenon and its boundaries

Vatanen's article concerns delayed completions, cases in which a response starts before a clause-sized turn has reached a transition-relevance place and in which the initiating speaker cuts off but, after hearing some part of the response, subsequently completes her turn. Vatanen examines the grammatical, prosodic, and embodied resources used by speakers to achieve the linkage between the host and the delayed completion. Speakers can, for instance, provide a grammatically projected completion with pitch, loudness, and tempo fitted to the host and maintain body posture throughout. She shows that the work accomplished in the host is similar across the cases, and that the course of the sequence is also rather uniform. The host is typically an assertion that summarizes preceding talk, making it easier for the intervening turn to start before the host is complete, since the content is somewhat projectable. The intervening turn is typically non-aligning or disagreeing, and the delayed completion, as well as its overlap with the intervening turn, can be seen as a way for the initial speaker to insist on her viewpoint and her right to complete her turn.

7. Elizabeth Couper-Kuhlen and Marja Etelämäki, Linking clauses for linking actions: Transforming requests and offers into joint ventures

In their article, Couper-Kuhlen and Etelämäki describe a practice used by speakers of English and Finnish to transform requests and offers into joint ventures through a division-of-labor format. They argue that this is done by speakers of both languages using two schemata, both of which are associated with several dedicated structures. The structures are all made up of two clauses combined with conjunctions. Each of the clauses expresses a future action, one with the speaker (Self) as agent, expressing a commitment on his or her part, and the other with the recipient (Other) as agent, expressing a directive to the other (request or suggestion). The basic rationale for the use of the structures is shown to be a reduction of the deontic gradient: they are used in order to make the deontic situation more symmetric through a division of labor between the participants. The authors show that the alternate structures appear in different positions in extended sequences, so that deontically weaker forms appear earlier in sequences than stronger forms. Furthermore, the authors show that the division-of-labor structures are used in a number of different contexts: for example, they can be used by requestees to respond positively to a request, or by requesters to reduce the workload. The differences in Finnish and English structures are also explored, with reference to the grammatical resources of each language. All in all, the structures analyzed here are prime examples of the combining of actions and clauses.

8. Lauri Haapanen, Directly from interview to quotations? Quoting practices in written journalism

This paper discusses a more abstract notion of linkage than the other papers in the volume. Haapanen explores written direct quotations in journalistic publications. Journalism guidebooks usually recommend that even if the form of a quotation needs to be slightly modified, at least the meaning should be preserved. Nevertheless, Haapanen points out that instead of being verbatim, quotations in magazines can be substantially modified both in textual form and meaning. Using as data recordings from the original interview situations, published magazine copy, and prompted recall interviews with the journalists, Haapanen first shows how bits and pieces of the talk by the interviewee and even the interviewer herself are combined in quotations. He then explains the departures from the original talk in the quotations with reference to the media concept of the publication. Quotations must thus be understood not only as being formed by combining elements from the original interviews, but also as being themselves links between the original interview situation and the particular media concept of the publication. The media concept can be shown to be a relevant context within which the quotations can become actions (by conforming to the media concept) within an interactional public space.

Open questions and some answers

The open questions formulated prior to the symposium concern among other things problems of recognition, emergence, and distance. In the following we briefly expand on these problems and then outline how the contributions collected here address them.

THE PROBLEM OF RECOGNITION: DOES LINKAGE NEED TO BE EXPLICIT, OR CAN IT BE IMPLICIT?

The problem here is knowing when and how to speak of linkage if there is no formal marking of it. This is especially problematic in cases of non-adjacency. But even the notion of a formal 'mark' of linkage is worrisome, as dispensability, or "leaving something out", can also signal a link between two things (Schegloff 2010).

The articles in the volume deal with both quite explicit and more implicit linkages between linguistic units and social actions, in addition to showing that such linkages can take a variety of forms. The articles by Couper-Kuhlen & Etelämäki, Keevallik, and Koivisto deal with perhaps the most explicit and best-known linkages of all, since the combining of clauses and actions discussed in these papers involves the use of linguistic items such as conjunctions, whose primary function can be seen as the creation of a linkage. Couper-Kuhlen & Etelämäki show that what they call division-of-labor structures involve the linking of two clauses and two actions through the use of the English *and* and the Finnish *niin* 'so, and': a commitment by self is conjoined to a directive to the other, resulting in a clause combination. Keevallik, on the other hand, deals with the linking of both linguistic and bodily actions through the use of contrastive grammatical devices such as the Estonian *aga*, the Swedish *utan*, and the Finnish *vaan*, all of which could be glossed as 'but', as well as the Swedish *istället för* and its English equivalent *instead of*. Koivisto's article discusses the conjunction *vai*, which is also used as a final particle. Koivisto shows that the distinction between the conjunction and particle use is not clear-cut, and one can be transformed into the other enchronically, as *vai* is used incrementally to link TCUs which are formatted as questions or are used to do questioning.

The linkages discussed by Vatanen are just as explicit. Vatanen shows that speakers use grammatical as well as prosodic and embodied means of linking the delayed completion to their overlapped turn.

Yet another form of linkage is presented by Frick, whose paper deals with correspondences between a verbal and an embodied action, where the verbal action is a linguistic version of the upcoming non-verbal action.

Perhaps somewhat less explicit means of linking are discussed in the articles by Harjunpää and Merke. The translatory turns in Harjunpää's data are marked as such through formatting which, in addition to marking the turns as translations of something said earlier, reflects the participation frameworks they create. The student turns in Merke's data from a foreign language class are linked to grammatical points presented in class through questioning and challenging; linguistically, the turns are formatted with constructions that imply contrast and function to evoke conflicting states of affairs.

Haapanen's paper discusses the often very indirect correspondence between quotations in journalistic articles and the original talk in the interview on which the quotation is based. Haapanen shows that the quotation functions as a link between the original language of the interview and the particular media concept of the publication, as journalists format the quotations to reflect the aims of the publication and of the particular article in which the quotation appears.

As can be seen, the degree of explicitness of linking is not a simple matter. We might think of conjunctions and other lexico-syntactic means as the most explicit ways of achieving linkage, but papers in the volume show that prosody and embodied means can also be used to link an utterance or action to something that was said or done earlier, and can be quite explicit. Correspondences between announcing what one is going to be doing next and doing it are also ways to achieve linkage, although they may not be traditionally thought of as doing linking. The papers also introduce other means of achieving linkage that are not confined to the job of doing linking as traditionally understood, such as the use of 'free' NPs as a means of linking a translatory turn to an earlier turn which it is a translation of. Should these then, even if lexico-syntactic, be considered less explicit as linkers?

The problem of emergence: Do we speak of combinations and linkages as they emerge or only post-hoc? When two actions are linked, do they remain separate actions or fuse into one?

When linguists spot complex patterns in the data, the question arises as to how these patterns came into being. This is a linguistically relevant question, since many linguistic patterns are highly conventionalized and projectable. What appears post hoc to be a pre-planned complex structure in the data may have emerged in real time due to interactional contingencies. However, in other cases a complex structure can also have been projected from the beginning of its production. Should we speak of linkage in both cases?

The degree of conventionalization is related to the problem of whether linked actions remain as separate or fuse into one. A grammaticized pattern accomplishes more than the sum of its parts: the more grammaticized a complex pattern is, the more its parts are fused. But since grammaticization is a matter of degree, how should we handle cases that are only partly conventionalized?

In some of the papers, as in Vatanen's, there is clearly only one action. In her examples, the beginning of the overlapped turn and its delayed completion form one action, because neither of the parts could in their sequential positions be an action on their own.[2] In Harjunpää's and Merke's papers, on the other hand, there are clearly two social actions produced by two separate speakers. In these cases, the two actions do not form an action combination, and they can be analyzed as linked only post hoc.

However, some of the papers deal with complex social actions themselves consisting of other actions. For example, Couper-Kuhlen & Etelämäki argue for a construction-like pattern that is used to suggest a division of labor between the participants. The pattern consists of two clauses accomplishing actions, namely a directive and a commitment, which could be analyzed as separate actions. However, in its contexts of occurrence, the second part is projected either syntactically and/or prosodically, and furthermore the pattern itself accomplishes a single complex action, proposing a division of labor. The division-of-labor proposal is thus not an emergent result of local interactional contingencies, but a complex grammatical format for a complex social action.

More open in this respect are the phenomena dealt with by Frick, Keevallik, and Koivisto. Frick discusses cases where a speaker first announces an embodied action, and then does the action. In these instances, the first action (announcement) could be understood as projecting the following embodied action. Frick's cases could, however, also be analyzed as preliminaries (Schegloff 1980), the announcement being a preliminary for the physical action. If analyzed in this manner, the announcement and the physical action do not fuse into one, but remain as two separate actions in a sequentially unfolding project.

Keevallik shows how dance teachers perform an incorrect and a correct dance movement in succession, and link these movements with a verbal element (a conjunction or a preposition). It could be argued that this is a conventionalized grammatical pattern consisting of embodied and linguistic elements. This would be the case if the first part projected the second. However, Keevallik argues that the pattern evolves locally, and thus consists of two separate actions that can be analyzed as belonging to one unit only post hoc. Like Keevallik, Koivisto also shows how grammatical

---

2   It could be argued, though, that delayed completion of an overlapped turn is a social action, since it is doing something more than only completing an already on-going action. In a similar vein incrementing is a social action, as incrementally produced parts add something or modify the already on-going action. However, these are qualitatively different from the "main" action of a turn, because delayed completion or incrementing are actions that deal with the interaction itself.

patterns emerge locally in interaction, her patterns consisting of clauses linked with the Finnish word *vai*. *Vai* can be used as a conjunction, a turn-initial particle, and a turn-final question particle. Finnish speakers exploit its meaning potential for incrementally producing alternatives that post hoc can be analyzed as forming lists.

In sum, those clause and action combinations that accomplish one conventionalized action and are linked by grammatical elements, as in Couper-Kuhlen and Etelämäki's paper, are identified as complex already from the beginning of their production. However, grammatical linking elements such as conjunctions can also be used to bring about complex clauses and actions due to interactional contingencies, as is shown in Keevallik's and Koivisto's papers. In these cases, complex patterns can be analyzed as patterns only after their production. When seeing a complex pattern in interaction, an analyst cannot, therefore, make a priori assumptions about whether the pattern was projected or only appears as complex post hoc (Laury & Ono 2010). Instead, complex patterns with grammatical linking elements must be analyzed case by case.

The problem of distance: How far apart can two things be from one another and still be linked?

Most of the papers presented in this volume discuss linkages between clauses and actions that are directly adjacent to each other. However, it is not uncommon for things that are spatiotemporally apart to be linked together. Interlocutors can link their turns to earlier talk in a single conversation; for example, at the end of a telephone conversation, it is typical to make a link to the beginning of the call. It also not uncommon for people to make links in their talk to interactions that happened days or even years earlier: interaction between people who meet on a regular basis is a never-ending process. So under what conditions is it possible to link spatiotemporally distant things and how do we know that they are linked?

In particular, the papers by Merke and Haapanen in this volume show that items that are very far apart temporally can still be linked. Merke's students often link what is said in class to matters covered in earlier class sessions. And as Haapanen shows, what is said in an interview and in the journalistic quotation based on it are also quite far apart temporally, yet clearly linked. In both these cases the things being linked have content in common. We know they are linked because there are lexical and/or typographic marks of the linkage.

Besides linking actions that are spatiotemporally far apart, Merke's and Haapanen's papers also show that there are linkages between things that are qualitatively different. They show how language use functions as a link between particular and unique interactions and higher level social structures and norms: the challenging questions in Merke's paper link the classroom interactions to normative expectations, and the quotations in Haapanen's paper provide a link between the interview interactions and idealized media concepts of the particular publications. The last kind of linking goes beyond the scope of this book, but is nevertheless worth keeping in mind, because in the end, social structures and ideologies are built and realized in and through unique interactions and how we represent them.

Conclusion

Linking is far more diverse than has been traditionally thought. It concerns not only the use of conjunctions or even the presence of sequential adjacency. As the papers here suggest, there is no finite list of linking elements; instead the means for linking are wide open, making recognition an empirical question. Moreover, determining whether linkages are projected or emerge in real time must be decided in a context-sensitive fashion. There is a vast array of forms and formats that are ambiguous with respect to their degree of conventionalization, and therefore their projectability, and this ambiguity can be a resource for the speaker. Finally, although there is no limit on how far apart things can be and still be linked, adjacency still seems to be the default means for linkage. However, even adjacent elements are often marked as belonging together with explicit means. It is this aspect that many of the papers in this volume begin to explore.

References

Austin, J. L. 1962. *How to do things with words.* London: Oxford University Press.
Croft, William. 2001. *Radical construction grammar: Syntactic theory in typological perspective.* New York NY: Oxford University Press.
Dryer, Matthew S. 1997. Are grammatical relations universal? In Joan Bybee, John Haiman & Sandra Thompson (eds.), *Essays on language function and language type: Dedicated to T. Givon.* 115–143. Amsterdam: John Benjamins.
Goodwin, Marjorie H. 1990. *He-said-she-said: Talk as social organization among black children.* Bloomington: Indiana University Press.
Hakulinen, Auli, Maria Vilkuna, Riitta Korhonen, Vesa Koivisto, Tarja Riitta Heinonen & Irja Alho. 2004. *Iso suomen kielioppi* [Finnish Descriptive Grammar]. Helsinki: Finnish Literature Society.
Haspelmath, Martin. 2010a. Comparative concepts and descriptive categories in crosslinguistic studies. *Language* 86(3): 663–687.
Haspelmath, Martin. 2010b. The interplay between comparative concepts and descriptive categories (Reply to Newmeyer). *Language* 86(3): 696–699.
Helasvuo, Marja-Liisa. 2001. *Syntax in the making: The emergence of syntactic units in Finnish conversational discourse.* Studies in Discourse and Grammar 9. Amsterdam: John Benjamins.
Koivisto, Aino. 2011. *Sanomattakin selvää? Ja, että ja mutta puheenvuoron lopussa.* Ph.D. dissertation. University of Helsinki, Department of Finnish, Finno-Ugrian and Scandinavian Studies.
Laury, Ritva & Tsuyoshi Ono. 2010. Recursion in conversation: What speakers of Finnish and Japanese know how to do. In Harry van der Hulst (ed.), *Recursion and human language.* 69–92. Berlin: Mouton de Gruyter.
Laury, Ritva, Tsuyoshi Ono & Ryoko Suzuki. Forthcoming. Questioning the clause as a crosslinguistic unit in grammar and interaction. Submitted for publication in Tsuyoshi Ono, Ryoko Suzuki & Ritva Laury (eds.), Usage based and typological approaches to linguistic units, a special issue offered to *Studies in Language.*
Levinson, Stephen C. 2013. Action formation and ascription. In Jack Sidnell & Tanya

Stivers (eds.), *The handbook of conversation analysis*. 103–130. Malden MA: Wiley Blackwell.

Linell, Per. 2009. *Rethinking language, mind, and world dialogically: Interactional and contextual theories of human sense-making*. Charlotte NC: Information Age Publishing.

Matthiessen, Christian & Sandra A. Thompson. 1988. The structure of discourse and 'subordination'. In John Haiman & Sandra A. Thompson (eds.), *Clause Combining in Grammar and Discourse*. 275–329. Amsterdam: Benjamins.

Mulder, Jean & Sandra A. Thompson. 2008. The grammaticization of but as a final particle in English conversation. In Ritva Laury (ed.), *Studies of clause combining: The multifunctionality of conjunctions*. 179–204. Amsterdam: Benjamins.

Quirk, Randolph, Sidney Greenbaum, Geoffrey Leech & Jan Svartvik (eds.). 1985. *A comprehensive grammar of the English language*. London. Longman.

Sacks, Harvey. 1992a, b. *Lectures on conversation*, Volumes I & II. Oxford: Blackwell.

Schegloff, Emanuel A. 1980. Preliminaries to preliminaries: 'Can I ask you a question?'. *Sociological Inquiry* 50: 104–152.

Schegloff, Emanuel A. 1996. Turn organization: One intersection of grammar and interaction. In Elinor Ochs, Emanuel A. Schegloff & Sandra A. Thompson (eds.), *Interaction and grammar*. 52–133. Cambridge: Cambridge University Press.

Schegloff, Emanuel A. 2000. On granularity. *Annual Review of Sociology* 26: 715–720.

Schegloff, Emanuel A. 2007. *Sequence organization in interaction: A primer in conversation analysis*, Vol. 1. Cambridge: Cambridge University Press.

Schegloff, Emanuel A. 2010. On dispensability. *Research on Language and Social Interaction* 37(2): 95–149.

Thompson, Sandra A. Forthcoming. Understanding 'clause' as an emergent 'unit'. Submitted for publication in Tsuyoshi Ono, Ryoko Suzuki and Ritva Laury (eds.), Usage based and typological approaches to linguistic units, a special issue offered to *Studies in Language*.

Thompson, Sandra A. & Elizabeth Couper-Kuhlen. 2005. The clause as a locus of grammar and interaction. *Discourse Studies* 7: 481–505.

Linking of clauses and physical actions   I

Maria Frick
http://orcid.org/0000-0001-5089-5752

1. Combining physical actions and verbal announcements as "What I'm doing" combinations in everyday conversation[1]

Introduction

In everyday life, people go about performing physical deeds while engaging in conversation: They move or fiddle with physical objects, they take food from the table, and they get up and move around, engage in, for example, cooking, or leave the room—without saying a word about what they are physically doing. Once in a while, however, one's physical actions become the object of a verbal announcement. The object of this study is to investigate such combinations of verbal and physical actions, in which one announces what he or she is currently doing or is about to do. Extract (1) is from a conversation held by two adult sisters in Finnish and exemplifies the case:

(1) [sg437_40-50] (00:03:45)[2]
Two adult sisters, Jaana and Tuula, are talking about the pizza they have just eaten. They have just returned to the room and Jaana has sat down behind the table. Tuula walks behind her to her own chair.

```
01 Jaana:    .mhhh toi o justii semmone et mikä noille
             this is exactly the kind (of food) that

02           mukuloil[lekki käy.
             the kids like too.

03 Tuula:            [ei yhtään paskem°pih°.
                     not bad at all.
```

[1] I would like to thank the editors Elizabeth Couper-Kuhlen and Marja Etelämäki as well as the two anonymous reviewers for their invaluable comments on the first drafts of this paper.
[2] The video recordings are housed in the Conversation Data Archive at the Department of Finnish, Finno-Ugrian and Scandinavian studies, University of Helsinki: http://www.helsinki.fi/fus/research/ka.html, where they can be found under signum numbers 396, 409, 410 and 437. The signum number, file name, and time of the extract are indicated at the beginning of each example.

```
04            (2.6) ((Figure 1 - Tuula pulls her chair out, looks at the floor
              behind her chair and turns towards the oven next to her.))

→ Tuula:   mä      paa-n    noi      to-sta     noi   *uunii,
           1SG     put-1SG  DEM2.PL  DEM2-ELA   PRT   oven-ILL
           I'll put those in the oven
           ((* Figure 2 - opens oven))

06 Jaana:  tota,  (0.2) minkälaist jäts#kii siel (o)#.
           ehm,         what kind of ice cream do they have?
```

Figure 1 – line 04   Figure 2 – line 05

The two sisters in (1) are talking about the pizza they have just eaten. After an exchange of assessments that close the topic (lines 1–3), Tuula pulls out her chair as if intending to sit on it, but notices some pots and pans lying on the floor (line 4, Figure 1). She then turns towards the oven and makes an announcement (in line 5) about a physical action she is about to do: *mä paan noi tosta noi uunii* 'I'll put those in the oven'.[3] While uttering the last word *uunii* 'in the oven', she opens the oven (Figure 2). The recipient, Jaana, does not respond to this in any way, but initiates, instead, a new topic regarding the types of ice cream sold at the local store. While conversing on this topic (not shown here), Tuula places the pots and pans in the oven.

The study is based on a collection of 14 announcements that accompany the speaker's own physical actions, similar to the one in line 5 in (1). In the following, these will be referred to as *"What I'm doing" combinations*. The dataset has been collected from a total of approx. 6 hours of video recorded Finnish everyday conversation between adult friends and family members.

---

3 The English translations give only a rough idiomatic approximation of the meaning of the original utterance, and the non-Finnish-speaking reader is therefore advised to pay attention to the morphological gloss line provided under each target turn in the extracts. Note, for example, that Finnish does not make an obligatory distinction between simple and continuous tenses, or the present and future tense, and the English clauses *I put those in the oven, I am putting those in the oven, I will put those in the oven* and *I will be putting those in the oven* can thus all be expressed with the same Finnish clause *Mä paan noi uunii*.

The study falls in the field of interactional linguistics (see, e.g., Couper-Kuhlen & Selting 2001): it discusses the structural, sequential, and social interactional characteristics of this action combination. This contributes to on-going discussions about the linking of verbal and physical actions as well as to the more general discussion about action formation (see Schegloff 2007: 7–9) in interaction and about the formation of initial actions more specifically.

The pairings of announcements and physical actions are referred to as *action combinations* (see Ford 2002 and the introduction to the current volume). They comprise a declarative clause that announces a physical action performed by the utterer either during or immediately after the utterance. The structure of these action combinations is further elaborated on in the next section. Sequentially, the announcements that were chosen for the collection are *initial* in the sense that the turns of talk are not responsive to any prior turn in the conversation (although they may touch an on-going topic).[4] They are, however, sometimes positioned so that the physical action they formulate starts earlier than the verbal announcement. Although the announcements are initial, they are not necessarily *initiating*, because they do not call for any responsive action from the recipient. The sequential positioning and outcome of the action combinations is further discussed in the third section. Finally, in the last section, these action combinations are approached by looking at the consequences the actions have on the participants. This leads to the conclusion that the announcements function as an account for a social transgression.

The term *announcement* is widely used for an action whose main function is to deliver news, that is, to convey information that the recipient does not already know (see, e.g., Terasaki 2004 [1976]; Schegloff 2007: 37; Stevanovic & Peräkylä 2012). This definition works for those action combinations which are like the one in extract (1), where the announcement is made prior to the physical action: The recipient cannot know beforehand that Tuula is about to put the pots and pans in the oven, and the announcement is thus epistemic in nature (on epistemics in conversation, see, e.g., Heritage 2012b). For those action combinations, however, that are otherwise similar to these, but in which the timing is such that the recipients can observe the physical action while hearing the announcement that formulates it—and thus know what is happening—the definition based on known vs. unknown information is problematic. On the basis of these data, one cannot, therefore, claim that the motivation for announcements is purely epistemic in nature (it is for this same reason that these turns cannot be called informings).

Stivers and Rossano (2010: 17) give a broader characterisation of announcements, claiming that they "treat the information as relevant and consequential for their addressee". They (ibid.) also mention a type

---

4 Similar combinations of 1st person announcements and physical actions can be used as responses to directive actions. For example, as a response to her mother's offer *Tulkaa ottaa hei Anu ja Linda* 'Come have some (food), Anu and Linda' the daughter enters the room, announces *Jos mä ota meil Anun kans puoliks tommose* 'If I take one of those for Anu and me to share' (sg437). Second actions like this were not chosen for the collection.

of announcement that accounts for a person's physical action, namely departure from the setting: "I'm gonna get some more tea". Announcements that account for leaving the setting are, in fact, a common type of action combination in my data: 8 out of 14 cases involve speakers getting up and moving away from their prior physical position (e.g., away from the table they were sitting at).[5]

In some contexts, there is a fine line between announcements and directive actions. For example, in service encounters announcements of physical actions actually function as requests: In Finnish kiosk encounters first person announcements like *mä otan tän* 'I'll take this' are accompanied by the customer's physical action of taking something or giving something to the sales person, who responds with actions that advance the sale (see Sorjonen, Raevaara & Lappalainen 2009: 107–112). Unlike the ones in my data, those action combinations that are directive in nature create a strong relevance for the recipient to respond in a way that benefits the speaker (on the directiveness of announcements in another institutional setting, see Stevanovic & Peräkylä 2012). I will return to this question in the last section of the article and discuss the consequences and relevance of the mundane combinations of an announcement and physical action in the current data set for the recipients.

The action combination of "What I'm doing"

Kärkkäinen and Keisanen (2012) introduce the term *social action format*, by which they mean "conversational formats for enacting particular activities --- that encompass language, embodiment and space, and to various degrees also mobility". Basing their research on English and Finnish data, they introduce four formats for making concrete offers, all of which include two parts—identifying an object and offering it to the recipient—both of which may be performed either verbally or via embodiment (ibid). My investigation is an exploration of the different kinds of sequential and social interactional usages of such combinations of actions (see the last two sections of the article). First, however, I will discuss some of the structural characteristics of "What I'm doing" combinations. The next subsection focuses on the physical actions and their timing relative to the announcement, and the one after that on the grammar of the announcements.

Combining a physical action with its announcement

If most of our body movements and movements of objects are carried out without being verbalised, what about the ones that are announced? It is impossible to make broad generalisations on the basis of the limited data collection at hand, but in it, we find at least some of the possible types of "What I'm doing" combinations. Table 1 summarises the data and shows the timing of the two components of the 14 cases in the collection. I have first listed combinations in which the verbal announcement and physical action

---

5   Although in only four of these cases does the person actually leave the room.

take place at the same time, then the one example in which the physical action precedes the verbal announcement, and finally, ones in which the verbal announcement precedes the physical action.

Table 1

	Announcement	Physical action	Timing
1. sg437_60-70 (7:50)	mä siisti-n nyt vähän tä-ssä 1SG clear-1SG now a_little DEM1-INE että näyttä-ä tohon COMP look-3SG DEM2-ILL kamera-lle paremma-lle camera-ALL better-ALL I'm clearing this out a bit so it looks better for the camera	Moves objects on the table.	simultaneous
2. sg437_20-30 (1:50)	mä haluu (1.2) pippuri-a 1SG want-1SG pepper-PAR I want pepper	Takes pepper from a cabinet.	simultaneous
3. sg396 (2:50)	mä ota-n vähän vaa lissää 1SG take-1SG a_little just more I'll take just a little bit more	Takes salad from a bowl.	simultaneous
4. sg437_10-20 (7:37)	pan-na-an kahvikupi-t tonne put-PAS-4 coffee_cup-PL DEM2.LOC.ILL odottele-ma-an wait-INF-ILL We'll put the coffee cups to wait here	Moves coffee cups to another spot on the table.	simultaneous
5. sg437_1-10 (0:98)	jos pan-is vaikka tuo-hon if put-COND.3 for_instance DEM2-ILL How about I put it for instance here	Moves a candle to another spot on the table.	simultaneous
6. sg396 (4:20)	mä ota-n tä-n patongi-n 1SG take-1SG DEM1-GEN baguette-GEN pala-n pois piece-GEN away I'm taking this piece of baguette	Raises his body. Reaches over someone. Grabs a piece of bread from the table.	physical action, then announcement
7. sg437_40-50 (3:45)	mä paa-n noi to-sta noi 1SG put-1SG DEM2.PL DEM1-ELA DEM2.PL uuni-i oven-ILL I'll put those in the oven from over there	Turns towards the kitchen counter. Opens oven. Puts pots and pans in the oven.	announcement, then physical action
8. sg437_1-10 (8:51)	mä pistä-n noi vähä syrjemmä-lle 1SG put-1SG DEM2 a_little aside-ALL I'll put those aside	Gets up. Moves objects on the table.	announcement, then physical action
9. sg437_1-10 (8:12)	mä kato-n to-ta (1.0) 1SG look-1SG DEM2-PAR meijän ruoka(--) 1PL.GEN food(--) I'll have a look at our food –	Gets up. Moves to the kitchen counter. Looks in the oven.	announcement, then physical action
10. sg437_10-20 (7:37)	mä-ki voi-si-n nyt syy-ä 1SG-CLI can-COND-1SG now eat-INF I could eat now too	Gets up. Clears the table. Sets the table. Takes food. Starts eating.	announcement, then physical action

11. sg410 (4:32)	voi vit(h)tu mää lähde-n anteeks vaa PRT cunt 1SG go-1SG sorry PRT (0.6) suitseta-ma smoke-INF⁶ Oh fuck, I'm leaving for a smoke	Gets up. Leaves the room.	announcement, then physical action
12. Sg409 (2:10)	mä voi-n vie-dä tä-n nyt 1SG can-1SG take-INF DEM1-GEN now (ulos) (out) I can take this (out) now	Gets up. Moves to another side of the room. Takes something from a table. Leaves the room.	announcement, then physical action
13. sg410 (5:39)	hei Sari mu-n täyty-y muuten hey [1NAMEF] 1SG-GEN must-3SG by_the_way näyttä-ä show-INF Hey Sari, by the way, I must show you	Leans forward and places her glass on the table. Gets up. Leaves the room. Returns with a pair of shoes in her hand. Shows them to Sari.	announcement, then physical action
14. sg 437_30-40 (7:40)	ni Rina (.) me käy-dä-än PRT [1nameF] 1PL go-PAS-4 tupaka-lla nytte cigarette-ADE now So Rina, we're going for a smoke now	A empties her glass, B wipes her mouth. Both get up. Both leave the room.	announcement, then physical action

We can see from Table 1 that there are five cases (numbers 1–5) in the data where the physical action only involves moving or taking something with one's hands. These actions take place during the announcement. The rest of the physical actions involve moving the whole of one's body. In one of the examples (number 6) the speaker announces taking a piece of bread immediately after he has grabbed it. In the majority of the examples (numbers 7–13) the announcement precedes the physical action it formulates, although some preparatory physical movement (e.g., getting up from one's seat) is started before or during the announcement. The last example (number 14) is the only one where the announcement is made fully before any physical movement starts (this may be because the announcement is made to a third person, the woman who is making the recording, who is just leaving the room).

By looking solely at the physical actions and their timing relative to the announcements, one could draw the conclusion that there are two variants of the action combination for "What I'm doing": 1) for accounting for one's on-going, manual, physical action (examples 1–6); and 2) for announcing an action one is about to do that requires moving one's whole body (examples 7–14). This is shown in Table 2.

6   The infinitive *suitsetama* is in Estonian. Codeswitching to Estonian is not uncommon in this conversation, in which the participants are Finns who live in Estonia (see, e.g., Frick 2013).

Table 2

Announcement	Physical action	Timing
1st person or impersonal present tense declarative clause	moving or taking objects with one's hands	simultaneous
1st person or impersonal present tense declarative clause	moving one's body away from the setting	announcement, then physical action

The latter variant could be said to be epistemically motivated in the way announcements are often thought to be—that the speaker informs the recipient about something the recipient does not know (see, e.g., Terasaki 2004 [1976]; Schegloff 2007: 37). But this leaves us with unsolved problems: If the motivation for the combination is epistemic, why do the recipients not respond with a news receipt token? And: What is the motivation for the first variant of the combination, where the recipient can already see, and thus know, what the speaker is doing? These questions will be addressed in the last two sections of the article, and the conclusion will be drawn that people have other reasons besides epistemic ones for using "What I'm doing" combinations. Another fact that cannot be overlooked is that within the first part there is a good deal of syntactic variation in how the announcements are made. This will be the topic of the next subsection.

SYNTAX OF THE ANNOUNCEMENTS

All of the announcements in the data collection are made with declarative clauses, but different persons, moods, modalities, and clause types are used. According to Hakulinen et al. (VISK § 887), declarative clauses can be used in all persons and moods and clause types in Finnish. Most announcements in the collection are made with transitive or intransitive clauses in which there is congruence between the subject and predicate. Seven of these clauses are in 1st person singular, indicative mood and with no modal verb. Most of these turns are rather simple clauses, but as can be seen from (2), "What I'm doing" combinations can be accompanied by an account.

(2) [sg437_60-70] (00:07:50)

```
mä    siisti-n    nyt   vähän     tä-ssä    että näyttä-ä to-hon
1SG   clear-1SG   now   a_little  DEM1-INE  COMP look-3SG  DEM2-ILL
```
I'm clearing this out a bit so it looks

```
kamera-lle     paremma-lle
camera-ALL     better-ALL
```
better for the camera

One of the announcements, extract (3), includes affective markers that are reactive to prior turns in the conversation. This will be discussed later, when the extract will be shown in context as extract (17).

(3) [sg 410] (00:04:16)

```
voi vit(h)tu mää lähde-n  anteeks vaa (0.6) suitseta-ma
PRT cunt       1SG go-1SG sorry   PRT         smoke-INF
oh fuck, I'm leaving for a smoke
```

In two of the clauses, (4) and (5), the agent of the action announced is a first person plural group 'we'. In both cases, the predicate verb is in the passive, which is commonly used as a first person plural form in colloquial Finnish. In (4), there is a subject pronoun *me* ('we') accompanying the verb, and the agent of the announced action excludes the recipient.

(4) [sg 437_30-40] (00:07:40)

```
ni  Rina    (.) me  käy-dä-än  tupaka-lla     nytte
PRT 1NAMEF      1PL go-PAS-4   cigarette-ADE  now
so Rina, we're going for a smoke now
```

In example (5), there is no explicit subject. Although in this case it is the speaker who performs the action alone, the action announced can be interpreted as facilitating a joint activity (a shared meal) and the first person plural form as including the recipient.[7]

(5) [sg437_10-20] (00:07:37)

```
pan-na-an    kahvikupi-t   tonne       odottele-ma-an
put-PAS-4    coffee_cup-PL DEM2.LOC.ILL wait-INF-ILL
we'll put the coffee cups to wait here
```

In the following case, (6), a so-called generic third person form that lacks person reference (Laitinen 2006; Couper-Kuhlen & Etelämäki 2015) is used for announcing the speaker's own physical action. In this case, the clause starts with *jos* 'if' (see Laury 2012), and the predicate is in the conditional mood.

(6) [sg437_1-10] (00.00:98)

```
jos pan-is    vaikka        tuo-hon
if  put-COND  for_instance  DEM2-ILL
how about I put it for instance here[8]
```

---

7 Morphological passives without an accompanying subject are also commonly used as first person plural imperatives (cf. *let's* in English) (see Lauranto 2014). In this case (5), however, the turn cannot have a directive interpretation, since the speaker has clearly already begun to carry out the physical action that she verbally describes.

8 Literally: 'if zero-person would put'.

The syntax of (6) is similar to what Laury (op.cit.) and Couper-Kuhlen & Etelämäki (op.cit.) have found to be used in proposals of joint future action by the speaker and the recipient. In (6), it is, however, the speaker alone who performs the physical action. Unlike actual proposals, the passive and zero-person "proposals to oneself" do not lead to any response from the participants, and can therefore be treated as announcements about the speaker's plans (VISK § 1659). Unlike proposals, announcements are not something that other participants have to commit to (see further discussion in section 4). The conditional mood is said to be one of "planning, foretelling and imagining" (VISK § 1592). This gives (6) the interpretation that the speaker is planning (or foreseeing or imagining) what it would be like if the objects in her hand were in another place. She is announcing her plans while carrying them out. In another instance, (7), where the conditional mood is used, the physical action will be carried out later.

(7) [sg437_10-20] (00:07:37)

```
mä-ki      voi-si-n         nyt    syy-ä
1SG-CLI    can-COND-1SG     now    eat-INF
```
I could eat now too

In this example (7) there is an overt 1st person singular subject and a modal verb *voisin* 'I could'. The verb *voida* can be used to express dynamic, deontic or epistemic modality, and it is not always clear which one is meant (VISK § 1566). The same modal verb *voida* 'can' is used in the indicative mood in (8).

(8) [sg 409] (00:02:10)

```
mä   voi-n      vie-dä      tä-n       nyt    (ulos)
1SG  can-1SG    take-INF    DEM1-GEN   now    (out)
```
I can take this (out) now

As in the case of the conditional clauses, it is impossible to distinguish the action performed by the modal clauses (7) and (8) on purely syntactic grounds. In another context, the participants could well interpret a clause like (7) as a request (cf. VISK § 1660) and the one in (8) as an offer. Had they led to such interpretations, their responses would be different (see further discussion in sections 3 and 4).

Other modal verbs used in the data are *täytyä* and *pitää*, which indicate necessity and are used with a specific clause type with a genitive subject and no congruence between the subject and verb, the verb being always in 3rd person singular (VISK § 906, § 1574). In (9) there is an overt 1st person singular subject.

(9) [sg 410] (00:05:39)

```
hei   Sari      mu-n      täyty-y    muuten        näyttä-ä
hey   [1NAMEF]  1SG-GEN   must-3SG   by_the_way    show-INF
```
hey Sari, by the way, I must show you

Is it a coincidence that the last example, which expresses necessity, starts with an attention-seeking particle (cf. VISK § 858) *hei*? The *hei* in this extract marks a turn that initiates a new topic and an interactional project that is independent of the prior talk. A sudden change of topic is dispreferred in conversation (see, e.g., Jefferson 1984; Laury 2005), and the necessive verb acts as an account for the speaker's action: "I'm doing this, because I have to". In the section about social actions, I will return to the question of accounting in relation to the "What I'm doing" combination.

This section has addressed the syntactic variation of the announcements in "What I'm doing" combinations. The action of announcing cannot, however, be identified solely on the basis of syntax. Studies of institutional conversations have shown that declarative clauses in the 1st, 2nd, or 3rd person can be used as directives (Sorjonen 2001: 108–111; Sorjonen, Raevaara & Lappalainen 2009: 107–112; Stevanovic & Peräkylä 2012). By looking at the responses, one can, however, see that participants treat announcements differently than directives. Directives call for a commitment on the part of the recipient, which is seen in the responsive turns (ibid.), while announcements are not necessarily responded to at all (Couper-Kuhlen, p.c.; Stivers & Rossano 2010: 17–18). The following section clarifies this by showing how "What I'm doing" combinations are sequentially positioned.

How "What I'm doing" combinations relate to talk that precedes and follows

The fourteen examples of "What I'm doing" combinations chosen for the current collection are all sequentially initial, meaning that they are not second pair parts or otherwise responsive to a prior action. Some of them are, however, related to a prior topic, while others seem to be quite independent. Likewise, what follows the "What I'm doing" combination is not responsive, but can be related to it, or, in other cases is totally independent of it. Examples of this will be treated in the following. In the following extract (10), there are two instances of a "What I'm doing" combination that is related to preceding talk and followed by talk that is related to it. Extract (10) is from the same conversation as extract (1). The two adult sisters have baked pizza, and Tuula's daughter has come into the kitchen to take some. There has been talk about the pizza with the daughter a few turns earlier.

(10) [sg437_10-20] (00:07:37)

```
01 Jaana:   nij ja sitten ni, (.) #ä#,
            and then ehm

02          (0.4)

03          kuulin että sinäkin tykkäät täst tämmösest näin
            I heard that you also like this,
```

```
04            että: <et ku on noita,
              you know when there's like

05            mhhhhh maustekkurkun suikaleita ja sitten ni siihe

06            smeta#naa ja hunajaa pääl#le?
              slices of pickled cucumber with sour cream and honey on top.

07            (1.4)

→ Tuula:      mä-ki   vo-isi-n       nyt  syy-ä,
              1SG-CLI can-COND-1SG   now  eat-INF
              I could eat now too.

09            (3.8) ((Figure 3 - Tuula drinks, puts her cup down, starts moving her body))

10 Tuula:     .mt @kun kahvit  on  juo-tu      nin nyt* >syö#-dä-än#<@;
                  when coffee-PL AUX drink-PPPC PRT now  eat-PAS-4
              now that we've had the coffee, now let's eat.
              ((getting up, *raises index finger))

11 Jaana:     =jip,
              yeah

12            (0.4) ((Tuula gets up))

13 Tuula:     mm,
              mm

14            (1.8) ((Figure 4 - Tuula grabs coffee cups and moves them))

→ Tuula:      pan-na-an    kahvikupi-t     tonne      odottele-ma-an
              put-PASS-4   coffee_cup-PL   DEM2.LOC.ILL wait-INF-ILL
              we'll put the coffee cups to wait here.

16            ↑tää on sun↑,
              this is yours

17            (1.0) ((Tuula places coffee cups in another spot))

18 Tuula:     .mts mikä on lähempänä ↑tota;
              which is closer

19            (.)

20            ja sit tää on mun.
              and then this is mine

21            (0.6)

22 Jaana:     .mt eiku toi on lähempänä tota mun paik°kaa°,
              no, that one is closer to my seat.

              (2.0)
```

Figure 3 – line 09    *Figure 4 – line 14*

In line 8 Tuula announces that she could eat too. She then starts making physical movements and actions that prepare her for getting up and leaving the table (cf. Laurier 2008; Siromaa 2013): She finishes her coffee and puts the cup down, and starts moving her body (line 9, Figure 3). This "What I'm doing" combination is topically related to the talk about the daughter taking pizza, and to the fact that she is currently doing it. This is also marked grammatically with a clitic *-ki* 'too' in *mäki (voisin nyt syyä)* 'I too (could eat)'. The action combination is, however, not related to the immediately preceding verbal turns, such as Jaana's telling (in lines 1–6) about how she has heard that Tuula likes pickled onions. It is topically related to what follows, namely Tuula's own turn (in line 10) where she continues talk about starting to eat.

Tuula's proposal (in line 10) is responded to by Jaana (in line 11) with *jip* 'yeah'. After this, Tuula gets up and grabs the coffee cups on the table (Figure 4, line 14). A second "What I'm doing" combination occurs when Tuula announces *Pannaan kahvikupit tonne odottelemaan* 'Let's put the coffee cups to wait here' (line 15) and places the cups in another spot. This turn, which talks about moving coffee cups aside, has a weak topical link to the prior one (line 10), which talked about finishing up the coffees. It also yields further talk, namely a sequence about which cup is whose (lines 16–22).

These two examples in extract (10) show two different ways in which following talk can be related to a "What I'm doing" combination: 1) by the first speaker continuing on the topic (line 8) or 2) by a sequence being initiated on the same topic (line 15). The relation to prior talk in both the cases is topical. These "What I'm doing" combinations are topically related to what precedes them in a conversation, and are followed by talk that is related to them. It is noteworthy that these relations are not always present. Announcements are an action type that does not make a response relevant (Couper-Kuhlen, p.c.; see also Stivers & Rossano 2010: 17–18). There is no expectation for the participants to respond to "What I'm doing" combinations.

The next examples of "What I'm doing" combinations are fully independent from the preceding and following talk. They are not (topically or otherwise) related to either the preceding or the following talk. Extract (11) is from a dinner party with five friends, who are just starting to take food from the dishes on the table. Akseli is taking salad, but the discussion (in lines 8–13 and 15–17) is about the main dish, chicken.

(11) [sg 396] (00:02:50)

```
01  Riku:    (--)  ((Akseli starts taking salad))

02  Taavi:   leipää ja
             bread and

03  Akseli:  ↑vähän meil on loistavaa en mä (.)
             ymmärtänytkään
             this is fantastic, I never thought

04  Taavi:   et
             that/no

05  Riku:    £et [nii£
             no you didn't

06  Taavi:       [£et nii et nii ei s(h)iin oo mit(h)ään
                  no you didn't no you didn't there's nothing

07           ihmeell(h)istä£
             special about this

08  Riku:    ehh heh (.) nii Taavi mitä [tää on
             so Taavi, what is this

09  Taavi:                               [siis siin on (0.3)
                                          well there's

10           >siis< maustamattomia (0.2) noita kanan (0.2)
             unseasoned chicken

11           filesuikaleita (0.2) sit mä ostin (0.2)
                                             Lindmannilta
             filet slices, and then from Lindman's I bought

12           ↑tietysti Porvoossa kun ↑ollaan niin (.)
             Lindmannilta
13           ostin semmosta oliivitahnaa,
             from Lindman's of course, now that we're in Porvoo, I bought this olive paste

→   Akseli:  °mä ota-n    vähän   vaa  lissää°
             1SG take-1SG little  just more
             I'll take just a little bit more.
             ((Figure 5 - continuing to take salad))

15  Taavi:   sit pistin siihen ola- oliivitahnaa=puristin yhen
             then I put the olive paste in, added one

16           valkosipulin kynnen=sitä tuli ihan reilusti (0.2)
             clove of garlic, that was plenty

17           #joo# maistatte kohta
             you'll taste it soon.
```

Figure 5 – line 14

In extract (11), line 14, Akseli, who has been taking salad from a bowl throughout the extract, produces a "What I'm doing" combination: *Mä otan vähän vaan lissää* 'I'll take just a little bit more'. There has been no mention of the salad before this, and none following the action combination (until ca. 40 turns later, when Lauri offers Riku the salad).

Another free-standing "What I'm doing" combination is shown in extract (12), where the physical action involves leaving the setting altogether. Extract (12) is from a conversation between two friends preparing to watch a football game on television. Marja is holding a sheet of game scores and examining it.

(12) [sg 409_Jalkapallo1] (00:02:10)
Two friends watching a football game on television. Marja is examining a score sheet.

```
01  Marja:   mut joka tapauskes (sillai et) Ranska on out.
             but anyways, France is out.

02           (.)

03  Oona:    ihanaa.
             wonderful

04           (4.0) ((Figure 6 - Oona stands up and moves to the other side of
                   the room, her back to Marja. Marja folds open the program sheet on
                   her lap and starts examining it.))

→   Oona:    mä voi-n  vie-dä   *tä-n      nyt   (ulos)
             1SG can-1SG take-INF DEM1-GEN  now    out
             I can take this (out) now.
             ((*Oona grabs something from a table))

06           (2.0) ((Oona leaves the room))

07  Marja:   mä (kirju/ottasin) hei siin.
             I wrote these here / I could write these here.⁹
```

9 The utterance can be understood as partly Finnish and partly Estonian, and the translation depends on this interpretation. The participants are Finns living in Estonia.

Figure 6 – line 4

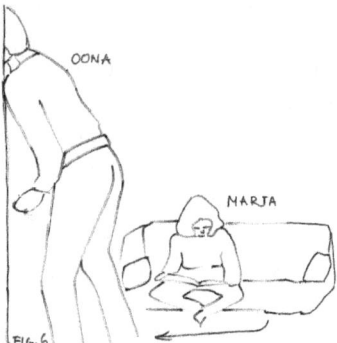

The "What I'm doing" combination in (12) starts with Oona's physical actions as she gets up from her seat and walks to the other side of the room (Figure 6, line 4). After this she produces an announcement (line 5) about a physical action: *Mä voin viedä tän nyt ulos* 'I can take this out now' and grabs something from a table. The women have been talking about game scores, which Marja sees on a sheet of paper she is reading. There is no talk between the participants during the "What I'm doing" combination, and after it, Marja starts a new sequence about the scores she has written on the sheet (line 7).

Oona's announcement in (12) *Mä voin viedä tän nyt ulos* 'I can take this out now' is syntactically formulated like an offer—it includes a 1st person singular modal verb *voin*, and, therefore, the impression the clause leaves is that Oona's action will benefit the recipient. The recipient, however, does not respond to it in a way that would be preferred for an offer (cf. Davidson 1984; Tainio 1995; Kärkkäinen & Keisanen 2012: 592). Nor does the speaker herself pursue a response to the offer by expanding or reformulating it (cf. ibid). Instead, she acts on it. The example should therefore be viewed as similar to the other examples where a person leaves the conversational setting and, while doing so, announces a physical action that serves as an account for leaving.

The examples in this section have shown that "What I'm doing" combinations can be related to preceding talk topically, and that they can yield further talk in the form of a recipient or the speaker him- or herself continuing on the topic, but that neither of these is necessary: "What I'm doing" combinations can be independent and free-standing.

If no recipient response is expected, why, then, do people announce their physical actions so that others can hear? The next section will address this question: What do "What I'm doing" combinations do, what is achieved by them socially?

Social actions of "What I'm doing" combinations

Researchers have addressed the question of the relation between syntactic form and social action formation, and Heritage (2012a), for instance, has shown that declarative clauses can be used as questions and interrogative clauses as assertions. How, then, do people recognise social actions? Heritage's work investigates the role of epistemics in action formation and recognition, but there are other aspects to it than that (see, e.g., Sidnell 2012: 54). Couper-Kuhlen (2014) has introduced a model for distinguishing directive-commissive actions based on the agency and beneficiary roles of the participants: An offer is about a future act which benefits the recipient and is carried out by the speaker, and a request about one that is carried out by the recipient for the benefit of the speaker. The grammatical forms used for directive-commissive actions in English range from imperatives and interrogatives to declarative clauses (ibid.).

The verbal parts of the "What I'm doing" combinations investigated in this paper are all declarative clauses, which, according to Hakulinen et al. (VISK § 887), have no prototypical speech-act function. The line between one action and another is not always clear, and although the main action of the utterances in the combinations is announcing, the same syntactic forms can be used, for example, in offers, proposals, and requests. For instance, Stevanovic & Peräkylä (2012) show examples of Finnish turns that are formulated as announcements, but that have implicit deontic consequences for the recipient. In their examples, this is evident also in the recipient responses, which, unlike in most of my examples, are similar to responses to proposals and requests (ibid.). In the previous section, the sequential characteristics of "What I'm doing" combinations were investigated, and the conclusion was drawn that, unlike directive actions, these announcements do not call for a response at all.

The cases in my data cannot be explained by epistemics or beneficiary roles alone. The announcements in the data are not made only to inform the recipient of something—the recipients can themselves often see and thus know what the physical action is, and they do not respond with news receipt tokens. Some of the physical actions announced, like extract (13), benefit the speaker, who is also the actor, but many do not. Extract (13) was shown in context in extract (10). It is an example of a "What I'm doing" combination where the announced action benefits the speaker: The speaker will get herself food.

(13) [sg437_10-20] (00:07:37)

```
08   Tuula:   mä-ki   vo-isi-n      nyt  syy-ä,
              1SG-CLI can-COND-1SG  now  eat-INF
              I could eat now too.
```

The data also show examples of "What I'm doing" combinations that are done for the benefit of a third party, namely ones where Tuula clears the table of things that are in front of the camera. This benefits whoever is recording the conversation and later using the video. In extract (14) Jaana is telling Tuula about some people who were supposed to come and visit her.

(14) [sg437_60-70] (00:07:50)
Two adult sisters in Tuula's kitchen. Jaana is telling about people who were going to come visit her.

```
01  Jaana:   .mthh (0.2) mut se et ee- (.) ei ne nyt
02           sitten tuuk#kaan#.
             but they won't be coming after all.

03  Tuula:   °nii°,
             Yeah.

04           (3.0) ((Figure 7 - Tuula takes the plates on the table and moves them aside.))

05  Jaana:   se et ku Elina tekee nii, (0.4)  [lyhen- ]
             you know when Elina works sho-

→   Tuula:                                    [mä siisti-n
                                               1SG  clear-1SG
                                               I'm clearing

→            nyt vähän    tä-ssä    että näyttä-ä tohon
             now a_little DEM1-INE  COMP look-3SG  DEM2.ILL
             this out so that it looks

             kamera-lle  paremma-lle
             camera-ALL  better-ALL
             better for the camera.

09           (0.8) ((Tuula continues arranging objects))

10  Jaana:   .hhhh nin ni tota toi, (0.6) Elina tekee
                        you know Elina works

11           lyhennettyy työ#päivää# sillon °ni°,
             shorter days then so
```
((Tuula continues arranging objects))

```
12           (6.4) ((Tuula continues arranging objects))
```

Figure 7 – line 04

In extract (14) Tuula's "What I'm doing" combination includes an account for why she is carrying out the physical action—clearing the table—*että näyttää tohon kameralle paremmalle* 'so it looks better for the camera'. Tuula names the camera (instead of the co-present participant or the viewer of the video) as the beneficiary of her action, which reveals that the viewer of the film is not the addressee, but could well be an intended beneficiary of the action. A more indirect benefit for the speaker can be seen in that tidying up shows the person in a good light: as someone who cares for how things look.

According to Couper-Kuhlen (2014), requests are actions that advocate future activities to be carried out by the recipient that will primarily benefit the speaker. They thus happen at the 'cost' of the recipient. In many of the "What I'm doing" combinations, the physical action is also such that it benefits the speaker and happens at the cost of the recipient. These actions are, however, different from the activities advocated by requests. Namely, the physical actions in "What I'm doing" combinations are carried out by the speaker, not the recipient. The 'cost' the recipient has to bear is thus not the trouble of doing something or giving something away. Instead, in many of the examples in the current collection, the physical actions have to do with either the speaker taking something the recipient could have had (e.g., food from a shared dish), or the speaker committing a social transgression such as leaving the conversational setting.

One of the extracts where the speaker uses a "What I'm doing" combination when taking something that the recipients could have is (11), the target line of which is repeated here as (15). The turn is from a setting where five friends are sitting at a dinner table and have just started to take food from the dishes on the table. The speaker, Akseli, is the first one to take salad, and he has already taken a few spoonfuls:

(15) [sg396] (00:02:50)

```
14  Akseli:  °mä   ota-n     vähän     vaa   lissää°
             1SG   take-1SG  a_little  just  more
             I'll take just a little bit more.
```

With his turn, Akseli announces that he's taking some more salad although he already has some on his plate. The words *vähän vaan* 'just a little' in this context imply that there is, in his mind, something wrong in taking a lot of salad. They mitigate the transgression: Taking a little is not as bad as taking a lot. The turn is uttered in a quiet voice, which can be a sign of the delicateness of the matter (cf. Lerner 2013: 96). The wrongfulness of taking a lot of salad is explainable by the fact that there is only a limited amount in the bowl, and that the others have not yet had any. In fact, a couple of minutes later, when the bowl has reached the last person at the table, the insufficient amount of the salad becomes a topic: see extract (16).

(16) [sg396] (00:05:00)
The almost empty salad bowl reaches Taavi, who is the host of the evening for his four friends (the sixth participant, Pete, has not arrived yet).

```
Taavi:  tätä salaattii on niin vähän
        there's so little of this salad.

Riku:   tai siis oli
        You mean there was.

Taavi:  mä oon pahoillani
        I'm sorry.

Lauri:  ei [se mitään
        it's alright.

Riku:      [ei se mitään
           it's fine.

Lauri:  kaikki on saanu.
        everybody got some.

Aapo:   nii. (.) paitsi Pete mut se nyt ei
        yeah, except Pete, but he doesn't.

Lauri:  sitä ei lasketa
        he doesn't count.
```

When the salad bowl reaches Taavi just before extract (16), there is almost nothing left in it. Taavi takes the blame for the shortage, but at this point it also could be claimed that Akseli's action of taking a large amount in (15) has actually happened at the cost of the others. There is little left for the host, and none for the last guest, who is yet to arrive.

Another type of "What I'm doing" combinations that happen at the 'cost' of the recipient(s) are the ones where someone leaves the setting. This type of announcement has been mentioned by Stivers & Rossano (2010: 17). Goodwin (1987) and Schegloff (1992) discuss an event where a participant accounts for her departure with a turn "Need some more ice". In their example, the announcement is made at a sequential juncture point, after a storytelling (ibid). The storytelling Goodwin and Schegloff describe is one that has gone wrong (ibid). Although the turn is formulated as self-talk, not related to the ongoing conversation, its sequential positioning after a storytelling gone wrong is not coincidental, according to Schegloff (ibid). A "What I'm doing" combination is seen in extract (17) where the "unilateral departure" (see Goodwin 1987; Dersley & Wootton 2001) of one of the participants is somewhat similar to the one in Goodwin and Schegloff's example. It is a reaction to something in the preceding interaction, marked by a particle and an expletive at the beginning of the turn (see VISK § 856), in line 7. In extract (17), one of the participants, Mikko, sums up the gist (line 5) of a story told by Elo. Because of the nature of the sum-up, Mikko is called 'suggestive' by Elo. Extract (17) is from a gathering of four friends.

Elo is sitting on an armchair, Mikko and Maija on a couch, and Sari on the floor in front of the couch.

(17) [sg410 Koti-ilta1] (00:04:32)
Four friends at Elo's place. Elo is finishing a storytelling.

```
01  Elo:     ja siis se oli tosi hauska me lähettii pesee rumimmat
             it was really funny we went and washed all the ugliest
02           munat sitte.
             eggs then.

03  Maija:   [nii.
             yeah.

04  Elo:     [uuestaa käyttöön.
             to use them again.

05  Mikko:   £Maijan m(h)unat uudest(h)aan käyt(h)töön he he£
             to use Maija's eggs again.

06  Elo:     he he

→   Mikko:   £voi vit(h)tu mää lähde-n anteeks vaa.£
              PRT  cunt      1SG  leave-1SG sorry    PRT
             oh fuck I'm sorry, I'm leaving.
             ((Figure 8 - Mikko gets up, Sari raises her body))

08  Elo:     miten sä oot noin kaksmielinen taas.
             how come you're so suggestive again.

→   Mikko:   suitset(a-ma).
             smoke-INF
             to smoke
             ((Sari gets up.))

10  Mikko:   no mä oon aina kaksmieline.
             well I'm always suggestive.
             ((Mikko leaves the room.))

11           (3.0) ((Sari moves to the other side of the room to adjust the camera))
```

Figure 8 – line 07

Extract (17) starts from the end of a storytelling by Elo about how she and some of her friends (including at least co-present Maija, possibly also Mikko) had painted Easter eggs, and then washed the ugliest ones to paint them again (lines 1–2 and 4). Mikko repeats a part of this turn and its increment (in line 5): *Maijan munat uudestaan käyttöön* 'to use Maija's eggs again'. Mikko's turn is uttered with a smile and laughter, which hints at non-seriousness. According to Elo's interpretation (in line 8), the turn is *kaksimielinen* 'suggestive', which is probably based on the fact that *munat* can mean 'eggs', but also 'testicles'. Mikko produces a "What I'm doing" combination (in lines 7 and 9) by announcing, again smiling and laughing: *Voi vittu mä lähen anteeks vaan. Suitsetama.* 'Oh fuck I'm sorry, I'm leaving. To smoke', getting up (Figure 8) while producing the turn, and leaving the room.

The announcement starts with the interjection *voi* and an expletive, which mark its reactivity to a preceding utterance or the speaker's affect (see VISK § 856). Regardless of its reactive nature, the turn is not responsive in the sense that it would form the second pair part of any first.[10] It is possibly a general reaction to the lewdness of the conversation at this point. When Mikko starts getting up (in line 5), Sari moves (possibly in order to get out of Mikko's way, but Mikko chooses to take another route). When Mikko leaves the setting (in line 9), Sari also gets up and follows him to the other side of the room, where she starts another physical activity (line 11). A new, unrelated topic is initiated by Maija after a pause.

In the end of line 7 Mikko apologises. According to Schegloff (2005), an apology marks something in the preceding interaction as the source of the apology. This source is thus treated by the speaker as a (potential) complainable, regardless of the fact that none of the participants actually complain about the matter. Schegloff (2005: 461) describes the apologising speaker's position as follows: "I noticed that something untoward or problematic has happened, or is happening or is about to happen, which affects you (the recipient[s]) which could be taken to warrant a complaint; I take responsibility; and I apologize." In extract (17) the turn (in line 7) thus does more than a plain announcement would; a plain announcement would only show recognition of an action that affects the recipients (cf. Stevanovic & Peräkylä 2012). However, the particle *vaan* that follows the apology in extract (17) (line 7) diminishes it (see VISK § 828), toning it down to a fake apology that shows that the speaker recognises the complainability of the matter but does not take responsibility for it. This is in line with the speaker's stance at the beginning of the turn a): the reaction to something 'wrong' in the preceding interaction, followed by b) the announcement and physical action that is the consequence of that 'wrongness' and can be accounted for by the 'wrongness'. Since leaving the setting is justified, there is no reason to be truly apologetic about it.

In doctor-patient interaction, doctors may also give what have been called "online explanations" (Heritage & Stivers 1999). Explaining procedures in the form of 1st person announcements or requests reduces

---

10 Turns that were responsive to a first pair part were not included in the collection.

patients' uncertainty when facing unfamiliar and even painful courses of action during the physician's examination, and they have even been found to correlate with fewer suits against malpractice (ibid. Robinson & Stivers 2001). The everyday situations of the conversations studied here are quite different from doctor-patient encounters, but similarities can be seen in how announcements of one's future actions show acknowledgement of the possible harm the actions might do to the recipient, and also the potential complainability of those actions.

Schegloff (2005) also states that complaints may occur when another participant finds that the agent of the transgression does not orient towards the complainability of the matter. The announcements show such orientation, and no actual complaints occur in the data after "What I'm doing" combinations.[11] Extract (18) shows, however, a case where the recipient treats the "What I'm doing" combination as something she has a say in. The conversation is the one where two middle-aged women are conversing in Tuula's kitchen. At this point, the person who is doing the recording has briefly entered the room.

(18) [sg 437_30-40] (00:07:40)
Two middle aged sisters conversing in Tuula's kitchen. A younger relative, Rina (who is doing the recording), has briefly entered the kitchen. Jaana is in the middle of a storytelling.

```
01  Jaana:    .hhhhhh ni, (0.4) se että sillon ku mä
                                so it was when I
02            tulin sieltä linja-autoasemalta sinne
              came from the bus station to
03            toiselle puolelle et mistä n[e,
              the other side where they

04  Tuula:                                [meill_on
05            Rina koht sulle kommentti ku Ja-, (.)
              Rina, we'll have a comment for you
06            Jaana lopettaa;
              after Jaana finishes.
```

((20 lines omitted: storytelling sequence))

```
→   Tuula:   ni ↑Rina. (.) me käydä-än tupakalla    ny[tte?
             PRT 1NAMEF    1PL go-PAS-4 cigarette-ADE now
             so, Rina, we're going for a smoke now.

29  Rina:                                            [oke?
                                                     okay.

30           (0.8)
```

11 The dataset is too small to determine whether this is a regularity or a coincidence. The former would indicate that a "What I'm doing" combination is sufficient to mark the speaker's awareness of and responsibility for the complainable matter. Further research on a larger dataset is required to determine if this is the case.

31	Rina:	käykää n<u>o</u>psaa sitte.
		don't be long then.
		((leaving the room))
32		(.)
33	Tuula:	joo.
		no we won't.
34		(1.0) ((Tuula raises her glass))
35	Tuula:	korkeintaa v<u>ii</u>s minuuttii.
		five minutes maximum.
36		(4.4) ((Tuula finishes her drink, Jaana wipes her mouth, both get up))
37	Tuula:	>se o< määräys.
		that's an order.
38		(0.6)
39	Jaana:	kr[mh.
40	Tuula:	[@(-) nopsaa sitteh@.
		don't be long then.
41	Jaana:	khe,
42		((Tuula and Jaana leave the room))

The particle *ni* in the beginning of the "What I'm doing" combination in extract (18), line 28, ties the turn to a previous line in the conversation (see VISK § 811), which is Tuula's informing (lines 4–6) that the women will have something to say to Rina after Jaana has finished her story. This informing implies that Rina, who mainly stays in another room during the recording, should not leave the kitchen before hearing the announcement. The informing also prepares the recipient for something that will be addressed to her, something of relative importance. In line 28, Tuula announces that she and Jaana will go out to smoke. Rina's complying response *oke* 'okay' (line 29) shows that she treats the "What I'm doing" combination as something that has consequences for her (cf. Stevanovic & Peräkylä 2012: 304). She further produces a turn (line 31) in the imperative form, telling Tuula and Jaana not to stay for long.

Rina's deontic rights (see Stevanovic 2013) over Tuula's and Jaana's plan to go out to smoke is based on her role as the person who is recording the conversation: The participants' leaving the room will result in a gap in the recorded conversation. Furthermore, the informing by Tuula (lines 4–6) indicates that, in Tuula's view, the matter announced will be of special importance to the recipient, and that she is aware that it will affect Rina. This does not yet mean that Tuula is assigning Rina the same deontic authority (see Stevanovic & Peräkylä 2012; Stevanovic 2013) as Rina takes for herself by telling the women not to stay for long. In fact, Tuula evaluates Rina's action by naming it an 'order' (line 37) and by mimicking (cf. Couper-Kuhlen 1996) Rina's turn (line 40). This can be seen as an indirect criticism of Rina's words (cf. Couper-Kuhlen 1996: 391), that is, an indication of Tuula's disalignment with the deontic stance Rina has taken. This extract supports Stevanovic & Peräkylä's (2012) view that announcements are not merely epistemic actions but have a hint of deonticity to them. Since they have consequences for the recipient, the recipient may take a stance on them. Thus, at least in some cases, the social transgressions of "What I'm doing" combinations can be explicitly negotiated.

The examples in this section have shown that "What I'm doing" combinations are used when the physical action in question is a social transgression. In this particular dataset, there are cases where the speaker takes something from a shared source (a shared dish in the dinner table) and ones where he or she leaves the setting. Indications that these actions are treated as accountable by the participants are found in the mitigated wording of the announcement, apologies, and negotiations over the deontic rights of the participants. The announcement part of the combination accounts (see, e.g., Heritage 1988) for the social transgression of the physical action part. By saying aloud something that is often obvious for the recipients, who can see the physical action, the speaker displays that he or she is acting consciously. Compared to an apology, by which the speaker notices the act, acknowledges that it affects the recipient and could be taken to warrant a complaint, takes responsibility and apologises (Schegloff 2005: 461), a person who accounts for their actions goes only part of the way by recognising the wrongful act.

Summary and conclusions

The purpose of this study was to investigate occasions in mundane conversations when people make an announcement about something physical they are doing or are about to do. The study showed that declarative clauses are combined with simultaneous or following physical actions within the social action of treating the physical action as accountable and departing from social norms. These combinations of a verbal and a physical action were named "What I'm doing" combinations. The data collection included examples of people moving objects on a table, taking food from a table, and leaving their seats for different reasons, such as to bring, look at, or take things, or to go outside to smoke.

The first task was to explore the linguistic and embodied design of the combinations. The analysis showed that physical actions that involved moving or taking something with one's hands are typically announced during the physical movement, while ones that involved moving the whole body are typically announced at a moment when some physical movement (e.g., raising the body) has already started, but the announced action itself has not.

The study also expands our knowledge of the grammar and use of announcements in interaction. The announcements in the data collection are made with declarative clauses. Most common are transitive and intransitive clauses[12] in the 1st person singular or plural form, indicative mood and without a modal verb. Clauses with generic third person are also used. Some announcements are in the conditional mood and some include a modal verb or are of the necessive clause type.

The second task was to explore the sequential usage of the combinations. The combinations chosen for the collection were initial, i.e., non-responsive, yet some of the examples were related to preceding talk topically or as an affective reaction to it. Some examples, again, were independent of prior talk. Also, there may be talk that follows "What I'm doing" combinations and is topically related to it, but it was noted that the combinations do not occur as a first pair part of an adjacency pair, that is, they do not call for a response. In conclusion, the announcements in "What I'm doing" combinations can be positioned at topical or sequential junctures, they can initiate new sequences, or they can be free-standing (not related to talk that precedes or follows).

The third and final task was to investigate the social actions of the combinations. In the literature, announcements have often been explained with reference to epistemicity. This study shows, however, that people have motivations for using them other than merely informing the recipient about something they assume the recipient does not know. Why would they otherwise use announcements of the type 'I'm moving these cups a bit' or 'I'm leaving' when the recipient can very well see what the speaker is doing? And why would there be no cases in the dataset where the recipient responds with a news receipt token? Instead, there is often no response to a "What I'm doing" combination. Response relevance is typical of directive actions, which have to do with the beneficiary and agency roles of the participants (see Couper-Kuhlen 2014). Although some of the physical actions in the combinations benefit the speaker and some happen at the 'cost' of the recipient, beneficiary roles alone do not explain the combinations. Instead, the data show that the physical actions in "What I'm doing" combinations are treated as accountable, as departures from social norms, and the announcements are actions that account for them.

References

Couper-Kuhlen, Elizabeth. 1996. The prosody of repetition: On quoting and mimicry. In Elizabeth Couper-Kuhlen & Margret Selting (eds.), *Prosody in conversation: Interactional studies.* 366–405. Cambridge: Cambridge University Press.

Couper-Kuhlen, Elizabeth. 2014. What does grammar tell us about action? *Pragmatics* 24(3): 623–647.

---

12 See, e.g., Hakulinen et al. (VISK § 891) for a description of the Finnish clause types.

Couper-Kuhlen, Elizabeth & Marja Etelämäki. 2015. Nominated actions and their targeted agents in Finnish conversational directives. *Journal of Pragmatics* 78: 7–24.

Couper-Kuhlen, Elizabeth & Margaret Selting. 2001. Introducing interactional linguistics. In Margret Selting & Elizabeth Couper-Kuhlen (eds.), *Studies in interactional linguistics.* 1–22. New York: John Benjamins.

Davidson, Judy. 1984. Subsequent versions of invitations, offers, requests, and proposals dealing with potential or actual rejection. In Max Atkinson & John Heritage (eds.), *Structures of social action: Studies in conversation analysis.* 102–128. Cambridge: Cambridge University Press.

Dersley, Ian & Anthony J. Wootton. 2001. In the heat of the sequence: Interactional features preceding walkouts from argumentative talk. *Language in Society* 30: 611–638.

Ford, Cecilia E. 2002. Denial and the construction of conversational turns. In Joan L. Bybee (ed.), *Complex sentences in grammar and discourse: Essays in honor of Sandra A. Thompson.* 61–78. Amsterdam: John Benjamins.

Frick, Maria. 2013. *Emergent bilingual constructions: Finnish-Estonian codeswitching in interaction.* Ph.D. dissertation. University of Helsinki, Department of Finnish, Finno-Ugrian and Scandinavian studies.

Goodwin, Charles. 1987. Unilateral departure. In Graham Button & John R.E. Lee (eds.), *Talk and social organisation.* 206–216. Clevedon: Multilingual Matters.

Heritage, John. 1988. Explanations as accounts: A conversation analytic perspective. In Charles Antaki (ed.), *Analysing everyday explanation: A casebook of methods.* 127–144. Thousand Oaks: Sage.

Heritage, John. 2012a. Epistemics in action: Action formation and territories of knowledge. *Research on Language and Social Interaction* 45: 1–29.

Heritage, John. 2012b. Epistemics in conversation. In Jack Sidnell & Tanya Stivers (eds.), *The Handbook of Conversation Analysis.* 370–394. Chistester: John Wiley & Sons, Ltd.

Heritage, John & Tanya Stivers. 1999. Online commentary in acute medical visits: A method of shaping patient expectations. *Social Science & Medicine* 49(11): 1501–1517.

Jefferson, Gail. 1984. Stepwise transition out of topic. In Max Atkinson & John Heritage (eds.), *Structures of social action: Studies in conversation analysis.* 191–222. Cambridge: Cambridge University Press.

Kärkkäinen, Elise & Tiina Keisanen. 2012. Linguistic and embodied formats for making (concrete) offers. *Discourse Studies* 14(5): 587–611.

Laitinen, Lea. 2006. Zero person in Finnish: A grammatical resource for construing human reference. In Marja-Liisa & Lyle Campbell (eds.), *Grammar from the human perspective. Case, space and person in Finnish.* 209–231. Amsterdam: Benjamins.

Lauranto, Yrjö. 2014. *Imperatiivi, käsky, direktiivi. Arkikeskustelun vaihtokauppakielioppia.* Helsinki: Suomalaisen Kirjallisuuden Seura.

Laurier, Eric. 2008. Drinking up: Conversational resources of the café. *Language & Communication* 28(2): 165–181.

Laury, Ritva. 2005. Dialogic syntax and the emergence of topics in interaction. *TRANEL (Traveaux Neuchâtelois Linguistiques)* 41: 165–189.

Laury, Ritva. 2012. Syntactically non-integrated Finnish *jos* 'if'-conditional clauses as directives. *Discourse Processes* 49: 213–242.

Lerner, Gene H. 2013. On the place of hesitating in delicate formulations: A turn-constructional infrastructure for collaborative indiscretion. In Makoto Hayashi, Geoffrey Raymond & Jack Sidnell (eds.), *Conversational repair and human understanding.* 95–134. Cambridge: Cambridge University Press.

Robinson, Jeffrey D. & Tanya Stivers. 2001. Achieving activity transitions in physician-patient encounters: From history taking to physical examination. *Human Communication Research* 27(2): 253–298.

Schegloff, Emanuel A. 1992. In another context. In Alessandro Duranti & Charles Goodwin (eds.), *Rethinking context: Language as an interactive phenomenon.* 193–227. Cambridge: Cambridge University Press.

Schegloff, Emanuel A. 2005. On complainability. *Social Problems* 52(4): 449–476.

Schegloff, Emanuel A. 2007. *Sequence organization in interaction: A primer in conversation analysis.* Cambridge: Cambridge University Press.

Sidnell, Jack. 2012. Declaratives, questioning, defeasibility. *Research on Language and Social Interaction* 45(1): 53–60.

Siromaa, Maarit. 2013. Monitoimintatilanteiden järjestäminen henkilökunnan taukotilassa. [Organising multiaction situations in a staff break room]. Presentation at Keskusteluntutkimuksen päivät, Tampere 17.–18.1.2013.

Sorjonen, Marja-Leena. 2001. *Responding in conversation: A study of response particles in Finnish.* Amsterdam: Benjamins.

Sorjonen, Marja-Leena, Liisa Raevaara & Hanna Lappalainen. 2009. Mä otan tän. Käynnin syyn esittämisen tavat kioskilla. In Hanna Lappalainen & Liisa Raevaara (eds.), *Kieli kioskilla: Tutkimuksia kioskiasioinnin rutiineista.* 90–119. Helsinki: Suomalaisen Kirjallisuuden Seura.

Stevanovic, Melisa. 2013. *Deontic rights in interaction: A conversation analytic study on authority and cooperation.* Helsinki: University of Helsinki.

Stevanovic, Melisa & Anssi Peräkylä. 2012. Deontic authority in interaction: The right to announce, propose, and decide. *Research on Language and Social Interaction* 45(3): 297–321.

Stivers, Tanya & Federico Rossano. 2010. Mobilizing response. *Research on Language and Social Interaction* 43(1): 3–31.

Tainio, Liisa. 1995. Preferenssijäsennys. In Liisa Tainio (ed.), *Keskustelunanalyysin perusteet.* 93–110. Tampere: Vastapaino.

Terasaki, Alene Kiku. 2004 [1976]. Pre-announcement sequences in conversation. In Gene H. Lerner (ed.), *Conversation analysis: Studies from the first generation.* 171–224. Amsterdam: John Benjamins.

VISK = Auli Hakulinen, Maria Vilkuna, Riitta Korhonen, Vesa Koivisto, Tarja Riitta Heinonen & Irja Alho. 2004. *Iso suomen kielioppi.* Helsinki: Suomalaisen Kirjallisuuden Seura. http://scripta.kotus.fi/visk URN:ISBN:978-952-5446-35-7 (visited 6 March, 2014.)

Leelo Keevallik
http://orcid.org/0000-0003-2175-8710

2. Linking performances: The temporality of contrastive grammar[1]

Introduction

Using videotaped records of settings where an embodied skill is being taught, this paper investigates how dance teachers build action in real time. In instructive activities such as dance and piano classes, the correct and the incorrect versions are often performed in close succession in order to enable comparison between the two. Ultimately, the incorrect version is to be replaced by the correct one by the students. In order to capture the difference between right and wrong in an activity that evolves in time, re-performing is an efficient method of reference (Keevallik 2013a) as well as of strategically enhanced contrast (Keevallik 2010a). Contrasted performances serve to present a salient pedagogical point for the students. The current paper looks into one practice for bringing about a combination of performances, focusing on grammatical devices that mark a contrast. Similar to other papers in this volume, the study thus targets the linking of actions, but here the actions are physical performances rather than spoken utterances. However, it will be argued that these verbal-bodily practices also help us discover the role of language in human action. They disclose the essentially temporal and indexical nature of grammar.

Several studies on language in interaction have already made a strong case that grammar emerges in time and that language structures are accomplished, revised, and negotiated in real-time interaction (Auer 2009). Language structures enable projection, i.e., a display of where the speaker-actor is heading and approximately how much time it will take for her to come to completion. On the other hand, in the more ethnomethodological tradition, researchers have demonstrated the crucial relevance of timing of language use in environments such as airline cockpits (Nevile 2007), archaeological excavations (Goodwin 2002), offices (Hindmarsh & Heath 2000), and while driving in a car (Haddington & Keisanen 2009). Instructions, directives, announcements, and other verbal actions have to be precisely placed in

---

[1] The study was financed by Riksbankens Jubileumsfond's project "The bodily component of grammar" and profited from a generous research stay at the Center of Excellence in Intersubjectivity in Interaction, Helsinki University.

time in order to achieve adequate and safe physical action. Instruction in an embodied skill furthermore constitutes an interesting arena for indexicality, as the speaking actors regularly refer to their own bodies in action. This gives them simultaneous control of both the reference and the referent and requires especially fine-tuned coordination of the two. The tempo of talk and physical performance can be mutually adjusted and manipulated for pedagogical purposes.

In embodied instruction interesting patterns emerge in terms of the temporal coordination of language and the performing body (Weeks 1996; Haviland 2007; Keevallik 2013b; 2015). The current paper targets one of them: a pattern of two embodied performances combined by what we are used to considering essentially grammatical devices, namely conjunctions and prepositions. Conjunctions have been a major research topic in interactional linguistics and conversation analysis, since they regularly function as pragmatic markers that structure and project action. It has been demonstrated how conjunctions such as *because* (Couper-Kuhlen 1996) and *and* in English (Heritage & Sorjonen 1994) as well as complementizers such as *et* in Estonian and *et(tä)* in Finnish (Keevallik 2008; Laury & Seppänen 2008) combine actions within and across turns. Speakers deploy grammatical linking devices for specific interactional aims. Recently also the turn-final usage of conjunctions has been scrutinized, demonstrating their capacity to tacitly prompt inferences (Mulder & Thompson 2008; Koivisto 2012). Prepositions such as *than* can be used alone in a turn with the strategic aim to elicit a specific extension by a prior speaker (Koshik 2002: 291–298; Lerner 2004). Here we will look at instances where contrastive conjunctions and prepositions indeed project a continuation, but the projection is not realized in the stream of talk: they are followed by silence. Instead of operating on talk, these concise grammatical devices accomplish a relationship between two performances. They are indexically tied to the performing body.

Traditionally, deictics have been classified as linguistic items that achieve their meaning in time and space. It has been claimed that they commit a speaker to setting up a frame of reference around herself (Saeed 1997: 173), and that they anchor language in the real world by "pointing" at variables along some of its dimensions (Verschueren 1999: 18). The present paper argues that "pointing" is a broader affordance of grammar, showing that conjunctions and prepositions can be used indexically to pinpoint moments and events in time. The items presented here basically refer to the current movement by the body, therefore being parallel to time deixis, such as *now*, or space deixis, such as *here*, but additionally drawing attention to the specific bodily transition of proceeding to a contrastive performance.

Conjunctions are used in a number of ways in dance teaching. One regular pattern is the cross-linguistic use of 'and' to coordinate the start of a practice. In fact, the coordinating 'and' can be used in several kinds of physical actions, similar to the count 'one two three'. They can both be used to guarantee that the participants start moving or apply force simultaneously. Other conjunctions that occur in the dance data are *eller*, Swedish 'or', which is used to introduce an alternative, and *nii*, Estonian 'so', *så*, Swedish 'so', which are used to accomplish transfers between related subsections of an activity (Keevallik 2010b). The focus here will be on contrasting devices, such as *aga* 'but' in Estonian, *utan* 'but' and *istället för* 'instead of' in Swedish, and *instead of* in English.[2] The Estonian (and Finnish) data do not reveal a pattern that would correspond to 'instead of' in the other two languages. The paper aims to make a cross-linguistic argument showing that contrastive grammatical devices can be used at points where the demonstration currently performed by the body is undergoing a qualitative transition. Here, contrastive items are deployed not to combine clauses, as has been claimed in grammars for a long time, but to mark a shift in the communicative meaning of the evolving embodied performance. By closely looking at these linguistic-bodily patterns we see how grammar is intimately tied to the temporally unfolding multimodal interaction as well as to local sense-making here and now. Grammatical regularities are useful beyond talk and verbal modality.

When contrasting a correct and an incorrect movement in the dance classes there are basically two options: When the correct one has been presented, it is possible to go on to present the incorrect one as a contrast, or the other way round. This ordering of performances can make a pedagogical difference as well as a grammatical one, as will be shown in the Swedish data. Different linking items may work for different temporal orders in instructional settings. In the following, the two options and the actual consequences of the emerging bodily-verbal practice are discussed separately.

The data

The main body of the data comes from 38 hours of video recorded group classes of different kinds of dances: lindy hop, balboa, step, and ballet. The groups range from 6 to 60 students and there are altogether 17 teachers in the recordings. Three of the teachers speak in Estonian (9h) and these recordings were made in Estonia. The rest of the recordings were carried out in Sweden, where six teachers speak in Swedish (13h), and ten in English (15h). One teacher couple gives one class in Swedish and one in English; there is only one native speaker in the English data. All the teachers have signed a formal consent for the research purposes, and the camera as well as the analysis focuses on them. The students were informed orally (sometimes also by signs at the doors) at the beginning of every class and could opt out of the recording at any moment. As can be judged from the recordings, there are a range of differences between the pedagogical cultures in Estonia and Sweden. In the Swedish settings the teachers tend to talk and demonstrate simultaneously, while in the Estonian classes the teacher is often a commentating onlooker. As the practice described here involves the simultaneous deployment of language and the body, the Estonian teachers

---

2   Swedish and English make a wide use of prepositions, while Estonian and Finnish only have a few, and traditionally rely on postpositions.

do not use it as frequently. The collection includes 17 cases, but unfortunately there is only a single case in Estonian (presented below).

The complex actions in focus in the current study are accomplished either during joint practice in the dance class or during extended teacher turns, so-called instructive segments (Broth & Keevallik 2014). During these segments the students' bodily practice has been stopped, and the students are standing in lines or in a circle and watching the teacher(s). During these extended turns teachers may deal with a number of pedagogical issues. The syntactic-bodily structures that emerge may be either corrective or present new tasks for practice.

In addition to the main data, a relevant case in Finnish was found from the conversation corpus at the Helsinki Center of Excellence in Intersubjectivity in Interaction.[3] It comes from a one-to-one piano class that is organized in a different way in terms of turn-taking. The switches between the teacher and the students are much more frequent and flexible, as the teacher only has one student to attend to. In addition, playing the piano involves predominantly hands and arms, which is why instruction, at least in the current case, focuses on these body parts. The presentation of contrastive performances, however, displays identical linguistic practice deployed in real time.

Transition after incorrect performance

When instructing, dance teachers may perform a version of a dance or a step that is not recommended. This is often done in an exaggerated manner, as a caricature, in order to enhance the salience of the mistake for the observing students. At the completion of this incorrect version the teachers may opt to continue by showing the correct one. This will be illustrated in the current section of the paper.

In excerpt (1) a lindy hop teacher couple performs an incorrect version of a step called Side-by-Side Charleston in lines 2–6. During the performance the partners are visibly disengaged from each other, they slouch and stare straight ahead, as shown in Figure 1. The male teacher who performs the lead dancer role (Lead) assesses the current behavior as *inte så mycket att föredra* 'not really preferable'. He then introduces the contrasting version by uttering *utan* 'but', which is the grammatically required conjunction after a negative clause in Swedish. He simultaneously turns his gaze to his partner, as shown in Figure 2. During the second version of the dance step the partners are proudly looking at each other, producing appreciative sounds (lines 12, 14). They snap to the rhythm of the dance and perform a perfectly engaged version of Side-by-Side Charleston.

Transcription conventions can be found in the front matter of the volume. Figures are marked with # and number in the transcript.

---

3   The author is indebted to Aino Koivisto for finding this case.

(1) Swedish conjunction *utan* 'but'

```
1  Lead:    gör  man  Side-+by-Side  Charleston.
            does one  NAME           NAME
            if you do Side-by-Side Charleston
                          +connects with partner

2           *(0.3)
            *incorrect performance*

3  Lead:    så kanske -
            so probably
            probably -

4           (0.3)

5  Lead:    det här är då   kanske inte#1 så mycket att föredra:.
            this is then maybe    not     so much   to  prefer
            this is probably not to be preferr:ed really.

6           (0.4)*

7  Lead:    +utan+,
            but
            +turns head toward F+

8           *(0.7)
            *correct performance ((continues throughout the excerpt))

9  Follow:  mmm, ((snap in the middle))

10 Lead:    #2ex:ak:t.
            ex:ac:tly.

11          (0.7)

12 Lead:    uh,

13          (0.2)

14 Follow:  haa
```

Figure 1 – line 5

Figure 2 – line 10

The incorrect version is performed during lines 2–6. The correct one starts on line 8 and continues beyond the end of the extract. The dancing is constant and the rhythm is maintained throughout. The contrastive conjunction is produced at the boundary between the two versions. Notably, the eight-beat step sequence called Side-by-Side Charleston is repeated three times during the excerpt and the switch to a preferable version is done in the middle of the second one. Thus, the conjunction is not actually produced at a step boundary, it is occasioned by the pedagogical project and finely timed to the change in dance style. The lead utters *utan* at exactly the moment when he transforms his performance by straightening up his body and turning his gaze to his partner, prompting her to do the same. A professional follow dancer can adjust to this almost immediately, thus achieving a change in the middle of the step pattern. The conjunction is thus applied at a relatively more abstract pedagogical project level, one that is not closely tied to the temporality and the logic of the dance. The teachers then produce appreciative *response cries* (Goffman 1981: 78–122) in lines 9, 12, and 14 while dancing in the recommended engaged style.

Importantly, there is no syntactic projection of further action at the end of line 5. The grammatical sentence has come to an end and the dance could be stopped, since the target step has already been performed once by that time. At that point the action sequence could evolve in a different direction, even though it is apparent that the instructive segment is not yet complete. There is some projection on the level of action; the teachers have not come to the completion of their extended turn but they could as well continue with additional demonstrations of sloppy performances, an invitation to the students to do something different, etc. The syntactic continuation initiated by *utan* is technically an increment, an add-on (Couper-Kuhlen & Ono 2007: 515). It is grammatically fitted to the prior and accomplishes a continuation, but it was not projected. At the same time, the teachers continue to dance.

Dance has a temporal structure of its own: it creates a rhythm that can persist for extended periods of time, and talk may be adjusted to this rhythm. In the current case, however, instructive talk simultaneously structures the dance demonstration. By indexing the contrastive performance with a contrastive conjunction, the dance is projected to proceed for a while, so that the contrast can be appreciated by the observers. In a verbal-only interaction in Swedish, the word *utan* would have projected another clause in this particular construction. In excerpt (1), there is no clause that follows but the unit of action is nevertheless not perceived as incomplete. The embodied performance brings it to a completion and the entire pattern results in a comprehensible whole. This is a recurrent practice in the instruction of embodied skills: units can be brought to completion by means of bodily demonstrations (Keevallik 2013b).

The first thing to notice about the above contrastive bodily displays is that language is used while the body is in mid-action. A contrastive item is uttered at the point when the body is already initiating the contrastive performance. In excerpt (1) the couple straightened up and brought their gaze to meet each other during the conjunction. The conjunction indexes a moment in time when the embodied performance is changing. This furthermore underlines the incremental emergence of grammar, as structure is built element-by-element while the participants are accomplishing actions also with their bodies. Grammar here emerges as a meta-comment on how to interpret what can be visibly perceived. It addresses the risk that visible information may not be sufficient or salient, as this is an instructive setting where not all the students possess expert vision yet. The conjunction functions as a signal on how to parse and understand the teachers' demonstration.

Excerpt (2) comes from the middle of joint practice in lindy hop. The students are trying out different styling of a step called Shake, and they move around the circle with the teachers performing in the middle. The lead teacher is explaining some playful variations of the step and encouraging students to explore the possibilities, as the ideology of the dance lindy hop encourages individual improvisation. He raises his shoulders high in line 1 while the students continue to practice, and some try out the suggested shoulder position. The lead then demonstrates the default position for the shoulders during lines 3–4, Figure 3, at the same time commenting that this is not always a recommendable posture (in the transcript it is nevertheless called "incorrect" for the sake of consistency throughout the paper). At the end of the pause in line 4 he bends his body forward, which implies the shoulders being as low as possible (as shown in Figure 4), and utters *utan* 'but' in this new recommended position. At the same time his hand finishes a fall to the knees.

(2) Swedish conjunction *utan* 'but'

```
1  Lead:   så våga      å    lek      med axlarna  också.
           so  dare:IMP  and  play:IMP with shoulders too
           so dare to play around with the shoulders too.

2          (0.9)

3  Lead:   +så att   de+  *inte  alltid  är   #3här.
           so  that  they  not   always  are  here
           so that they would not always be here.
           +lowers shoulders+
                          *incorrect performance*

4          (1.2)*+(0.4)
                +bends down, hand down+

5  Lead:   utan,+
           but
           but

6          *(2.7)#4*
           *correct performance*
```

```
7  Lead:    >ta     +med dem,<+ å  när man kommer upp  hit
            take:IMP along them     and when one come   up   here
            bring them along, and if you come up here
                    +raises the body+

8           så  kanske man  tar  upp  dem.
            PRT maybe  one  raise     them
            you may raise them.
```

Figure 3 – line 3   Figure 4 – line 6

Similar to excerpt (1), the syntactic-bodily unit before *utan* is brought to a close here. Line 3 is syntactically complete and the deictic *här* 'here' refers to the simultaneous shoulder position, which is also extended for quite a while into the pause. *Här* can thus also be understood as projecting the embodied demonstration. In any case, there is nothing at the end of line 3 or during 4 that would syntactically or pragmatically project a continuation beyond the current demonstration, especially because at least one recommendable variation has already been performed (in line 1). Nevertheless, the incipient structure initiated by *utan* is syntactically and semantically dependent on the prior (multimodal) unit. It is a type of continuation of the multimodal turn-constructional unit, an add-on. *Utan* indexes precisely the moment when the body can be observed to start doing something new. During the ensuing pause in talk the projection is realized by another embodied demonstration, a hunched version of the Shake. The syntactic-bodily unit is brought to a completion by the embodied performance during the pause in line 6.

The teacher shows the recommended Shake three times, and at the very end of the third time he glosses his current demonstration as *ta med dem* 'bring them (i.e., the shoulders) along'. Even though the anaphoric *dem* 'them' refers back to shoulders, this clause is not grammatically fitted to the earlier syntactic structure *så att de inte alltid är här utan* 'so that they would not always be here but'. Furthermore, 'bring them along' is produced quicker and lower than the talk before and after it, lending it a more parenthetical character. In any case, the talk in line 7 is not a continuation of any previous syntactic structure, and the focus of our interest, the conjunction *utan*, emerges as an index of the contrast between two embodied objects. The pattern with the contrastive conjunction ends up being a grammatically complete complex clause combination. However, the pattern includes bodily as well as spoken elements. Hence it is a multimodal complex structure involving two parts, both of them syntactic-bodily units. This structure is complete before the independent gloss that follows.

The conjunction is uttered during a transition between the two versions of the step, at a moment when the teacher has already bent his body slightly forward. He is on his way to the position that he is about to demonstrate but nevertheless performs a Shake in this mid-position to retain the rhythm of everybody's practice in the hall. The contrasting demonstrations are thus through-performed; the teacher continues to practice together with the students all through the excerpt while he changes the position of his shoulders from very high to very low. Language is used as a commentary and interpretive contextualization device that draws the students' attention to how the teacher's simultaneous embodied performance should be understood.

In the current Swedish data *utan* is only used to index a transition from incorrect to correct performance. This may well be a coincidence but it may also be related to the grammatical fact that the clause before *utan* has to be negated. *Utan* thus may well be a device for this specific type of transition from incorrect to correct in instructional activities. More generally, its meaning emerges in the temporal evolvement of actions: when an incorrect version is complete, there is an option to show a contrastive exemplar. To introduce this, the grammatical structure with a contrastive conjunction can be used. After or during the demonstration the speaker-performer can optionally comment on it, either in a grammatically fitting manner or not. By describing grammar in these terms, we adhere to a truly temporal and incremental understanding of language.

Example (3) is in Estonian and comes from a ballet class. The class is taught by a single teacher. In the example, she corrects the students after she has seen them perform an exercise at the barre in a slower and quicker version. The teacher first contextualizes the problem to *kui on kiire* 'when it is quick' and then demonstrates the incorrect version of a forward bend in lines 2–3, starting on *siis* 'then', finishing just before *selliseks* 'like this'. The demonstration of a sloppily arched spine (shown in Figure 5) continues into the pause. After 'like this', the utterance is syntactically complete and the teacher has also taken down her hand, as shown in the transcript (line 4). Only non-final prosody indicates that she may continue. The correct version of the bend is initiated on *aga* 'but' in line 4. The teacher starts to bend forward again, this time with a straight spine, as can be seen in Figure 6.

(3) Estonian conjunction *aga* 'but'

```
1  Teacher:   et    kui   on       kiire,  all:a:  (.)  üles, (.)
              that  when  be:3SG   quick   down         up
              when it is quick, dow:n: (.) up, (.)

2             et    *siis   ta   ei    läheks         natukeseks
              PRT   then    it   NEG   become:COND    little:TRA
              it should not become a little
```

```
3          (0.7)#5*
           *incorrect performance*

4          +selliseks+,    *aga:,
           like.this:TRA   but
           like this, but:,
           +hand down+

5          (1.5)#6
           *correct performance*

6          hoitud*,        a+ga  k+iire.
           control:PAS:PPC but   quick
           controlled but quick.
                                 +strike +strike
```

Figure 5 – line 3   Figure 6 – line 5

Similar to earlier examples, the turn continuation initiated by *aga* 'but' is not realized verbally. Instead, *aga* contextualizes the just initiated performance as a contrast to the prior, thus the correct one. The subsequent description *hoitud aga kiire* 'controlled but quick' that starts during the last part of the performance in line 6 is not grammatically fitted to the preceding syntactic structure. It nevertheless builds on earlier information, as it does not specify a subject or a full predicate. It contains only adjectives that describe the correct version. Simultaneously with the adjectives, the teacher raises her hands to the two beat gestures. The teacher has thereby stopped the bodily performance and now reassigns the body a subservient role in relation to the talk.

These power transformations between the talk and the body are recurrent in the multiactivity of teaching and dancing in dance classes, where an embodied activity is the subject of instruction. In contrast to the first two cases, the demonstrations in excerpt (3) are not accomplished during the ongoing dance but are fitted to the instructive talk by the teacher. Rhythm is not maintained in the excerpt. On the contrary, the teacher even slows down during the correct performance to enhance the observability of the 'controlled' nature of the movement. The emerging pattern is similar to the Swedish *utan* use: both contrastive conjunctions *utan* and *aga* index the just-beginning contrastive demonstration. However, there are no restrictions as to the polarity of the first clause for the Estonian *aga*.

Finally, the Finnish *vaan* 'but' can be used in a similar way to *utan*: it is deployed after negative clauses as a 'corrective conjunction' (Hakulinen et al. 2004: 1051–1052). Excerpt (4) shows two consecutive instances from a piano class. The teacher and the student are sitting at separate pianos. Unfortunately their hands are hidden from the camera, so the gestures can only be inferred from moving shoulders. The teacher has just criticized a note played by the student and in line 1 he explicitly advises against a hand movement that the student has done. On *viä* 'move/take' his hand moves, apparently in an incorrect manner. The student's initiation of playing is proof that also the contrastive correct version has been performed during line 3.

(4) Finnish conjunction *vaan* 'but'

```
1  Teacher:  s- (.) ä- älä   ny  ↑viä   sitä tänne sitä kättä
                    don't now take  this there this  hand:PAR
                    don't take the hand there

2             (0.2) >vaan<,
                    but

3             (0.2) ((shows the move without the piano))

4  Stud:      ((tests the movement by playing))

5  Teacher:  >kato<  (0.2)  se    mitä    mä  en      tee on
             look:IMP:2SG   that  what:PAR I  NEG:1SG do  is
             look (0.2) what I don't do is

6             et    mä   käännän  ranteen   (.)  >vaan<,
              that  I    twist:1SG wrist:GEN       but
              to twist the wrist (.) but

7             ((plays [2 sek.))

8  Stud:      [((plays 3 sek.))

9  Teacher:  mä   ↑avaan    (0.4)  ↑ton,
             I    open:1SG         that:GEN
             I open it.
```

However, the teacher is not satisfied and goes on with further instruction in lines 5–6. Again, he first produces a negative statement describing the incorrect wrist movement and then contrasts it with the correct one. This time the gloss of the correct movement in line 9 is syntactically matched to the previous syntax. Even though the precise timing of the demonstrations is inaccessible in this recording, the general contrastive performance pattern seems to be the same. The import of what is to be done is clear before the teacher's gloss, as the student starts playing (line 8) and implementing the advice already after the teacher's embodied demonstration (line 7).

We can thus see across three languages that contrastive conjunctions are used at transitions to a contrastive demonstration. In cases where we can judge the exact timing from the video recording, the conjunction is deployed precisely when the contrastive performance is launched. Uttering the conjunction is timed with the body moving into the demonstration. The prosody on the conjunction is always continuative, projecting more to come. There is no cut-off, however, which would mean that the unit is abandoned. In hindsight the structure that emerges is as follows (Figure 7): the body goes from incorrect to correct performance, with an optional transition period in between (such as moving into the new position); the talk has to contextualize the first performance as the incorrect one and then mark the beginning of the contrastive performance with a 'but'. The conjunction can be uttered during the transition or at the initiation of the correct movement. Pauses are possible before and after the conjunction, depending on the rhythm and nature of the performance. Thus, the temporal development of the entire complex structure is defined here by the performing body rather than language.

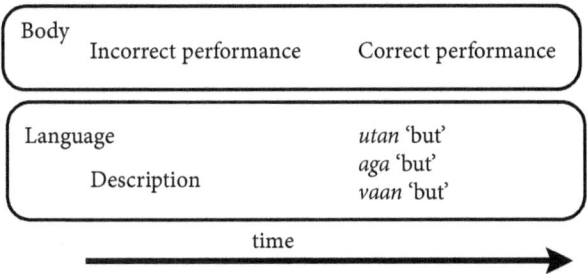

Figure 7

The whole gestalt must also be contextualized in relation to the ongoing task for dance practice. This may either be done before or during the first performance. The second performance can be accompanied by silence but it is also possible to gloss it simultaneously or after its termination, which was shown in excerpts (2, 3). The contrastive conjunction is regularly deployed at the beginning of the correct version, immediately classifying the incipient performance in terms of correctness and recommendability in contrast to what has been going on so far. The conjunction is therefore an account for what the body is performing, thus reflexive of the embodied action and explanatory for the students. Grammatical elements are used for indexing the temporal emergence of embodied action.

Transition after correct performance

There is an alternative pattern of contrasting performances that emerges when a correct performance is presented first. In the current data the incorrect performances that follow are all initiated with contrastive prepositions, English *instead of* or Swedish *istället för* 'instead of'.

In excerpt (5) the teacher illustrates the relevance of a strong body and strong arms during spinning in lindy hop. The correct performance is initiated during the deictic *såhär* 'like this' and terminated at the end of line 2. A student's response token *mm* in line 3 indicates that the instruction can be heard and seen as complete at this point, because it is produced with "agreeing" prosody. There is no projection of continuation; the result of correct tight posture during spinning has already been illustrated (Figure 8). During the preposition *istället för*, which initiates a turn increment, the teacher takes a couple of preparatory steps, and the incorrect performance starts on the beat after it. This performance is terminated when the teacher adds a tag *eller hur* 'isn't it?/true?'. With this addition she makes clear that the prior structure consisting of a preposition and an embodied performance is indeed complete.

(5) Swedish preposition *istället för* 'instead of'

```
1  Teacher:  (när)vi snurrar så blir resul+tatet så*här,
             when  we spin    so be:FUT result:DEF   like.this
             when we spin, the result is like this
                                                +preparation for the spin

2            (1.0)#8*
             *correct performance (spin)*



3  StudF:    mm,=

4  Teacher:  =+istället för,+
              instead of
             +regular dance steps+

5            *(2.8)#9*
             *incorrect performance: preparation and spin*

6  StudM:    ((unintelligible, starts slightly before and overlaps with the teacher))

7  Teacher:  eller +hur, det blir  jätteskillnad,visst [blir  det det.]
             or    how  it  be:FUT huge.difference sure  become it  this
             true? it makes a huge difference, right?
                   +last step

8  StudF:                                                  [((        ))]
```

Figure 8 – line 2

Figure 9 – line 5

The preposition *istället för* is used to launch the incorrect performance in contrast to what has been going on so far, the demonstration of a strong correct posture. Similar to the contrastive conjunctions above, this preposition functions as an index that the body is currently launching a different action. In the second performance the teacher's arms are hanging sloppily and her body is limp, as shown in Figure 9. For pedagogical salience the contrastive preposition is essential. *Istället för* is designedly incomplete and projects a continuation, claiming temporal space after it. This space is filled with an embodied demonstration.

The preposition *instead of* expresses contrast but more specifically suggests replacement of one element with another (on Swedish *istället för*, see, e.g., Teleman et al. 1999: 714). *Instead of* introduces the versions of performance that are to be suppressed and avoided by the students. Like conjunctions, this preposition-like contrastive marker can project a clausal or a phrasal unit in talk, depending on its context. At least in the data for this study, there does not seem to be any regularity in the performance itself in regard to whether it is framed as a "clause" or a "phrase". I therefore suggest that demonstrations, especially embodied ones, constitute a separate category with their own grammatical systematics. They can be projected by certain syntactic structures and incorporated into the syntagmatic structure of turns in idiosyncratic ways (Keevallik 2013b; 2014; see also Jääskeläinen 2013, who makes similar arguments on imitatives in the written language).

When it comes to the dual use of the human body, embodied demonstration and language production, there are other aspects that do not match the logic of verbal-only behavior. As can be observed in line 1 in the last extract (5), the performance starts slightly early during ongoing talk. This possibility for simultaneous production of speech and movement is an affordance that is different from merely verbal interaction, where sounds, words, and clauses by a single speaker have to be produced in a linear fashion. Accordingly, the contrastive preposition in line 4 is uttered in overlap with the steps in between the two performances. In this way, the grammatical device initiates a juxtaposed version and projects it during steps that are not yet demonstrating anything relevant for the pedagogical project at hand. Finally, the evaluating talk in line 7 starts in overlap with the very last steps of the incorrect performance. The teacher is already raising her hands to a gesture that supports her talk, and this is clearly not part of the dance. In short, it is possible to layer the demonstrating body and the discussing, describing, and juxtaposing oral channel in a variety of ways, only a subsection of which is the focus of the current study.

Lastly, there is a very similar case of *instead of* from a lindy hop class in English (excerpt 6).[4] The teacher here is explaining that a lead into a dance turn should be subtle. He is using a metaphor for that, *asking her* in line 1. On *ask-* he prepares the first performance by taking and lifting the follow teacher's hand. The lead into the Tuck-turn is carried out during line 3 (shown in Figure 10) and the follow accomplishes the turn during the pause. After

---

4   This case may be modeled on Swedish, as the teacher is a non-native speaker of English.

this demonstration the gestalt is complete and the couple almost comes to a standstill. Then the lead teacher launches into a contrasting performance by uttering *instead of* and at the same time preparing for another demonstration of a Tuck-turn, as shown in line 5. The first audible student reaction in line 7 is timed with the demonstration of the deficient lead, while the follow still has to go through with her turn. The turning itself is not the pedagogical focus here.

(6) English preposition *instead of*

```
1  Lead:    but I'm +only asking her,
                    +preparatory moves+

2           (0.3)+*(0.2)

3           would you do a #10Tuck-turn?

4           (1.5)*
                 *correct performance*

5           +instead of+,
            +preparatory moves+

6           *(3.1)#11

7  Stud:    mm,

8           (0.6)*
                 *incorrect performance*

9  Lead:    yeah,=

10 Stud:    =((laughter))
```

Figure 10 – line 3   Figure 11 – line 6

Characteristically for this activity setting, the incorrect version is done in an exaggerated manner, as a caricature (Figure 11), and an adequate response to a caricature is laughter. This is indeed what follows the demonstration. At the same time, the laughter is evidence of the students' understanding that the syntactic-bodily gestalt was complete, despite its rudimentary grammar. The gestalt is perceived as consisting of the preposition in combination with the preceding and following embodied demonstrations.

In summary, the general pattern of preposition use here is the same as the one involving conjunctions above. The prepositions index the moment in time when the body launches into a contrastive performance. Again, the temporality of the structure is defined by the body, i.e., the dance, and not the talk itself, provoking us to reconsider the role of grammar. The significant difference from the conjunction pattern is a reverse order of correct and incorrect performances. This has been schematically depicted in Figure 12.

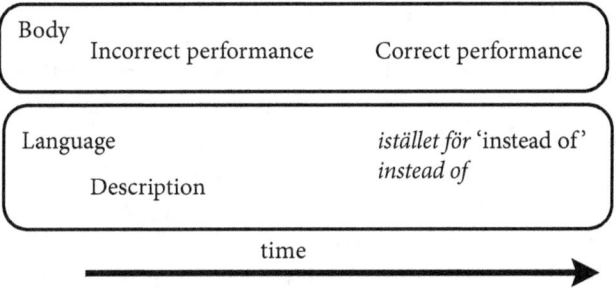

Figure 12

Indeed, there are instances in the current data with complex syntactic structures produced during the contrasted performances. Considerably longer projective segments of grammar may be used in transfers to incorrect performances, such as *det är inte* 'it's not', and *så att det inte blir*, Swe. 'so that it would not be'. Occasionally the teachers talk all the way through the complex bodily performances. However, even in these cases the contrastive items are timed with the changes in the body, they index a moment defined by the acting body. Thus, conjunctions and prepositions seem to work very similarly to deictic items that index space and time. They collaborate with the body to produce meaningful precision-timed action. When a correct performance is terminated and framed as the right thing to do, the speaker-actor can continue to present a contrast, which will inevitably be the incorrect one. 'Instead of' is one linguistic practice for locally indexing exactly that.

Conclusion

This paper argues for the temporal nature of grammar, looking at how a multimodal complex structure emerges in an embodied activity context in real time. Contrastive conjunctions and prepositions are usable for making a transition to a contrastive content, be it expressed in language or by the body. In fact, they regularly link clausal constructions with upcoming embodied actions, hence linking clause and action. It is shown how contrastive items are deployed in a timely manner, building emergent structures that involve both the grammar and the body. The contrastive items are uttered at the very moment when the second performance is incipient or already underway. They are used to index that the contribution of the body will from now on be contrasted with the prior, with what has been going on thus far.

Linear grammar can be layered with the evolving bodily performance in many ways. Embodied demonstrations are sometimes performed simultaneously and sometimes interchangeably with grammatical items. The contrastive items studied in this paper index relevant moments in the demonstrations. Conjunctions and prepositions are studied here in the versions where they project a continuation, and the projection is realized by the body. Grammar as a temporal phenomenon enables structures that cross-cut verbal and embodied modalities of sense-making. Many other grammatical items, in particular the conjunctions 'and', 'so', and 'but', could be studied in regard to their ability to coordinate emerging grammar with embodied actions in dance classes. Among the prepositions, 'from' is used to project a definition of one step out of a longer sequence in the dance. Ultimately, the above analysis shows how in real-life, real-time interaction, a paradigm of similarly behaving contrastive items may involve items that have traditionally been classified into different word-class paradigms, as either conjunctions or prepositions.

The choice between a conjunction and a preposition is not based on any internal rules of grammar in these instances, but on temporal considerations within the framework of the pedagogical activity. Teachers regularly perform both correct and incorrect versions to visualize mistakes, and the choice of the transition marker between these two depends on whether the just terminated performance was correct or incorrect. In case it was correct it can now be pedagogically enhanced by a contrastive caricature, and in case it was incorrect it has to be followed by a better illustration of the dance. The choice of the item is determined by the pedagogical task of the upcoming performance. By focusing on contrastive items the paper points to the indexicality of the lexicon beyond deictics and shows how these items firmly anchor the speech in the embodied behavior of an interacting human being.

References

Auer, Peter. 2009. On-line syntax: Thoughts on the temporality of spoken language. *Language Sciences* 31(1): 1–13.

Broth, Mathias & Leelo Keevallik. 2014. Getting ready to move as a couple: Accomplishing mobile formations in a dance class. *Space and Culture* 17(2): 107–121.

Couper-Kuhlen, Elizabeth. 1996. Intonation and clause combining in discourse: The case of because. *Pragmatics* 6(3): 389–426.

Couper-Kuhlen, Elizabeth & Tsuyoshi Ono. 2007. 'Incrementing' in conversation. A comparison of practices in English, German and Japanese. *Pragmatics* 17(4): 513–552.

Goffman, Erving. 1981. *Forms of talk*. Philadelphia: University of Pennsylvania Press.

Goodwin, Charles. 2002. Time in action. *Current Anthropology* 43: 19–35.

Haddington, Pentti & Tiina Keisanen. 2009. Location, mobility and the body as resources in selecting a route. *Journal of Pragmatics* 41(10): 1938–1961.

Hakulinen, Auli, Maria Vilkuna, Riitta Korhonen, Vesa Koivisto, Tarja Heinonen & Irja Alho. 2004. *Iso suomen kielioppi* [The comprehensive grammar of Finnish]. Helsinki: Finnish Literature Society.

Haviland, John B. 2007. Master speakers, master gesturers: A string quartet master class. In Susan D. Duncan, Elena T. Levy & Justine Cassell (eds.), *Gesture and the dynamic dimension of language: Essays in honor of David McNeill*. 147–172. Amsterdam/Philadelphia: John Benjamins.

Heritage, John & Marja-Leena Sorjonen. 1994. Constituting and maintaining activities across sequences: *And*-prefacing as a feature of question design. *Language in Society* 23(1): 1–29.

Hindmarsh, Jon & Christian Heath. 2000. Embodied reference: A study of deixis in workplace interaction. *Journal of Pragmatics* 32(12): 1855–1878.

Jääskeläinen, Anni. 2013. *Todisteena äänen kuva: Suomen kielen imitatiivikonstruktiot*. Ph.D. dissertation. University of Helsinki, Department of Finnish, Finno-Ugrian and Scandinavian Studies.

Keevallik, Leelo. 2008. Clause combining and sequenced actions: The Estonian complementizer and pragmatic particle et. In Ritva Laury (ed.), *Crosslinguistic studies of clause combining: The multifunctionality of conjunctions*. 125–152. Amsterdam/Philadelphia: John Benjamins.

Keevallik, Leelo. 2010a. Bodily quoting in dance correction. *Research on Language and Social Interaction* 43(4): 1–26.

Keevallik, Leelo. 2010b. Pro-adverbs of manner as markers of activity transition. *Studies in Language* 34(2): 350–381.

Keevallik, Leelo. 2013a. Decomposing dance movement and spatial deixis. In Pentti Haddington, Lorenza Mondada & Maurice Nevile (eds.), *Interaction and mobility: Language and the body in motion*. 345–370. Berlin/Boston: Walter De Gruyter.

Keevallik, Leelo. 2013b. The interdependence of bodily demonstrations and clausal syntax. *Research on Language and Social Interaction* 46(1): 1–21.

Keevallik, Leelo. 2014. Turn organization and bodily-vocal demonstrations. *Journal of Pragmatics* 65: 103–120.

Keevallik, Leelo. 2015. Coordinating the temporalities of talk and dance. In Arnulf Deppermann & Susanne Günthner (eds.), *Temporality in interaction*. 309–336. Amsterdam/Philadelphia: John Benjamins.

Koivisto, Aino. 2012. Discourse patterns for turn-final conjunctions. *Journal of Pragmatics* 44(10): 1254–1272.

Koshik, Irene. 2002. Designedly incomplete utterances: a pedagogical practice for eliciting knowledge displays in error correction sequences. *Research on Language and Social Interaction* 35(3): 277–309.

Laury, Ritva & Eeva-Leena Seppänen. 2008. Clause combining, interaction, evidentiality, participation structure, and the conjunction-particle continuum: The Finnish *että*. In Ritva Laury (ed.), *Crosslinguistic studies of clause combining: The multifunctionality of conjunctions*. 153–178. Amsterdam/Philadelphia: John Benjamins.

Lerner, Gene H. 2004. On the place of linguistic resources in the organization of talk-in-interaction: Grammar as action in prompting a speaker to elaborate. *Research on Language and Social Interaction* 37(2): 151–184.

Mulder, Jean & Sandra A. Thompson. 2008. The grammaticalization of 'but' as a final particle in English conversation. In Ritva Laury (ed.), *Crosslinguistic studies of clause combining: The multifunctionality of conjunctions*. 179–204. Amsterdam/Philadelphia: John Benjamins.

Nevile, Maurice. 2007. Action in time: Ensuring timeliness for collaborative work in the airline cockpit. *Language in Society* 36(2): 233–257.

Saeed, John I. 1997. *Semantics*. Oxford/Cambridge: Blackwell Publishers.

Teleman, Ulf, Staffan Hellberg & Erik Andersson (eds.). 1999. *Svenska akademiens grammatik* [Grammar of the swedish academy]. Stockholm: Nordstedt.

Verschueren, Jef. 1999. *Understanding pragmatics*. London: Arnold.

Weeks, Peter. 1996. A rehearsal of a Beethoven passage: An analysis of correction talk. *Research on Language and Social Interaction* 29(3): 247–290.

Linking of questions and answers II

Katariina Harjunpää
http://orcid.org/0000-0002-4586-1563

3. Mediated questions in multilingual conversation: Organizing participation through question design[1]

Introduction

This paper examines how speakers mediate questions from one language into another in multilingual conversations in Finnish and Brazilian Portuguese. When mediating others' questions, speakers engage in what is referred to as *bilingual brokering, ad hoc interpreting,* or *translation* of other's talk (Auer 1984a; Müller 1989; Tse 1996; Greer 2008; Del Torto 2008; Wilton 2009; Traverso 2012; Bolden 2012; Merlino 2012; Merlino & Mondada 2013; 2014; Kolehmainen et al. 2015). These mediators are lay bilinguals, not professional interpreters, and as the term *ad hoc* suggests, the mediating does not permeate the whole interactional event, but is only resorted to occasionally, and the need to mediate is locally negotiated (e.g., Müller 1989). Thus, in this context, the practices for mediating emerge endogenously from and within the unfolding courses of action (see Merlino & Mondada 2013; 2014).

The present study investigates the organization of mediating in the specific environment of asking questions in multilingual everyday conversation. In the cases examined, a speaker uses another language to redo a request for information or confirmation made by another speaker. This paper examines the unfolding of the action phase-by-phase. This includes how the speaker and recipient(s) orient to each other, what motivates their redoing of the question, and in particular, what type of pragmatic relations are established between the mediated questions and the prior question turns.

While the mediated questions address the recipient's lack of access to prior talk, they also embody a process of incorporating a prior speaker's talk in one's utterance (see C. Goodwin 2007). Taking a position as a relayer, or "translator", of others' words is yet a further, local interactional accomplishment (e.g., Merlino & Mondada 2014). To analyze the process at the level of conversational structures, the mediated questions are examined in terms of how they are designed as repetitions, or *resayings* of prior talk (see Sacks 1995: I 722; Schegloff 2004; Oh 2005; Rauniomaa 2008). The

[1] I would like to thank the editors of this volume and the anonymous reviewers for their valuable comments on earlier versions of this paper. The study has been supported by the Finland Distinguished Professor project "Grammar and Interaction: the linking of actions in speech and writing", funded by the Academy of Finland, and the Langnet Doctoral Programme. The research has been conducted within the Centre of Excellence in Research on Intersubjectivity in Interaction at the University of Helsinki.

particular type of resayings examined here involve switching the language and redoing an action that was initiated by another participant. The analysis focuses on how the turns are linked to their sources at the level of turn-design, action, and participation framework.

Let us consider the following question in Finnish and its resaying in Portuguese (extract 1) (for further analysis, see ex. 6):

(1) Ticket.FI

```
01 Raili:   kuinka +paljon  se  (.) maksaa    se   matka sielt
            how    much     DEM3    cost.3SG  DEM3 trip  there.from
            how much does it cost the trip from
                    +ANDRÉ RAISES HIS HEAD, TURNS GAZE>RAILI

02          Brasiliasta    tänne   (0.2)  edestakasi.
            [name].ELA     LOC.to         back.and.forth
            Brazil to here, and back

03          (1.0)

04 Sanna:   .mt quanto     é         pas↓sagem,
                how.much   be.3SG    ticket
                how much is ticket

05 André:   aam.  (0.6)  hh tuhat  (2.0)  kaksisataa.  (0.6)  euroa.
            ahn, (one) thousand, two hundred, euros
```

When André does not respond, Sanna steps in to render Raili's question understandable for André by producing a short and simple version of it in Portuguese. The position and composition of Sanna's turn also contribute to its being hearable as a translation of Raili's talk. The upcoming analyses of how this type of action is accomplished are concerned with question design, the relation of the first and second question, and the means of organizing participation. A distinction is made here between resayings that are designed to be heard as another *first* occasion of asking and those that are linked as a *second* saying of a question, as in the example under consideration. These distinct means to mediate questions relate in different ways to the prior speaker's action, reflecting different participation frameworks in the trajectory of the question.

Data and participants

The data consist of a total of 17 question–answer sequences involving a resaying of the question by a speaker other than the original questioner. The database has been created by collecting all these sequences from four video recordings (1.5–4 hours each, for a total of 9 hours) that were conducted in Finland and Brazil. The recordings consist of casual conversations with 4 to 13 participants which either occur at someone's home or at some other familiar place. These data have been extracted from a larger corpus of interactions in Finnish and Brazilian Portuguese.

The participants in each recording come from different cultural backgrounds. In fact, at least one participant is either not a fluent speaker of the languages used in the conversation, or does not speak one of the languages at all. Some of the participants also join the encounter as guests or visitors, relatively unknown to the hosts. This means that the data represent many features of both an intercultural encounter and a host-visitor setting. The person acting as a mediator in this data is usually a fluent bilingual and a key person in that s/he knows most of the participants and has been influential in organizing the gathering. However, others may sometimes engage in facilitating the interaction, as well.

To assist the reader, when presenting the participants a rough coding of linguistic repertoires has been provided. The participants' competences in Finnish and Portuguese are evaluated as fluent/some/none. Following the order of a first and second/other language, the capital letters F and P stand for fluent or good in Finnish and Portuguese respectively, and the small letters f and p refer to some skill in these languages. Moreover, some participants have a minus (-) after their small letter, which indicates only very basic skills in this language. As an illustration, Gaia (P/f) means that Gaia is a native Brazilian Portuguese speaker who knows some Finnish. When a participant does not speak the language at all, no letter is provided. It is noteworthy that when this occurs, the speaker is not a "non-native speaker", but simply not a speaker of a certain language. To distinguish the languages in the transcripts, stretches of talk in Finnish are written in italics. Morphological glosses are provided for focus turns. In addition, to ensure anonymity, the names of all the participants have been changed in the transcripts.

This study examines translatory turns both in Finnish and Portuguese, focusing on aspects of the verbal design of turns. Other features in the design of actions, such as embodied conduct, and especially gaze, are transcribed selectively and discussed in more detail when crucial for the analysis.

Coordinating participation in multiparty, multilingual interaction

Studies on interpreting in institutional settings have shown that while rendering talk in another language between the main participants, the interpreter engages in various types of coordinating work (e.g., Wadensjö 1998; Bolden 2000; Baraldi & Gavioli 2012; Merlino & Mondada 2013; Raymond 2014). Coordinating the interaction involves remedying the ruptures that occur in the unfolding of the conversation and in the participants' common ground. The lack of a shared language is intertwined with matters such as asymmetries related to the participants' institutional roles. Bridging the gaps involves varying ways of translation as well as distinct patterns of turn-taking and sequential organization that are typical of translatory interaction. An example of these is the dyadic clarification sequences between the interpreter and either of the main participants before translating (Bolden 2000)[2].

---

2   On patterns of turn-taking and sequential organization in interpreter-mediated interaction, see, e.g., Knapp & Knapp-Potthoff 1987, Müller 1989, Wadensjö 1998, Bolden 2000, Davidson 2002, and Baraldi & Gavioli 2012.

In contrast to the pre-arranged mode of interaction in the institutional setting, mediating in the mundane multilingual setting emerges within the unfolding of a casual multiparty conversation. The organization of turn-taking/allocation and recipient design in a multiparty situation is inherently complex (for example, see Sacks et al. 1974; C. Goodwin 1981; 1987; Egbert 1997; Lerner 2003; Mondada 2004; 2007), and it may involve further complexities in an asymmetric language constellation, as the participants have unevenly distributed opportunities to participate. The situation may engender particular mediating practices. For example, Bolden (2012) demonstrates that linguistic expertise allows "bilingual brokers" to step in and provide a repair solution in place of the trouble-turn speaker.

When participants ask and answer questions in the multilingual constellation, they may encounter difficulties both in addressing particular recipients and in acting as a recipient due to the lack of shared resources as well as to an asymmetric access to the on-going conversation. Moreover, there are often multiple potential recipients, some more easily available than others. For these reasons, mediating questions may involve additional adjusting and coordinating in terms of who participates in the sequence.

In the cases examined here, speakers pose questions that concern something in the epistemic domain (Heritage & Raymond 2005; Stivers & Rossano 2010; Heritage 2012) of the "other-language-speaking" participant, and these questions are then mediated to that participant. Nevertheless, the questions are not always posed to the final recipients in a straightforward manner. Tension can arise between the costs and benefits of what the questioner does in relation to the progression of the interaction and the social alignment between the participants. For instance, it may be problematic to pose a question by addressing the recipient in a language that s/he has no or limited access to. This would enhance that speaker's risk of highlighting the limited language competence of both her/himself and the recipient. Recruiting a translator may have the same result, and moreover, this often entails additional interactional work and a hitch in the progression of the conversation. It is also important to note that questions that concern co-participants do not always become redone in their language. Making the interactional effort to have a question mediated has, nevertheless, considerable benefits for the co-participants. On the one hand, the mediator is promoting the recipient's access to the conversation and her or his epistemic rights to speak for her/himself (Lerner 1996a: 316–318; Heritage & Raymond 2005; Heritage 2012; Bolden 2013). On the other hand, s/he encourages the questioner's access to the main source of information.

When a speaker produces a resaying of a question, s/he must calibrate the resaying within the action and participation framework (Goffman 1981; C. Goodwin 2007) created in the prior turn, maintaining or transforming who is addressed as a recipient and by what means. The resaying speaker attunes her/his actions with how the source speaker orients to the other-language-speaker as well as with the verbal and embodied signs of her/his involvement and understanding. Hence, engaging in mediating involves monitoring and manipulating the recipient's access and status in the interaction. In orienting to these aspects of *participation* (e.g., Goodwin & Goodwin 1992; 2004;

C. Goodwin 2007), the speakers come to produce different types of resayings. In particular, different configurations of participation entail differing circumstances for linking the turn to the "source" talk.

In the majority of the data on translatory intearctions which were the source for the data of this study, turns are not explicitly marked as translating prior talk. The contextualizing work is achieved through the design of the turns in positioning them within the unfolding courses of action and the participation framework. Let us now turn to analyze in detail the mediator's subtle coordination work in question–answer sequences.

From a question to a resaying in another language: three interactional trajectories

When speakers resay questions in another language, they modify them, most obviously by changing the language. Designing the turn for the particular recipient may involve various additional changes, such as replacing some expressions with more explicit ones. At the same time, the turns preserve some aspects of the structure of the prior saying. In examining the design of the resayings, the paper makes a distinction between *full* and *partial* resayings. Rather than a binary distinction, these are to be understood as two opposite ends on a continuum (Couper-Kuhlen 1996: 368). Examples of the two types are presented below. The complete sequences are examined later in the analysis.

a) Full resaying
Antti: käyköhän   täälä visakortti. → Toni: dá pra: (.)   pagar   com cartão visa   a↑qui,
        be.usable.3SG.Q.CLI here [name]card   be.possible.IMPS pay   with card   [name] here
        ((I wonder)) does a Visa card work here   is it possible to pay with a Visa card here

b) Partial resaying
Antti: ↑minkä   heimon   intiaani olet. → Toni: qua-qual tribo.
        what.GEN tribe.GEN indian   be.2SG   wh- which tribe
        (you) are an indian of what tribe   wh- which tribe

Full resayings recycle (with transformation) most of the elements from the prior saying and have a complete, initiating-like question design. By contrast, partial resayings provide only some key elements, perhaps a noun phrase or other minimal package to recapitulate talk by another speaker. This paper suggests that the full and partial resayings take different positions with regard to the prior other-language talk. In other words, they are designed to be heard as another *first* or as a *second* saying of a first pair part. The prior are instances of a speaker asking a question "for another first time," to borrow Garfinkel's (1967: 31–34; Heritage 1984: 124) apt wording. This means that a question is intelligible as an independent first doing, even though it derives from a similar other-language turn in prior talk (ex. a). First sayings are distinguished from turns that are designed to be heard as second sayings. The latter are turns that display their secondary position in repeating prior talk (ex. b). In other words, part of their doing is to indicate that they are second occasions. (Sacks 1995: I 722–723; Wong 2000; Schegloff 2004; Oh 2005; Local et al. 2010).[3]

All the resayings that are analyzed here occur either as adjacent to the original question turn or in close proximity to it, and enable the recipient's access to what was asked. By their design as first and second sayings, the resayings distribute the action of asking differently among the participants. The exact combination of elements in the resaying in relation to the source turn is "a vehicle for achieving the reflexivity of position and composition in conversation" (Schegloff 2004: 95; also 1996a). As a result of empirical analyses, the questions followed by resayings in the data can be divided into three recurrent trajectories during which a question becomes reproduced in another language (and eventually answered).

Table 1. Three trajectories from a question to a resaying

Recipient of the resaying during the original question	Format of resaying	Position of resaying	N=17
1) not addressed	full	first saying	6
2) indirectly addressed (topic initiating question)	partial	second saying	5
3) addressed (follow-up question)	partial	second saying	4
other			2[3]

The three types of questions are distinguished by three types of orientations to the future recipient of the resaying (henceforth "recipient RS"). As presented in Table 1, original questions of type 1 do not clearly make a response by the recipient RS relevant. By contrast, original questions of the latter two types create a projection for that participant's response even if it is indirect. Type 2 questions address her/him indirectly as a recipient of a topic-initiating question and type 3 follow-up questions address her/him directly, as the speaker of the talk that is being revisited by the follow-up question.

The resayings reflect the configurations of participation in the original questions. The resayings in type 1 treat the recipient RS as previously not having been involved in the conversation and as hearing the question for the first time. This is reflected in their design: they are done as full, another-first sayings, not dependent on the prior saying. In comparison, the resayings in type 2 and 3 treat the recipient as an already involved participant. They

---

3 In the prior studies, the term *resaying* has been used predominantly for turns hearable as second doings of a speaker's own prior talk. This term is used here to refer to both "another first" and "second" sayings because in both cases, the action that has begun in the initial saying is expanded by the resaying instead of being treated as previously abandoned.

4 The category "other" includes questions that address someone other than the future recipient of the resaying. After an answer has already been provided by someone else, the question is repeated to her/him as reported speech, mobilizing a second answer. These cases will be analyzed elsewhere (Harjunpää, in prep.).

are designed as partial, second sayings, dependent on a prior saying. As all language use, the design of the resayings is both context shaped and context renewing (e.g., Heritage 1984; Goodwin & Goodwin 1992; 2004). This means that speakers can utilize the design of the resaying strategically for re-shaping the situation. For instance, they can integrate the recipient in the conversation by resaying a question *as if* it had been addressed to her/him even though this might have not been the case (see ex. 5).

A summary of the findings and a discussion on the implications of the linking phenomena for translatory interaction are provided at the end of the paper.

RESAYING OF A QUESTION AS A *FIRST* SAYING

In the first group of cases, the original question does not target the other-language-speaking participant as a recipient even though the question concerns a matter in her/his area of knowledge or expertise. The speaker of the resaying turns to her/him to seek information or confirmation in order to be able to respond to the question, and thus repeats the question. Although the question is reproduced in another language, the fact that there was a prior saying does not become visible in the design of the resaying. Instead, the speaker passes on the question as her/his own inquiry.

Extract (2) is an example of a question redone as another first saying. This example is the same one presented in (a) above, but here it occurs in the larger context. A Finnish man, Antti (F), is visiting his son, Toni (F/P), in Brazil. Sauli (F/P) has invited them to have lunch in a restaurant owned by his friends. Antti asks whether it is possible to pay with a credit card. Cíntia (P), the waitress and restaurant owner, is just arriving at the table.

Focus turns: Q=question, RQ=resaying of a question, A=answer, RA=resaying of an answer

(2) Visa card.BR

```
01  Antti:   Q  +käyköhän      täällä  visakortti.
                be.usable.3SG.Q.CLI here  [name].card
                ((I wonder)) does a Visa card work here
                   +GAZE>SAULI

02           A  (1.0) SAULI NODS

03  Toni:    RQ #1 +dá pra:  (.)  pagar com cartão visa a↑qui,
                   be.possible.IMPS pay.INF PREP card  [name] here
                   is it possible to pay with Visa card here
                   +GAZE>CÍNTIA
```

Cíntia
Antti   GAZE Toni
  GAZE
     Sauli
(behind Cíntia)

81

```
04  Cíntia:     A    com certe*za.
                     of course
                         *TONI STARTS NODDING

05  Toni:      RA   +mmh (.)    joo.
                                yes
               +GAZE>ANTTI

06  Antti:       °joo°.* (.) °hyvä°.
                 yes          good
                       *TONI STOPS NODDING
```

Antti's inquiry concerns an issue under Cíntia's authority because she works at the restaurant. However, Antti directs the turn to Sauli through gaze. Sauli responds by nodding (line 2), but Toni does not see this gestural response. Toni proceeds to ask Cíntia, who is just about to sit down at the table to chat with them (frame #1). Toni returns Cíntia's affirmation to Antti at line 5. The exchange resembles a basic case of interpreting, with Toni providing translations of the question and the answer. However, as the question did not target Cíntia, Toni's turn at line 3 is his own inquiry. Toni seeks information from Cíntia in order to provide a response to Antti, not primarily to facilitate a contact between them. Even though Toni's turn is motivated by Antti's question, it serves as another (first) instantiation of a question regarding paying. The design (line 3) as a full, first saying makes it intelligible to Cíntia without Antti's talk as its context. This does not imply that Cíntia does not recognize, at least retrospectively, that the question she answered was part of a larger project. This may become evident when Toni returns Cíntia's affirmative answer to Antti by nodding immediately after her turn. Despite formulating it as an independent question, Toni still facilitates the interaction in that his turn allows Cíntia (who possesses the required knowledge and authority) to offer an answer to the inquiry, which she would not have otherwise been able to manage due to the language choice.

The wording "another first time" was used by Garfinkel (1967: 31–34; see Heritage 1984: 124) in his discussion of studying practical actions. The main idea is that the organization of social conduct is a contingent accomplishment. Thus, rather than reproducing ready-made rules, actors rely on situated methods to recognize and produce accountable action. This means that on each new occasion, with each set of circumstances and contingencies, rules are applied for another first time.

During a stretch of conversation, speakers may produce their turns as new, or first, occasions of some conversational action, or as second with regard to an action already in progress (Sacks 1995; Schegloff 2004; Local et al. 2010).[5] A turn can be marked as a second by *tying* it to a prior turn by means that are in line with the second position, such as anaphoric reference (Sacks 1995: I 150). However, speakers may also use situated methods to resist the secondess of the turn in second position. Goodwin & Goodwin (1987)

---

5   In multilingual interaction, reiterations of prior talk by the same speaker have been discussed in terms of language alternating first pair parts, so-called *non-first-firsts* (Auer 1984b; cf. Gumperz 1982: 78–79; see also Harjunpää & Mäkilähde 2016).

and M. H. Goodwin (1990) demonstrate how speakers use *format tying*, recycling the interlocutors' full turns, to counter their action. Heritage & Raymond (2005) discuss issues of firstness and secondness with regard to second assessments. When they produce second assessments, speakers may deliver them as firsts instead of merely going along with the prior one. By doing this, the second speaker reclaims the first-position assessment slot in order to convey primary epistemic rights to assessing something. Using "fully sentential" and "full-form" design in the second position contributes to disregarding a prior saying and claiming speakership as a "first author" (ibid. 18, 29) (see also Stivers 2005; Thompson et al. 2015: 139–199).

Toni's resaying in (2) can be regarded as a similar achievement, as the design of the resaying of the question disregards the prior question to some extent and conveys autonomous speakership instead of transmitting Antti's words. Consequently, the full design of the resaying does not display the speaker as a relayer of someone else's words. Such examples contrast with resayings that display a secondary position by being tied to their sources. The resayings that are tied to other speakers' talk (types 2 and 3) might be said to apply what Sacks refers to as "second speaker rules" (1995: I 150–153). Accordingly, the resayings of type 1 apply "first speaker rules".

The independent design of a resaying in the next extract deviates from the original question to the extent that it results in a misunderstanding. Simo (F/p-) and Leena (F/p-) as well as their children have been invited to a barbecue at the home of Ulla and Teppo (both F/P). Their housekeeper, Clarice (P), has left the table and gone to another room. Prior to the extract, Simo has asked how long Clarice has worked for them, and at line 1, he asks whether she takes the bus to come to work. His question appears to prepare for talk about an on-going bus strike by checking whether Ulla and Seppo might know about the current situation through Clarice.

(3) Bus strike.BR⁶

```
01  Simo:      liikkuuks hän bussilla.
               does she take the bus

02  Ulla:      ↑joo-o↑,
               yes

03  Simo:  Q   mites t- onks täällä bussit nyt ajossa. (.)
                                                       Sorocabassa.
               how.CLI be.3SG.Q  here    bus.PL  now  run.INE
               what about are the buses here now running in Sorocaba

04  Teppo: A   kyl ne=
               yes they

05  Ulla:  RQ  =a:::h OS ÔNIBUS ESTÃO DE GREVE H↑OJE OU↑ NÃO.
               ((TO CLARICE IN ANOTHER ROOM))
                       ART.PL  bus    be.3PL  PREP  strike  today   or   NEG
               aaah are the buses on strike today or not
```

6   Leena's simultaneous turns to her son have been omitted.

```
06              (0.6)

07   Ulla:      Clarice.

08   Clarice:  A  hoje  não  ta↑va  nã↑o.    (.) só    sei         an↑teontem        (pois)
                  today  NEG   be.3SG.PST NEG      only  know.1SG  day.before.yesterday PRT
                  today were not                     (I) only know of the day before yesterday

09   Ulla:     RA toissapäivänä          oli?
                  day.before.yesterday   be.3SG.PST
                  the day before yesterday were

10              (0.2)

11   Simo:     aam (.) Limeirassa on (.) ollu se lakko.
               uhm     in Limeira there has   been the strike

12              (0.6)

13   Simo:     kai se on n- ollu täälläki.
               ((I)) assume it has been here too

14   Teppo:    [on.
                yes

15   Ulla:     [o:li yks päivä vaan.
                yes just for one day

16   Simo:     ai yks päivä vaan.
               oh just for one day
```

When Simo hears that Clarice takes the bus to come to work, he asks whether the buses are running at the moment (line 3). He does not explicate that the buses might not run due to a strike. Nonetheless, Ulla's formulation of the question to Clarice (line 5), 'are the buses on strike today or not,' suggests that she is aware of the strike and assumes it to be behind Simo's inquiry. Ulla requests information from Clarice in order to provide an answer for Simo. Ulla's autonomous speakership is reflected in her manner of basing the resaying on her own background knowledge: the specification of time *hoje*, 'today,' and the reference to the strike, which Simo did not make explicit in his original question. Clarice thus ultimately answers an inquiry about buses *on strike today* instead of buses *running* (see lines 3 and 5). When Ulla reproduces the 'day before yesterday' from Clarice's turn in Finnish (line 9) and ties the answer to Simo's question by repeating the verb *olla*, 'to be,' (*toissapäivänä oli*, 'the day before yesterday were'), a misunderstanding is created. This can be seen in Simo's account for his question (line 14). He "reveals" the cause for asking about the buses by offering the strike as something new in this conversation, although he does mark it as possibly generally known by using the demonstrative pronoun *se* (Laury 1997): *se lakko*, 'the strike'. At line 16, Simo expresses uncertainty regarding whether the strike also involves the town they are visiting, thereby displaying that he has *not* understood that the buses were on strike 'the day before yesterday.'

To conclude, Ulla does not ask Clarice the same thing that Simo asked Ulla, and this leads to incoherence in the way the answer is returned to Simo in the main sequence. The resaying of the answer inherits its "proposition" concerning the strike from the sequence between Ulla and Clarice. This occurs even though the interactional project has been to acquire information to answer Simo's question. The turn at line 9 reveals something important about the sequential embedding of translated answers. It is difficult to draw a line between the speaker providing an answer as her/himself with newly acquired information and as a mediator of an answer provided by another (Müller 1989: 722). However, structural contingencies seem to occur in the sequential slot for producing an answer. The resaying is inclined both towards repeating the prior answer turn as well as towards fitting as a response to the original question.[7] This provides the logic of the misunderstanding in this extract. This type of example makes it easier to see what is achieved and how in the cases that do maintain coherence between sequences in two languages, as happens in the majority of question-answer sequences in the data. Mediating questions and answers successfully requires embedding the language-alternating turns in the larger sequence. In the case of translating answers, this means selecting a form of resaying that fits as an answer to the original question.

The point of departure for the resayings in this section is the need to acquire information or confirmation from a previously unaddressed participant in order to respond to the original question. Thus the resaying of the question is done from the position of an unknowing recipient who addresses a new recipient, initiating a particular type of "side sequence within an on-going sequence" (Jefferson 1972). These resayings occur in full format, being designed as self-contained first sayings. They do not display the original question as their source by establishing a link to it in their design. After acquiring the information from the third party, the resaying speaker may return smoothly to the main sequence to act as a respondent. In the cases analyzed, the recipient RS could not have volunteered to provide a response because s/he did not share the language, and furthermore, because they were not nearby, or were just arriving at the scene. Nevertheless, these are not the only situations in which questions are produced as another firsts, as the data also involve resayings as firsts that are delivered for such recipients who may understand the other language to some extent and who have been co-present all along.

Let us now move on to examine resayings that are produced as second sayings of the prior question, and thus display their translatory nature through their design. The section begins by discussing how the speaker of the original question makes the other-language-speaker's response possibly relevant.

---

7   See related observations in Wadensjö's (2010: 23) study on interpreting yes/no questions during a court trial. In her cases, matching a translated answer to the questioner's yes/no question seems to conflict with orienting to re-presenting all aspects of the defendant's answer.

SECOND SAYING OF A TOPIC-INITIATING QUESTION

In the cases of the previous section, participants inquire about matters in the epistemic domain of other-language-speaking participants without targeting them in the question. Their contribution to the issue at hand is made relevant by a speaker who repeats the question to them in order to be able to respond. In comparison, the cases in this section involve original questions that make a contribution by the recipient RS possibly relevant. The questioners initiate talk on a topic that concerns the recipient RS by referring to her/him in third person.

With third-person reference to a co-participant, an individual is being talked about, but at the same time, her/his presence in the speech situation is oriented to (Hanks 1990: 226; Levinson 1988). This transposition of roles can have specific interactional purposes, as in achieving something more than referring or addressing (Schegloff 1996b; Lerner 2003). According to Seppänen (1998: 127, 211), forms of third-person reference can be regarded as ways to offer specific participant roles to the person referred to. Seppänen (ibid.126) cites Sacks (1995 I: 573), who finds that a third-person reference can be used to not specify who should take the next turn. This is also what the third-person reference seems to achieve in questions that become mediated.

The third-person reference in the original question can be interpreted by the participants as indirectly targeting the referred-to person as the recipient.[8] The design is ambiguous in the sense that it leaves unspecified whether that participant is selected as the next speaker or whether it invites a possible mediator to step in. Approaching the recipient indirectly may be regarded as the speaker's method for dealing with the situation of not sharing linguistic resources with a potential recipient.[9] However, the indirectness also entails interactional contingencies to be dealt with in the translatory turns, as is demonstrated in the following examples. As second sayings, type 2 resayings establish a link to prior talk more clearly than the "firsts" discussed in the previous section.

In (4), Raili (F) is walking into her living room, where a visitor from Brazil, André (P/f-), and his host, Márcio (P/f), are seated on a couch. In frame #1, André is fiddling with his cell phone while Raili bypasses him and the camera. Raili goes to sit down further away, next to her daughter, Sanna (F/P).While walking, Raili inquires about the time of André's first visit to Finland. In frame #2, André looks at Raili, who is now close to Sanna (outside of the camera view). After a while, André asks *mitä*, 'what'.

---

8   By *targeted recipient*, I refer to a participant who has been invited to act as a recipient in an indirect way. I do not mean targeting by an implied message, as discussed in Goffman (1981: 134) and Levinson (1988: 210–221).

9   For a summary of research on primary parties' choice of indirect versus direct addressing in institutional contexts of interpreting, see Paulsen Christensen (2008).

(4) A year ago.FI

```
01 Raili:    Q #1 oliks      se    nii että  (.) André   oli     *täälä   (.)
               be.3SG.PST.Q.CLI DEM3  so    COMP     [name]   be.3SG.PST here
               was it so that André was here
                                                                  *ANDRÉ LIFTS HIS GAZE
```

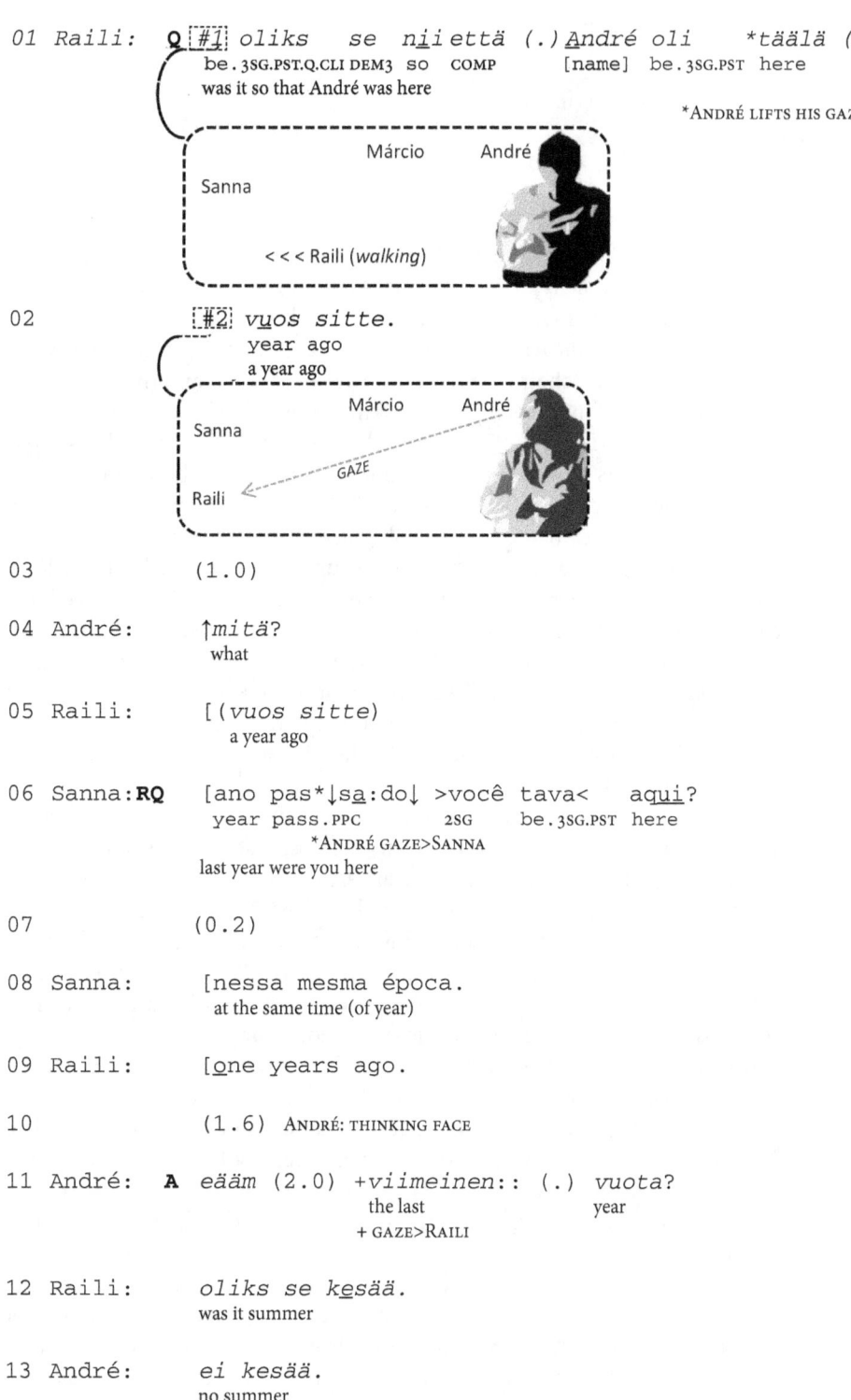

```
02            #2 vuos sitte.
                  year ago
                  a year ago

03           (1.0)

04 André:    ↑mitä?
              what

05 Raili:    [(vuos sitte)
               a year ago

06 Sanna: RQ [ano pas*↓sa:do↓ >você tava<   aqui?
              year pass.PPC       2SG   be.3SG.PST here
                     *ANDRÉ GAZE>SANNA
              last year were you here

07           (0.2)

08 Sanna:    [nessa mesma época.
              at the same time (of year)

09 Raili:    [one years ago.

10           (1.6)  ANDRÉ: THINKING FACE

11 André:  A eääm (2.0) +viimeinen::  (.)  vuota?
                         the last              year
                        + GAZE>RAILI

12 Raili:    oliks se kesää.
              was it summer

13 André:    ei kesää.
              no summer
```

```
14                    (0.4)

15   Andre:           ää

16   Márcio:          syksyllä.
                      in the fall

17   André:           syksyllä:: ja::,
                      in the fall and
```

In addition to André, both his hosts, Sanna and Márcio, have access to the information that is needed to answer Raili's question. By referring to André by his first name, Raili leaves the possibility for Sanna to answer and continue to talk *about* André, all the more because Raili is facing her while walking towards the chair next to her. However, after a pause (line 3), André takes the turn and initiates repair by asking *mitä,* 'what.'

According to Drew (1997), open-class repair initiators such as *what* indicate problems of a sequential character, a lack of fit between the turn and its sequential context (see Haakana 2011 for Finnish). It seems that here a problem arises from the initial ambiguity of André's participant status. When Raili begins to speak, André is occupied with his cell phone. Raili does not ensure his availability as a recipient, such as by waiting to catch his gaze (C. Goodwin 1981; Rossano 2012). Moreover, she refers to him in the third person. Thus, at the beginning of Raili's turn, André's recipient status has not been not clearly established. André most likely responds to hearing his name as a summons for him to respond. By first shifting his gaze to Raili and then initiating repair in Finnish, he displays some access to the turn as well as its relevance for him.

André has initiated repair on Raili's turn, but Sanna also intervenes to provide a repair solution. This confirms the observations by Bolden (2012) and Müller (1989: 724) that linguistic expertise provides a license for a third party to take a turn in place of the original speaker. At lines 5 and 6, Raili and Sanna simultaneously display their different understandings of the problem by offering different solutions to it. Raili repeats only the time reference in Finnish. Sanna begins by providing a time reference in Portuguese (line 6 *ano passado,* 'last year') and continues with more comprehensive facilitating. The turn is marked as asking by the rising intonation in >*você tava< aqui?,* 'were you here' (Morães 1998: 183–187). At line 9, Raili provides another temporal noun phrase in English. To conclude, Raili and Sanna vacillate between orientations to what their recipient does not have access to, to one item in a certain language, or to the whole question. Even though they orient to "saying the same thing" as in the original question, they accomplish it differently.

Schegloff (2004) investigates the modification of turns in which speakers are "saying the same thing" as in a prior turn. The speakers modify what was said by leaving out and adding elements in the resaying. A case in point is Raili's turn on line 5, where only an appropriately modified version of the trouble source is provided after open-class repair initiation (ibid: 95–99, 127). Schegloff further reports that the elements that the speaker dispenses with vary from turn-initial discourse markers to central grammatical constituents of a prior utterance. The resulting design signals to the recipient how the turn relates to prior talk as a second saying (see also Oh 2005; Rauniomaa 2008: 81–96; Local et al. 2010).

Even though Sanna formulates the resaying as a question at line 6, the turn design displays that it is not her independent question, but a second doing of Raili's turn. Raili has indicated some prior knowledge on the matter by the beginning the question with 'was it so that', but Sanna dispenses with the framing in the resaying. The initial *ano passado* occurs without a preposition or an article (*no* [PREP+ART] *ano passado*). It follows that the rest of the turn is syntactically only loosely integrated with the circumstances explicated by the turn-initial 'last year.' In Brazilian Portuguese, temporal adjuncts in this position typically mark relations with prior utterances (e.g., Pontes 1987: 18; Conceição de Paiva 2008). By launching the resaying with the last element of Raili's turn in this manner, Sanna displays an operation on the prior turn. By the modification, Sanna preserves and transforms structures from Raili's prior turn to construct an action that relates to it in a specific way (see C. Goodwin 2007; 2013); the design works in positioning her turn as a second saying.

The fact that the referred-to participant's answer is treated as absent and thus interactionally problematic indicates that s/he is not treated as a non-participant but as a targeted recipient. The conclusion is that speaking about a participant in the third person is not intended to exclude her/him, but to deal with the language barrier and the possible need for mediation. In example (4), as in most cases of initial indirect addressing, the third-person reference in the original question is changed into the second person in the resaying, disambiguating the recipient.

As will be demonstrated in the following extract, even in situations where the original questioner could be interpreted as merely referring to a co-participant, a third-person reference may be treated as targeting her/him. In the extract, Leena's (F/p-) family is visiting Ulla's (F/P) home. Leena is walking around with the baby in her arms (outside of the camera view) while Ulla and Clarice (P) are seated at a table side-by-side. Clarice asks about Leena's baby.

(5) Breast milk.BR

```
01 Clarice:Q  +°a menina mama    o quê ↑peito [m-°
              ART girl   feed.3SG ART what breast
              the girl takes what, breast
              +GLANCES AT LEENA/BABY WHILE POINTING WITH INDEX AND LITTLE
              FINGER, HAND ON CHIN

02 Ulla:                                         [ahn?

03 Clarice:Q  +*a menina dela    mama    o quê (.) l↑eite
              ART girl   PREP+3SG feed.3SG ART what      milk
              what does her girl take, milk
              +GLANCES AT LEENA/BABY, POINTS WITH INDEX FINGER AND HEAD
              *ULLA HEAD AND GAZE>LEENA/BABY
```

89

```
04              #1 mama↑deira p↑eito que que é;=
                   feeding.bottle  breast    what COMP be.3SG
                   feeding bottle breast what is it
```

```
05 Ulla:RQ  =↑tis*siäks  se    syö     #vai::#
              breast.PAR.Q.CLI DEM3 eat.3SG   or
              ((is)) breast ((what)) she takes or
                    *CLARICE GAZE>LEENA
```

```
06 Leena:A   +°mm°
             +NODS
```

```
07 Ulla:RA   +*peito.
                breast
             +HEAD AND GAZE>CLARÍCE
                *CLARICE GAZE>ULLA
```

```
08           (0.4)   CLARÍCE NODS
```

```
09           (5.6)
```

```
10 Ulla:     mas é muito pequeninino meu #deus do céu#,
             but good god (she) is so small
```

In the beginning of her turn at line 1, Clarice glances at Leena's direction, otherwise gazing at Ulla. Covering her mouth with her hand, Clarice asks about the baby girl's feeding. Ulla does not hear her at first, and Clarice reformulates the question (line 3), now referring to "her" baby girl instead of speaking directly about the baby.[10] Clarice points at Leena and the baby for the second time with her index finger and head, while her hand is still covering her mouth. Again, Clarice only glances at the direction she is pointing at during *a menina*, 'the girl,' in the beginning of the turn. Clarice's gaze towards Ulla, her bodily posture and quiet voice, all signal a withdrawal into a dyadic exchange with Ulla rather than a targeting of Leena. However, from *a menina* at line 3, Ulla steadily gazes at Leena during Clarice's question. Ulla holds her gaze until she receives Leena's answer (line 6), whereas Clarice sustains gaze towards Leena only after the onset of Ulla's resaying (from line 5 to 7).

Ulla's resaying (line 5 *tissiäks se syö*) presents breast feeding as the expected answer to be confirmed; the object is fronted and the question

---

10 The possible different uses of a name versus pronominal reference to the recipient RS in a question that becomes mediated is an interesting issue that goes, however, beyond the scope of this paper.

clitic is attached to the noun instead of the verb (cf. *syöks se tissiä*, 'does she take breast ((milk))'). In other words, the noun is placed in focus (ISK § 1690). The answer option that Ulla anticipates might be either her own conjecture, or stem from the formulation of Clarice's question. This extract resembles the "first sayings" discussed at the beginning of the present paper, as Clarice's question is addressed to Ulla, and in the resaying, Ulla requests Leena's confirmation in order to answer Clarice. However, as the question is *about* Leena, it also enables treating her as the targeted recipient. Ulla's sustained gaze towards Leena (lines 3–6) instead of the questioner works to engage her in the conversation by making visible an orientation to her. Moreover, the design of her resaying presents the question as having been derived from the on-going conversation with Clarice. The placement of the noun in turn-initial position, which indicates that it is not new, but rather contrastive/focused with regard to something prior, creates a link to that stretch of conversation. The particular contextual circumstances enable Ulla to use pronominal tying. By referring to the baby by a pronoun (line 5 *se*, DEM3), she orients to the baby already being the focus of Leena's attention. Using the locally subsequent reference form (Schegloff 1996b: 481) in this position also contributes to the secondness of the turn by *not* introducing a new referent by a fuller name. After Ulla's resaying, Leena joins the others at the table, and they continue discussing children.

In the first extract of this section (4), repair initiation provides a slot for redoing the question. The reformulation of the question appears as a response in itself (see Linell 2009: 180). It is tied to the conversation as a second saying, shaped by the specific interactional environment: the initiation of repair and configurations of the participation framework. In (5), the resaying is not offered as a solution to a problem in understanding. Nonetheless, it occurs in a situation where the questioner does not have the linguistic resources to address the person talked about directly. The original question could have been treated as talking about the mother and the baby without addressing them. However, the question also introduced an opportunity for the bilingual speaker to integrate the talked-about participant in the conversation.

In both cases, a question initiates a topic concerning a co-participant by referring to her/him in the third person. This offers an opportunity for a bilingual speaker to redirect the question. On the one hand, the participants balance between the limited access of the recipient RS to what was said, and on the other, to her/his potential recipient status. With regard to the resaying, there is a need to disambiguate whose question it is (who has, in Goffmanian terms, the *principal* speaker role). The resayings are tailored to these situational contingencies by (most often) disambiguating the recipient and by systematically relating the resaying to prior talk through turn-design. This is achieved particularly through lexical choices and word order in the turn-initial position, which display a link to the prior turn. It can therefore be concluded that speakers do not design translatory turns to solve language-related problems of understanding only, but also to solve matters related to the organization of sequences in specific participation frameworks.

Second saying of a follow-up question

The question turns discussed in this section address the recipient of the resaying in the most direct manner of all the cases examined. They are follow-up questions, which by their nature target a prior speaker as their recipient (Lerner 2003). Consequently, the resayings occur in a position where the recipient RS is treated as being involved in prior talk. It is suggested that the partial resayings display an interpretation of such a framework and make use of it by producing partial, minimal repeats of a few key elements from prior talk as translations. By selectively preserving parts of a prior first pair part the speakers succeed in marking the resaying as a second saying.

In some of the follow-up questions, the recipient is addressed with a second-person reference that is accompanied by gaze towards the referred-to person. The combination of these explicit methods of addressing clearly designates the recipient (C. Goodwin 1981; Lerner 1996b; 2003). Yet a follow-up question can also potentially select a recipient without using explicit addressing methods. By virtue of requesting further information, the question suggests that the turn is being yielded to the prior speaker. This makes her/him the only eligible respondent, which means that the participant has been *tacitly addressed* as the next speaker (Lerner 2003: 190).

Example (6) demonstrates the contextual circumstances that a follow-up question creates for its resaying. Prior to the extract, Raili (F) has inquired about André's (P/f-) last trip to Finland (ex. 4). Raili and Sanna (F/P) are sitting at a distance from André, away from the view of the camera. The sequence has closed, and André concentrates on his cell phone. Raili continues the conversation by inquiring about the ticket prices for flights between Brazil and Finland.

(6) Ticket.FI

```
01 Raili: Q   kuinka +paljon se  (.) maksaa   se   matka sielt
              how     much    DEM3    cost.3SG DEM3 trip  there.from
              how much does it cost, the trip from
                    +ANDRÉ RAISES HIS HEAD, TURNS GAZE>RAILI


02            Brasiliasta tänne  (0.2)  edestakasi.
              [name].ELA   here.to      back.and.forth
              Brazil to here, and back


03            (1.0)

04 Sanna:RQ   .mt quanto é        pas↓sagem,
                  how.much be.3SG ticket
                  how much is ticket


05 André: A   aam. (0.6) hh tuhat (2.0) kaksisataa. (0.6) euroa.
              ahn, (one) thousand, two hundred, euros
```

All Raili's co-participants travel between the two countries and they are aware of the ticket prices. However, as André was the last person to discuss his visits to Finland, he is the likely recipient of Raili's further question on the topic (see Lerner 2003: 190). After no response (see gap at line 3), Sanna repeats the question. She merely states *quanto é passagem*, 'how much is ticket,' without mentioning a roundtrip or explicating the destinations. Her turn relies on the prior saying in its recipient selection and in assuming the knowledge of which tickets are being talked about as shared.

In addition to the blunt wording, the resaying has "downgraded" prosody. Local et al. (2010: 143) examine the prosodic formulation of turns in which a speaker re-delivers a turn that was for some reason not taken up by a recipient. They claim for cases of retrieving a prior turn[11] that prosodic downgrading is a reference to the first attempt. The prosodic design makes the existence of a first saying relevant for the interpretation of the current turn. In a similar manner, the prosody of Sanna's turn marks it as not posing an entirely new question to André but rather delivering a second saying of Raili's question. With this design, Sanna's turn achieves a decoding of the question without being in conflict with her own access to the information on ticket prices. In accordance with this participation framework, André maintains Raili as the questioner instead of Sanna, as is indicated by his choice of responding in Finnish (see Auer 1984a).

What is referred to as *tying techniques* (Sacks 1995: I 716–747) work on the basis of invoking a search by the hearer to determine what is being tied to. Although one of the most typical tying techniques is anaphoric reference (ibid. 722), in translatory turns, locating an item in prior talk through an anaphoric reference may not be possible. This is because the speaker cannot assume the recipient's access to prior mentions. However, pronominal tying devices do sometimes occur in tying to a prior saying, as in some cases of type 2. They are nevertheless not a primary tying device, as demonstrated by the examples. Other techniques that are used especially in turn-initial position appear to be translation-oriented, such as producing lexical key elements in turn-initial position to display an operation on prior talk. The resayings in type 3 consist of even more concise resayings. It is suggested that the partial format of a resaying itself functions as one type of tying device by invoking the not fully accessible, other-language talk as its source. A selective repetition of elements in a second saying can function to display doing a similar thing as in a prior turn, as evidenced by studies on "dispensability" (e.g., Schegloff 2004; Oh 2005).

In the following extract, Gaia (P/f) first announces to the others that she is "Indian," referring to her indigenous descent. After some turns of collective searching for the correct term in Finnish, Antti (F) makes a specifying question (line 7). Antti's son, Toni (F/P), delivers the translatory turn in the form of an interrogative noun phrase.

---

11 For Local, Auer & Drew (2010) "retrievals" and "redoings" are turns in which the speaker repeats something that has been intercepted by another speaker and that create a link to the prior saying. In contrast, "resuscitated" turns are new attempts that are constructed without orientation to the prior saying. See also Curl (2005).

(7) Tribe.BR

```
01 Gaia:    minä olen intia. (0.4)  india.
            I am intia                india

02 Cíntia:  índ[ia.
            indian

03 Toni:        [intia[ani.
                 indian

04 Antti:              [↑intiaani. (.) ai   [↑jaa,
                        indian               oh really

05 Cíntia:                                   [↑índia e uma paulista. hehe
                                              an indian and a paulista¹²

06 Sauli:   mheh

07 Antti: Q jaa. ↑minkä  heimon   intiaani <olet>.
            PRT  what.GEN tribe.GEN indian   be.2SG
            oh, you are an indian of what tribe

08              (0.6)  ANTTI, SAULI AND TONI LOOKING AT GAIA

09 Toni:RQ  qua- qual tribo.
            wh-  which tribe
            wh- which tribe

10          (1.0)

11 Gaia: A  eem (0.4) tupi caiabi.

12          (0.4)

13 Antti:   °tupi°.

14 Toni:    tupi caiabi.

15 Antti:   joo.
            right
```

Gaia does not immediately answer Antti's question (see line 8), and Toni comes in to produce a noun phrase that consists of an interrogative word *qual,* 'which,' and *tribo,* 'tribe' (line 9). As Toni has been a recipient of Gaia's general announcement, in principle, he could also pose this

---

12 *paulista*=native of the state of São Paulo in Brazil

question himself. However, Toni's turn must be interpreted as orienting to the conditional relevance that was created by Antti's question. It is unlikely that Toni would simply disregard the first pair part that has projected an answer by Gaia (line 7). This turn is clearly directed to her by gaze and second-person reference, and it is even distinctly articulated. In this position, Toni's turn qualifies the first pair part in order to deal with the lack of response (Schegloff 2007: 15).

When Toni delivers the resaying (line 9), he makes use of the sequential position after Antti's follow-up question and of Gaia's established position as the recipient of that turn. Toni does not reproduce the whole question, but delivers a partial resaying in the form of a noun phrase. A resaying that is formulated in a phrasal format is not self-contained in delivering an action like the questions in type 1 (or Antti's turn at line 7). By leaving so much implicit, the turn becomes pragmatically and semantically dependent on the context. Despite being dependent, the turn does not need to be regarded as lacking something. On the contrary, producing a turn in a phrasal format is one means of using a sequential position as a resource for relating the current turn to the action in prior turns (Mazeland 2013: 489; see also Schegloff 1996a; 2004; Helasvuo 2001; Ford et al. 2013: 26–40; C. Goodwin 2007, 2013). By delivering the resaying with an interrogative phrasal design after a turn that is lacking a response, the mediating speaker may tie his turn as a second saying of the prior question.

In this and in the prior example, the original question is followed by the recipient RS gazing at the speaker in silence. The lack of a response reveals an interactional problem in a way somewhat similar to open-class repair initiators produced by a recipient. Both leave the problem undefined and convey that "the difficulty affects or permeates the (repairable) prior turn as a whole" (Drew 1997: 98). Indeed, the partial resayings do not seem to point to a specific, linguistic trouble-item in the prior talk. However, they also do not repeat the whole turn – in fact, the analysis reveals that a partial design differs from formulating a whole new question. Despite dispensing with various elements from the prior saying, the resayings contain a sufficient number of response-mobilizing features (see Stivers & Rossano 2010) to function as second sayings of questions. Instead of merely repairing ones, the turns provide concise versions of the prior questions. They summarize, or encapsulate, the "gist" of talk in a manner that appears to be typical of mundane translatory practices.

Jefferson (1972: 295–296) argued that a conversational repeat is "a conversational object identifiable whether or not one has heard something twice in succession". Evidently she points to the same issue that Sacks (1995: I 723) raises in saying that it can be a part of a doing to show that it is a redoing. This distinguishes conversational repetition from the mere occurrence of two or more similar items in some stretch of talk. Likewise, second sayings work retrospectively to mark a turn as a second, which indicates the existence of a first (Oh 2005: 278). When speakers deliver a translatory resaying of a question with a phrasal or otherwise minimal design, they dispense with the design that made the prior saying a sequence-initiating first pair part. As no "first" by the same speaker is available, the design of a second saying may evoke the immediately prior other-language talk as its source, even when it is only faintly accessible to the recipient.

In conclusion, the partial resaying establishes a frame of participation in which the action of asking is to be understood as being distributed between two speakers. As they inhabit a sequential position by means of timing and turn design, the second sayings succeed in marking the question as one that is derived from someone's earlier talk. Simultaneously, the turn is rendered understandable as a translation by linking to the source. By contrast, signaling this type of position is not necessarily a concern for a speaker who is resaying a question for his own purposes, as in the case of type 1 resayings.

Discussion and conclusions

This study has analyzed instances of questions that were reformulated by another speaker in another language, and eventually answered. The division of the three trajectories from a question to a resaying (Table 1) is presented here again, updated with details that have been introduced and discussed in the analyses of data extracts.

Table 2. Three trajectories from a question to a resaying

Recipient of the resaying during the original question	Format of resaying	Position of resaying
1) not addressed -not actively involved in the conversation	full -not tied to prior saying by means of turn design	first saying -self-contained, intelligible independently of the prior saying
2) indirectly addressed (topic-initiating question) -newly involved	partial -tied by fronted, turn-initial elements	second saying -reacts to contingencies related to recipient selection and/or repair initiation
3) addressed (follow-up question) -prior speaker	partial -tied by phrasal or otherwise minimal design	second saying -recapitulates the original question with a few key elements

In the original questions, three types of orientations to the recipient RS were identified: no addressing, indirect addressing as a new recipient, and direct addressing as a prior speaker. This analysis has presented evidence to demonstrate how the speaker of the resaying orients to the recipient RS's current involvement in the interaction when producing the resaying. In other words, this paper has examined how recipient selection/design as part of the "pragmatic nature of the stretch of talk to be translated" (Traverso 2012: 151) may affect how the talk becomes translated.

Questions that do not target the other-language speaker (type 1) are forwarded to her/him by the speaker of the resaying to seek information or confirmation so as to respond to the question. Even though the resaying forwards a question to a new recipient, being "second" is not clearly displayed by its design. Thus, the resaying appears as another first saying, virtually independent of the prior saying.

The two other types of questions are treated as inviting a response from the recipient RS, and their difference lies in how and when the response by that participant becomes projected in the unfolding of the asking. The questions that target the recipient RS indirectly (type 2) initiate talk about her/him with a third-person reference. Investigation of the data suggests that speakers may use the ambiguity between referring and addressing as a strategy to deal with the challenge of not fully sharing linguistic resources with the co-participant. The resayings of these questions work to consolidate the recipient's status by disambiguating recipient selection and by linking the turn to the prior question, orienting to the recipient as already having been targeted by the prior speaker. In comparison, the follow-up questions (type 3) designate the recipient in the original question. The recipient RS is addressed as a prior speaker whose talk is being followed up by the question. The resayings maintain the recipient selection and rely on the recipient's established status when recapitulating the prior question. Accordingly, type 2 cases typically involve some negotiation of the development of the sequence, whereas type 3 cases allow more straightforward minimal resayings.

In contrast to the "another first" sayings, the partial resayings of type 2 and 3 evoke a search for a source in prior talk, that is, for how they are *linked* to preceding talk. The resayings in type 2 contain fronted, turn-initial elements that signal a relation to what was just said, such as that of focus or contrast. By a design that invokes the prior talk as the contextual background, the speakers create an effect of tying to prior turns, even when the recipient does not have direct access to that talk. In comparison, the resayings of type 3 are more straightforward. They consist of noun phrases or clauses of a minimal size for conveying a summarized version of the prior question. The phrasal or otherwise minimal design makes the turns dependent on (linked to) the context in their interpretation, relying on the projected action trajectory and participation framework.

The data suggest that mediating a question as a full or as a partial resaying renders the action of asking socially meaningful in two different ways. This process involves means of linking to prior talk, and clauses. The full resayings recycle whole interrogative clauses and become hearable as first occasions of asking. The full design allows for the re-said question to be heard "for another first time," as if the speaker were initiating a whole new sequence with a new recipient, even though s/he is taking a side-step from the main sequence. The design might even be said to de-link the question from its origin in order to produce an independent action. In contrast, the partial resayings recycle parts of clauses (or phrases) and this establishes a link with the prior interrogative clauses. In other words, these structures, which could perhaps be described as "symbiotic" (Auer 2014) with prior talk, display to the recipient that the speaker is operating on a prior turn, and this is how they become understandable as second sayings. Recipients display their understanding, for instance, by directing their the answer to the original speaker, or by an embodied orientation to her/him after the completed sequence, as in moving closer and making her/himself available for further interaction.

The analysis of how participants ask about matters in the epistemic domain of the other-language-speaking participant suggested that establishing recipiency in these situations poses challenges for both the non-understanding recipient and for the speaker. In the majority of cases, the speakers do not approach the recipient RS directly. Instead, they either do not address that participant (type 1), or they do so in an indirect way (type 2). The questions that do address the recipient RS directly rely on her/his involvement in the prior sequence. In short, the speakers' strategies are to ask someone else, to target indirectly, or to seize the moment in conversational time by exploiting the co-participant's current status in the unfolding sequence and participation framework.

The complexity of approaching a recipient in the multiparty, multilingual situation described here gives rise to varying practical solutions for mediating. In addition to negotiating who will participate in the first place, there is a need to organize the position of the mediator. This aspect is especially interesting from the point of view of a speaker's methods for displaying that they are *translating* the prior talk. In the present data, a secondary speaker role is signaled by producing a partial resaying. By contrast, a primary speaker role is achieved by a full resaying. This indicates that providing a full version of a question and accordingly, producing a "faithful" translation (complete, as close as possible), may be in conflict with the need to indicate that one is translating. For instance, regarding knowledge status, the speakers cannot rely on an institutional role as a supposedly neutral participant when translating questions that they know the answer to. In the cases with resayings as full, first sayings, the speakers are actually asking questions on their own behalf, in order to answer the original questions. By comparison, speakers producing second sayings of questions may be either unknowing or knowing participants. One way they can adjust the design of the question resaying with their knowledge status is by designing a question to be heard as a second saying of another speaker's turn, which is linked to that turn through the dispensing of elements that would mark it as a first. As a result, the speaker does not lay claim to the status of a first speaker and a genuine questioner, but to that of a relayer of another's question.

When a speaker engages in mediating, s/he does not assume an imposed role of an intermediary, but adopts a position with regard to the prior action by particular, situated means. One way of making the process visible to the recipient is through linking to the prior talk. The comparison of full and partial resayings has revealed that the partial resayings may function to display the turn's translatory nature. For this reason, this study proposes that mundane interactional motivations account for why lay speakers produce translations in the form of partial resayings. Their translatory turns resemble what have been regarded as *reduced* renditions in professional interpreting (Wadensjö 1998: 106–108). Here we might discover "good organizational reasons" for what may be a "bad practice" (Garfinkel 1967:186–207, see also

Meyer et al. 2010)[13] from the viewpoint of institutional interpreting. Whereas the present study examines everyday conversation, the findings intersect with research on professional interpreting, which has demonstrated how the interpreters' turns also achieve positioning work in systematic modes of interpreting (Wadensjö 1998; 2010; Bolden 2000; Mason 2009; Baraldi & Gavioli 2012).

Conversational data that contain translatory talk offer an interesting perspective on action ascription; they allow us to observe how a prior action is re-presented by another speaker. Through the position and composition of the resaying, speakers may establish different types of links and levels of sameness between what they are saying and another speaker's talk. By designing a resaying as a first or as a second saying of a question, the speaker relates the resaying to the original question in a particular way. Besides mediating a request for information, the resaying of another's question also, and centrally, enables the re-positioning of all the actors involved.

References

Auer, Peter. 1984a. *Bilingual conversation*. Amsterdam/Philadelphia: John Benjamins Publishing Company.
Auer, Peter. 1984b. On the meaning of conversational code-switching. In Peter Auer & Aldo di Luzio (eds.), *Interpretive sociolinguistics*. 87–112. Türbingen, Germany: Narr.
Auer, Peter. 2014. Syntactic structures and their symbiotic guests. Notes on analepsis from the perspective of online syntax. *Pragmatics* 24(3): 533–560.
Baraldi, Claudio & Laura Gavioli (eds.). 2012. *Coordinating participation in dialogue interpreting*. Amsterdam/Philadelphia: John Benjamin's Publishing Company.
Bolden, Galina. 2000. Toward understanding practices of medical interpreting: Interpreters' involvement in history taking. *Discourse Studies* 2(4): 387–419.
Bolden, Galina. 2012. Across languages and cultures: Brokering problems of understanding in conversational repair. *Language in Society* 41(1): 97–121.
Bolden, Galina. 2013. Unpacking "self". Repair and epistemics in conversation. *Social Psychology Quarterly* 76(4): 314–342.
Conceição de Paiva da, Maria. 2008. Ordem não marcada de circunstanciais locativos e temporais. In Sebastião Votre & Cláudia Roncarati (eds.), *Anthony Julius Naro e a lingüística no Brasil. Uma homenagem acadêmica*. 254–264. Rio de Janeiro: 7letras.
Couper-Kuhlen, Elizabeth. 1996. The prosody of repetition. In Elizabeth Couper-Kuhlen & Margret Selting (eds.), *Prosody in conversation. Interactional studies*. 366–405. Cambridge: Cambridge University Press.
Curl, Traci S. 2005. Practices in other-initiated repair resolution: The phonetic differentiation of repetitions. *Discourse Processes* 39(1): 1–43.
Davidson, Brad. 2002. A model for the construction of conversational ground in interpreted discourse. *Journal of Pragmatics* 34(9): 273–300.
Del Torto, Lisa. 2008. Once a broker, always a broker: Non-professional interpreting as identity accomplishment in multigenerational Italian-English bilingual family interaction. *Multilingua* 27(1/2): 77–97.

---

13 I would like to thank Jörg Bergmann for ideas and discussion regarding this matter.

Drew, Paul. 1997. 'Open' class repair initiators in response to sequential sources of troubles in conversation. *Journal of Pragmatics* 28(1): 69–101.

Egbert, Maria M. 1997. Schisming: The collaborative transformation from a single conversation to multiple conversations. *Research on Language and Social Interaction* 30(1): 1–51.

Ford, Cecilia E., Barbara A. Fox & Sandra A. Thompson. 2013. Units and/or action trajectories? The language of grammatical categories and the language of social action. In Beatrice Szczepek Reed & Geoffrey Raymond (eds.), *Units of talk – Units of action*. 13–55. Amsterdam/Philadelphia: John Benjamins Publishing Company.

Garfinkel, Harold. 1967. *Studies in ethnomethodology*. Englewood Cliffs NJ: Prentice-Hall.

Goffman, Erving. 1981. *Forms of talk*. Philadelphia: University of Pennsylvania Press.

Goodwin, Charles. 1981. *Conversational organization: Interaction between speakers and hearers*. New York: New York Academic Press.

Goodwin, Charles. 1987. Forgetfulness as an interactive resource. *Social Psychology Quarterly* 50(2): 115–131.

Goodwin, Charles. 2007. Interactive footing. In Elizabeth Holt & Rebecca Clift (eds.), *Reporting talk: Reported speech in interaction*. 16–46. Cambridge: Cambridge University Press.

Goodwin, Charles. 2013. The co-operative, transformative organization of human action and knowledge. *Journal of Pragmatics* 46(1): 8–23.

Goodwin, Charles & Marjorie Harness Goodwin. 1992. Context, activity and participation. In Peter Peter & Aldo di Luzio (eds.), *The contextualization of language*. 77–99. Amsterdam/Philadelphia: John Benjamin's Publishing Company.

Goodwin, Charles & Marjorie Harness Goodwin. 2004. Participation. In Alessandro Duranti (ed.), *A companion to linguistic anthropology*. 222–244. Malden MA: Blackwell.

Goodwin, Marjorie Harness. 1990. *She-said-he-said: Talk as social organization among black children*. Bloomington: Indiana University Press.

Goodwin, Marjorie Harness & Charles Goodwin. 1987. Children's arguing. In Susan Philips, Susan Steele & Christine Tanz (eds.), *Language, gender, and sex in comparative perspective*. 200–248. Cambridge: Cambridge University Press.

Greer, Tim. 2008. Accomplishing difference in bilingual interaction: Translation as backwards-oriented medium repair. *Multilingua* 27(1/2): 99–127.

Gumperz John. 1982. *Discourse strategies*. Cambridge: Cambridge University Press.

Haakana, Markku. 2011. *Mitä* ja muut avoimet korjausaloitteet. *Virittäjä* 115: 36–67.

Hanks, William. 1990. *Referential practice: Language and lived space among the Maya*. Chicago & London: University of Chicago Press.

Harjunpää, Katariina (in preparation): *Turn-design for bilingual mediating. Translation in everyday conversation*. Ph.D. dissertation.

Harjunpää, Katariina & Aleksi Mäkilähde. 2016. Reiteration: at the intersection of code-switching and translation. *Multilingua* 35(2): 163–201.

Helasvuo, Marja-Liisa. 2001. *Syntax in the making. The emergence of syntactic units in Finnish conversation*. Amsterdam/Philadelphia: John Benjamins Publishing Company.

Heritage, John. 1984. *Garfinkel and ethnomethodology*. Cambridge: Polity Press.

Heritage, John. 2012. Epistemics in action: Action formation and territories of knowledge. *Research on Language and Social Interaction* 45(1): 1–29.

Heritage, John & Geoffrey Raymond. 2005. The terms of agreement: Indexing epistemic authority and subordination in talk-in-interaction. *Social Psychology Quarterly* 68(1): 15–38.

ISK=*Iso suomen kielioppi* [The Comprehensive Grammar of Finnish] 2004: Auli Hakulinen, Maria Vilkuna, Riitta Korhonen, Vesa Koivisto, Tarja Riitta Heinonen & Irja Alho (eds.). Helsinki: Finnish Literature Society.

Jefferson, Gail. 1972. Side sequences. In David Sudnow (ed.), *Studies in social interaction.* 294–333. New York: Free Press.

Knapp-Potthoff, Annelie & Karlfried Knapp. 1987. The man (or woman) in the middle: Discoursal aspects of non-professional interpreting. In Karlfried Knapp, Werner Enninger & Annelie Knapp-Potthoff (eds.), *Analyzing intercultural communication.* 181–211. Berlin: Mouton de Gruyter.

Kolehmainen, Leena, Kaisa Koskinen & Helka Riionheimo. 2015. Arjen näkymätön kääntäminen. Translatorisen toiminnan jatkumot. *Virittäjä* 2015(3): 372–400.

Laury, Ritva. 1997. *Demonstratives in interaction. The emergence of a definite article in Finnish.* Amsterdam/Philadelphia: John Benjamin's Publishing Company.

Lerner, Gene H. 1996a. Finding 'face' in the preference structures of talk-in-interaction. *Social Psychology Quarterly* 59: 303–21.

Lerner, Gene H. 1996b. On the place of linguistic resources in the organization of talk-in-interaction: 'Second person' reference in multi-party conversation. *Pragmatics* 6(3): 281–294.

Lerner, Gene H. 2003. Selecting next speaker: The context-sensitive operation of a context-free organization. *Language in Society* 32(2): 177–201.

Levinson, Stephen. 1988. Putting linguistics on a proper footing: Explorations in Goffman's concepts of participation. In Paul Drew & Anthony Wootton (eds.), *Erving Goffman: An interdisciplinary appreciation.* 161–227. Oxford: Polity Press.

Linell, Per. 2009. *Rethinking language, mind, and world dialogically: Interactional and contextual theories of human sense-making.* Charlotte NC: Information Age Publishing.

Local, John, Peter Auer & Paul Drew. 2010. Retrieving, redoing and resuscitating turns in conversation. In Dagmar Barth-Weingarten, Elisabeth Reber & Margret Selting (eds.), *Prosody in interaction* (Studies in discourse and grammar 23). 131–160. Amsterdam/Philadelphia: John Benjamin's Publishing Company.

Mason, Ian. 2009. Role, positioning and discourse in face-to-face interpreting. In Raquel de Pedro Ricoy, Isabelle Pérez & Christine Wilson (eds.), *Interpreting an translating in public service settings. Policy, practice, pedagogy.* 52–73. New York: Routledge.

Mazeland, Harry. 2013. Grammar in conversation. In Jack Sidnell & Tanya Stivers (eds.), *The handbook of conversation analysis.* 475–491. Malden/Oxford: John Wiley & Sons.

Merlino, Sara. 2012. *Négocier la transition de la parole du traduit au traducteur: l'organisation séquentielle et multimodale de la traduction orale.* Ph.D. dissertation. Université Lumière Lyon II, France & Università degli Studi di Torino, Italy.

Merlino, Sara & Lorenza Mondada. 2013. La traduction comme pratique multiforme imbriquée dans l'activité située. In Danielle Londei & Laura Santone (eds.), *Entre linguistique et anthropologie. Observations de terrain, modèles d'analyse et expériences d'écriture.* 205–232. Bern: Transversales/Peter Lang.

Merlino, Sara & Lorenza Mondada. 2014. Identités fluides dans le travail interactionnel du traducteur improvisé. In Lucca Greco, Lorenza Mondada & Patrick Renaud (eds.), *Identités en interaction.* 87–114. Limonges: Lambert Lucas.

Meyer, Bernd, Birte Pawlack & Ortrun Kliche. 2010. Family interpreters in hospitals: Good reasons for bad practice?. *mediAzioni* 10, http://mediazioni.sitlec.unibo.it

Mondada, Lorenza. 2004. Ways of 'doing being plurilingual' in international work meetings. In Rod Gardner & Johannes Wagner (eds.), *Second language conversations.* 27–60. London: Continuum.

Mondada, Lorenza. 2007. Multimodal resources for turn-taking: Pointing and the emergence of possible next speakers. *Discourse Studies* 9(2): 194–225.

Morães, João Antônio de. 1998. Intonation in Brazilian Portuguese. In Daniel Hirst & Albert Di Cristo (eds.), *Intonation systems. A survey of twenty languages.* 179–194. Cambridge: Cambridge University Press.

Müller, Frank. 1989. Translation in bilingual conversation: Pragmatic aspects of translatory interaction. *Journal of Pragmatics* 13(5): 713–739.
Oh, Sun-Young. 2005. English zero anaphora as an interactional resource. *Research on Language and Social Interaction* 38(3): 267–302.
Paulsen Christensen, Tina. 2008. Judges' deviations from norm-based direct speech in court. *Interpreting* 10(1): 99–127.
Pontes, Eunice. 1987. *O tópico no Português do Brasil*. Campinas: Pontes editores.
Rauniomaa, Mirka. 2008. *Recovery through repetition. Returning to prior talk and taking a stance in American-English and Finnish conversations*. Ph.D. dissertation. Oulu: University of Oulu Press.
Raymond, Chase Wesley. 2014. Epistemic brokering in the interpreter-mediated medical visit: Negotiating 'patient's side' and 'doctor's side' knowledge. *Research on Language and Social Interaction* 47(4): 426–446.
Rossano, Federico. 2012. *Gaze behaviour in face-to-face interaction*. Ph.D. dissertation. Max Planck Institute for Psycholinguistics Series.
Sacks, Harvey. 1995. *Lectures on conversation*. Volumes I and II. Oxford/Cambridge: Blackwell Publishing.
Sacks, Harvey, Emanuel A. Schegloff & Gail Jefferson. 1974. A simplest systematics for the organization of turn-taking for conversation. *Language* 50(4): 696–735.
Schegloff, Emanuel A. 1996a. Turn organization: one intersection of grammar and interaction. In Elinor Ochs, Emanuel A. Schegloff & Sandra A. Thompson (eds.), *Interaction and grammar*. 52–133. Cambridge: Cambridge University Press.
Schegloff, Emanuel A. 1996b. Some practices for referring to persons in talk-in-interaction: A partial sketch of a systematics. In Barbara Fox (ed.), *Studies in anaphora*. 437–485. Amsterdam/Philadelphia: John Benjamins Publishing Company.
Schegloff, Emanuel A. 2004. On dispensability. *Research on Language and Social Interaction* 37(2): 95–149.
Schegloff, Emanuel A. 2007. *Sequence organization in interaction: Volume 1: A primer in conversation analysis*. Cambridge: Cambridge University Press.
Schegloff, Emanuel A. & Harvey Sacks. 1973. Opening up closings. *Semiotica* 8(4): 289–327.
Seppänen, Eeva-Leena. 1998. *Läsnäolon pronominit: tämä, tuo, se ja hän viittaamassa keskustelun osallistujaan*. Helsinki: Finnish Literature Society.
Stivers, Tanya. 2005. Modified repeats: One method for asserting primary rights from second position. *Research on Language and Social Interaction* 38(2): 131–158.
Stivers, Tanya & Federico Rossano. 2010. Mobilizing response. *Research on Language and Social Interaction* 43: 3–31.
Thompson Sandra A., Barbara A. Fox & Elizabeth Couper-Kuhlen. 2015. *Grammar in everyday talk: Building responsive actions*. Cambridge: Cambridge University Press.
Traverso, Véronique. 2012. Ad hoc-interpreting in multilingual work meetings: Who translates for whom? In Claudio Baraldi & Laura Gavioli (eds.), *Coordinating participation in dialogue interpreting*. 149–176. Amsterdam/Philadlephia: John Benjamins Publishing Company.
Tse, Lucy. 1996. Language brokering in linguistic minority communities: The case of Chinese- and Vietnamese-American students. *The Bilingual Research Journal* 20 (3&4): 485–498.
Wadensjö, Cecilia. 1998. *Interpreting as interaction*. London/New York: Longman.
Wadensjö, Cecilia. 2010. On the production and elicitation of expanded yes/no questions in interpreted-mediated trials. In Mona Baker, Maeve Olohan & María Calzada Pérez (eds.), *Text and context. Essays on translation and interpreting in honour of Ian Mason*. 9–26. Manchester: St. Jerome Publishing.
Wilton, Antje. 2009. Interactional translation. In Kristin Bührig, Juliane House & Jan D. ten Thije (eds.), *Translational action and intercultural communication*. 80–109. Manchester: St. Jerome Publishing.

SAIJA MERKE
http://orcid.org/0000-0002-7860-0212

4. Tackling and establishing norms in classroom interaction: Student requests for clarification

Introduction

This article examines student-initiated question sequences in Finnish-as-foreign-language classroom interactions at the university level. The analysis will focus on sequence-initiating turns that function as requests for clarification but at the same time display that the student has previous knowledge of the academic subject, namely the Finnish language. Recent research in CA-for-SLA (Kasper & Wagner 2011; Pekarek Doehler 2013) discusses sequences in which students independently detect and introduce learnables and knowledge gaps to the classroom discussion (Majlesi & Broth 2012; *epistemic search sequences*, Jakonen & Morton 2015). The sequences in the present study are comparable to these types of epistemic search sequences. They are characterized first by the sequence being launched with a turn that detects a linguistic detail that does not meet the student's expectations towards previously discussed grammatical rules. Secondly, the design of the initiating turn displays the participant's epistemic access to the domain of Finnish. In addition, the sequence-initiating turn questions the correctness or coherence of new linguistic information as compared to already acquired linguistic knowledge.

In this sense, the linking that is discussed in this article concerns the relationship between previous knowledge and the current language study context. The link between these two states of affairs is the initiating turn, which is characterized by negation or the expression of contrast. The first example (1) illustrates this phenomenon. The student (S) addresses the teacher and evokes a competing meaning for the word *vaalea* 'blond'. The negation in the turn-initiating quotative implies a contradiction between information stated *la dernière fois* 'last time' and something that has just been said:

(1) poivre-et-sel

S: vous avez pas dit que c'était pour (>poivre-et-sel<)
   ↑la dernière fois,
   didn't you say that it was for greyish ↑last time,

The sequence-initiating turns to be analyzed function as questions, since they elicit an answer as a relevant next. They are all clausally formulated: they may be negatively formatted declaratives (*là dedans il y a pas un mot qui veut dire billet ou* 'Isn't there a word in there which means note or'), adversative declaratives (*mais la gare* ça *restera ouvert* 'but the station stays open'), or causal question-word interrogatives (*pourquoi* ça *se construit pas sur le même dessin* 'why isn't it constructed with the same pattern). In French, declaratives can be used as polar questions. In this specific context of sequence initiation in the foreign language classroom, they challenge or question the representation of a state of affairs.

AIM AND BACKGROUND OF THE STUDY
The primary aim of the study is to demonstrate that the learners' expectations for grammatical rules and their predictability are comparable to the expectations they have towards social norms and their moral dimension. When speakers are confronted with unanticipated behavior, they expect such behavior to be subsequently explained or corrected (Scott & Lyman 1968; Bergmann & Luckmann 1999). This same expectation can be observed when students are confronted with surprising grammatical phenomena.

In my data, students are able to assess a grammatical phenomenon as unexpected in at least two different contexts. The first is that the grammatical detail is neither in the range of the students' epistemic domain, nor has ever been topicalized or explained. The second context occurs when the phenomenon is in the students' epistemic domain, but epistemic access is hindered or complicated. The participants assess the unexpectedness of the phenomenon differently depending on how they evaluate their own epistemic access. For this reason, it is useful to distinguish between expectations regarding the academic subject and expectations towards the sequential development of the on-going interaction, which connect to the normativity of epistemic rights and responsibility.

A second aim of this analysis is to demonstrate that such epistemic search sequences enable speakers to tackle and establish norms of various types. The participants may revisit the normativity of an expectation, whether it concerns how grammar 'behaves' or the participants' ability to access a certain piece of linguistic knowledge. This study emphasizes the dynamics between 'given'/'acquired' and 'not-given'/'not-yet-acquired' knowledge and the potential of these sequences to initiate a learning process in interaction. The dynamics can be considered to be the prerequisite of constant adaption of new information to previously existing knowledge.

The normative character of expectations can be best illustrated in relation to the activity of repair or to accounts (Drew 2013; Enfield 2011: 290; Scott & Lyman 1968). The previously mentioned turn design (negation and expression of contrast) performs a type of repair initiation and therefore projects in the following the relevance of some type of repair or accounting from the recipient. The turn design helps the sequence format to emerge. In this format, participants develop a specific communicative project: an explanation that accounts for and addresses violations of an assumed norm (Mazeland 2013; Ford 2001).

The sequence-initiating turns focus on a surprising linguistic detail. By topicalizing and questioning the detail, the students display epistemic access. I will particularly emphasize the legitimacy of these initiating actions in the on-going classroom interaction as well as the reception of these turns, as the reception advances the establishment of normativity in actions. The sequence-initiating turns can be actions that claim a violation of norms. As such they may in themselves evoke moral issues (Bergmann & Luckmann 1999). When students disagree with the teacher's or their peers' claims concerning Finnish grammar or previously acquired knowledge, they display an awareness regarding their own state of knowledge. They indicate what they (already) know or what they *cannot* know yet. They therefore create their own norms and group-specific agreements and rules (cf. Günthner 1999: 211), both in the field of already acquired grammatical knowledge and during the process of learning a language together.

Data and methodological framework

The video data for this study were collected in a Finnish language class at a French university. This class is attended by a small group of young adults. The data consist of four hours of videotaped classroom interaction between first-year students of Finnish and their Finnish-speaking teacher.[1] The data include more than 35 question sequences. They vary in length from a few turns to discussions lasting several minutes and including several speakers. At the time of the recordings, the students had been attending Finnish classes four times a week for seven months.

The classroom discussion is predominantly conducted in a plenary form. The teacher stands between the group and the blackboard and leads the discussion. The plenary form alternates with sequences in which the group either compares exercises with each other or works in pairs.

Participation in classroom activity, especially in university plenary settings, demands specific interactional work from the students (on secondary school data, see Lehtimaja 2011). They have limited space to intervene without breaking the norms of interactional organization. One means to access the floor is to ask the teacher questions. Like teachers' questions, students' questions trigger three-part sequences (Merke 2012; for the classical IRE-scheme, see Sinclair & Coulthard 1975; Mehan 1979; on questions in CA, see Schegloff 2007; Steensig & Drew 2008, special issue). The responses to a question are, to a certain extent, projectable from the linguistic design of the question. The relation between these parts of a sequence may thus be described by the concept of *projection* (Hayashi 2004; Auer 2005; Pekarek Doehler 2011) and *type-conformity* (Raymond 2003). Negatively formatted declaratives that function as questions project two alternative responses, *non* 'no' or *si* 'yes', with *si* being the non-aligning option in this context (Kerbrat-Orecchioni 2001). *Pourquoi* 'why'-interrogatives, on the other hand, may evoke responses with an explicit explanation marker *parce*

---

[1] The data have been transcribed according to the Gail Jefferson transcription system (Sacks, Schegloff & Jefferson 1974) and glossed according to the Leipzig glossing rules.

que 'because'. The third turn in the sequence, the feed-back turn, belongs to the questioner. It signals whether or not the response was satisfactory.

Next turns in the sequence also reveal whether a participant is *aligning* or *non-aligning* with the prior turn. These concepts of alignment describe a form of linking action: whether an action counters or advances the ongoing interaction (Stivers 2008; Stivers et al. 2011). In this sense, an action that challenges the representation of a state of affairs can be categorised as non-aligning, because it initiates a side-sequence (Jefferson 1972) where the recipient is invited to clarify his/her representation, to account for it, or to explain it.

The article is organized as follows: in the next section, I will present the theoretical approach concerning the normative side of classroom interaction in order to identify norm violations later in the article. The first analytical section then examines the first position of the student-initiated question sequences. On the one hand, it shows the sequence format with sequence-initial negative declaratives, and on the other, a turn design that evokes contrast. I will discuss the potential of these sequence-initial turns for challenging and launching legitimate criticism of the teacher. In the following section, I will discuss the moral dimension of disappointed expectations in question sequences and its impact on learning. Finally, I will summarize my findings and present some concluding remarks.

Normative actions in classroom contexts

Classroom interaction is a type of institutional talk. The discourse situation is determined beforehand. This means that the place, time, and the duration of the interactions as well as a certain distribution of roles (representative of the institution versus lay person) create a constant that is rarely modified during the interaction. The interaction itself is therefore structured differently from everyday talk. Classroom interaction is characterised by a specific order of phases (*agenda*). Moreover, the different distribution of rights to talk or to introduce new topics creates asymmetry between the students and the teacher (Drew & Heritage 1992: 43).

The participant orientation to these external settings is displayed in the design of conduct (Drew & Heritage 1992: 43). Actions, behavior and activities that are not accounted for can be categorized as normative and belonging to the horizon of expectations and common knowledge. One important area of normativity in classroom interaction is the distribution of rights to *request* information and to *claim* knowledge (*epistemic primacy*, Stivers et al. 2011). Furthermore, the teacher as an expert is expected to be the most knowledgeable in the domain in question. Yet, as my data illustrate, students already display some knowledge concerning the study field. When students make a strong claim to knowledge and disagree with a teacher's claim, the teacher's expertise may be locally challenged.

In the extracts selected, students claim knowledge concerning Finnish grammar. They demonstrate that they do not agree with the presentation of a grammatical viewpoint (extract 1). At the same time, they can disapprove of the course of the ongoing interaction, disagree with the teacher, or with each other. In brief, student disagreement normally arises when something runs counter to their expectation.

The classroom context is the interpretational frame for these actions. This means that actions that disrupt the ongoing activity (the teacher's agenda) demand a higher degree of accountability than would be the case in everyday interaction. In addition, a student is part of the student collective, and therefore acting as an individual may become significant. This can be observed, for example, in accounts that occur subsequent to requests: these justify the request for clarification. (On classroom participation, see Koole 2003, 2007; Lehtimaja 2012: 42–45). At any rate, the existence of relevant norms in a classroom can only be revealed by the ongoing interaction and the speakers themselves. Asking a question is an expected action in the classroom (McHoul 1978; Drew & Heritage 1992: 26). However, the requests for clarification under focus are comparable to repair initiations in the sense that an unclear detail is pointed out and examined more closely.

Question turns always activate normative expectations or assumptions (Spranz-Fogasy 2005: 151 on *Kommunikationsideologien* and Peräkylä & Vehviläinen 2003 on *stocks of interactional knowledge*). Classroom participants have the expectation that questions will be understood and answered and that problems will be solved. An unanswered question may be commented on and evaluated as such by both the students and the teacher. Secondly, the question may reveal (untoward) assumptions about the speaker's understanding of a grammatical detail or assumptions about the addressee's previous claims, such that the teacher's actual explanations contradict some previous information. This concerns the assumption that "correct" information exists, an assumption that is relevant throughout the questioning activity.

Extracts (2) and (3) illustrate the sequential establishment of norms during epistemic search sequences. Excerpt (2) presents the whole context of extract (1). It illustrates a sequence that involves a problem in understanding, where the described normative design of conduct influences participants' *readiness to respond*. The example shows *how* participants introduce understanding problems to the interaction and to what *extent* problems in understanding are addressed. In this example, the participants opt not to continue the negotiations regarding an unclear lexeme and the problem remains unsolved.

The sequence in extract (2) begins with Lucie asking for a translation of the word for 'blond' *vaalea* (line 01), which is also used in compound color terms such as 'pink' *vaaleanpunainen* (literally 'light red') and 'light blue' *vaaleansininen*. Subsequently, Clarissa self-selects and claims some knowledge concerning the word (line 07).

(2) Blond

```
01    Lucie:  et ↑comment on dit bl<u>ond</u>,
                  and how do you say blond

02            (0.5)

03    Teach:  **vaa:lea.**

04    Lucie:  ((points with her pen))

05    Lucie:  ↑ah mais c'est marr<u>an</u>t en plus,
                  oh but that's even funny

06    Teach:  **va[a:lea.**

07 => Clari:     [vous avez pas dit que c'était pour (>poivre-et-sel<)
                  didn't you say it was for (greyish)

08 =>         ↑la dernière fois,
                  last time

09    Teach:  ↑quoi? que c'ét↑ait
                  what? that it was?

10    Clari:  (>poivre-et-s<u>el</u><)
                  (>greyish<)

11            (0.5)

12    Clari:  *donc il y avait avait des cheveux ↑gris ↓euh c'est
                  so there was was grey hair? uhm it's
      David   *((shifts gaze to Clarissa, smiles))

13    Clari:  c'était cl<u>air</u> [c'est:::::     ]
                  it was bright i::t's

14    Lucie:                  [non si c'est mm]
                                  no yes it's mm

15    Clari:  [c'était qu<u>oi</u> c'était euh
                  what was it it was uh

16    Lucie:  [c'est (---------------)]
                  it's (---)

17    Clari:  (**armaass**) non je pas ((gazes down))
                  (**armaass**) no I don't know

18    Teach:  je me souviens plus?
                  I don't remember anymore?
```

```
19    Clari:  (bon) c'est pas grave.
              (well) never mind

20            (1.0)

21    Teach:  °qu'est-ce que £j'ai raconté°£
              °what £have I said£°
```

In line 07 Clarissa asks a follow-up question that is formatted as a declarative. In French, the turn design projects either a *non* 'no' or a *si* 'yes' (Kerbrat-Orecchioni 2001), with a preference for the *si*, which has the same polarity as the subordinate clause (*que c'était pour poivre-et-sel* 'that it was for greyish').

However, Clarissa's request for clarification is not clear to the teacher. This is evident from the teacher's repair initiator (line 09) and Clarissa's multiple subsequent repairs. Clarissa estimates that the teacher's present answer to Lucie (line 03) contradicts the teacher's prior talk and checks the correctness of her understanding. She formulates her request for clarification as a quotation, which refers to the teacher's own talk, *vous avez pas dit* 'didn't you say'.

The teacher apparently does not understand the last part of Clarissa's turn (*poivre-et-sel* 'greyish', line 07), as she partially repeats Clarissa's turn (line 09). The problem might be connected to Clarissa's articulation and/or the fact that the teacher is not a native speaker of French. David, who is sitting next to Clarissa, displays some understanding, as he turns his gaze to Clarissa and smiles. Lucie responds to the question (line 14) and indicates that she can make sense of Clarissa's turn. She apparently tries to recollect what color they were talking about the other day. In any case, Lucie's turn remains opaque and no one addresses the teacher to paraphrase or to repeat the unclear item in Clarissa's turn. As Clarissa's question includes a quotation of the teacher's prior talk, the teacher is the only targeted participant and she is expected to answer the question. As the teacher does not claim understanding at any point, the repair actions continue over several turns and are afforded more space than the original question itself.

This sequence ends when Clarissa withdraws her gaze after her fourth try (she is apparently using the Finnish word for 'grey' "*harmaa*", line 17) and when the teacher identifies the problem as a lack of recollection and suggests that she is trying to remember (line 21). The nature of the problem is not specified. In the end, the teacher assumes responsibility for the comprehension problem as well as her own inability to solve it. The problem is, nonetheless, evaluated during the sequence by Clarissa as not being serious "*pas grave*" 'never mind' (line 19). In this case, the participants' normative expectation may be revealed by the redoing of repair initiations. Several attempts fail to solve the problem in understanding by initiating a repair sequence. This state of affairs may hinder the participants' pursuit of a satisfactory answer.

The third extract (3) illustrates how *access to knowledge* is treated normatively. The group is studying a Finnish text. An incorrect interpretation of case endings and stems leads to a misunderstanding. Gaëlle requests clarification (line 01) for the juxtaposition of two inner, local cases (inessive and illative), which for reasons of case congruence should be aligned. She spells out her problem (line 02): the use of local cases (which does not seem to correspond to the rules) is not clear to her. The item, *tietokoneen*, which Gaëlle interprets as an illative form, actually has a genitive marker (-n) and not an illative marker (-Vn). Her incorrect assumption is connected to the specific word type (lexemes ending with the vowel e, *tietokone*), which has a special stem (*tietokonee-*).

(3) Inessive and illative

```
01   Gaëlle:  pourquoi c'est ines‎sif et et et illatif ↓les deux, (.)
              why is there inessive and and illative both,

02            je comprends pas l'usage des cas locatifs ici,=
              I don't understand the use of local cases here,=

03   Lucie:   =mm ou ça,
              =where

04   Teach:   hh. [↑tietokonee-n käytö-s↑sä
                   computer-GEN    use-INE

05   Hélène:      [°mm°

06   Gaëlle:  mm

07   Hélène:  ↑mais c'est ↑pas un locatif,
              (to Gaëlle) but it's not a locative

08   Gaëlle:  de- ((looks at Hélène))

09   Lucie:   ((où))
              where

10   Teach:   >oui c'est pas un locatif<
              >yes it's not a locative<

11            [>pourquoi c'est pas,<]
               >why isn't it <

12   Hélène:  [(-----------------)  ]

13   Teach:   [pourquoi,          ]
               why

14   Lucie:   [ou ça un loca]tif
               where (should there be) a locative

15   Lucie :  °je vois pas°=
              ° I don't see (it)°=
```

```
16   Teach:    =£.HHH£

17   Hélène:   ((looks at the teacher))

18   Gaëlle:   °moi je comprends rien°
               °I don't understand anything°

19   Teach:    £des cas locatifs partout,£
               £locatives everywhere,£

20             ((laughter))

21   Teach:    tietokonee-n käytö-ssä mikä se on
               computer-GEN   use-INE   what it is
               the use of a computer, what is that

22             ((turns to write onto the blackboard))

23   Lucie:    ah non c'est c'est le parti- c'est l'accusa↑tif
               oh no it's it's a par- it's an accusative

24   Hélène:   c'est un accusatif singulier (---)
               (to Gaëlle) it's a singular accusative (---)

25   Teach:    (turns to the class)) joo:.
                                      ye:s.

26   Gaëlle:   ((looks into the book))

27   Gaëlle:   o::h. (.) ((leans back)) heh

28             ((laughter))

29   Lucie:    ((laughs, leans her head onto the table))

30   Hélène:   >£ne t'inquiète pas [j'ai fait l'erreur]
               (to Gaëlle) >£don't worry, I made that mistake

31   Lucie:                        [parce que---------]
                                   (to Gaëlle) because---

32   Hélène:   [tout au début en lisant la] phrase£<
               in the beginning when I read the sentence£<

33   Lucie:    [-------------------------](to Gaëlle)

34             (.)

35   Hélène:   £pareil.£
               £just the same.£

36   Teach:    oui: parce que c'est un mot avec e à la fin
               yes because it's a word ending with e
```

37	Hélène:	£ouais exactement oui °mm°£
		exactly yes °mm°£
38	Teach:	ça veut d<u>i</u>re déj<u>à</u> à la base d<u>a</u>ns s<u>on</u> radical=
		it means that already in its base in the stem=
39	Gaëlle:	=ah oui c'est vrai
		=oh that's right
40	Teach:	il a d<u>eu</u>x, e,
		it has got tw<u>o</u>, e,

In line 02 Gaëlle accounts for her question by pointing to a surprising phenomenon that is in contrast to a general rule: the alignment of two different local cases. The teacher initiates repair to clarify the unclear item (line 04), while a peer, Lucie, overtly claims that she cannot find the sentence that Gaëlle is talking about (lines 03, 14–15). Hélène then displays understanding (line 07). She claims independent access to knowledge when she corrects Gaëlle's false assumption *mais c'est pas un locatif* 'it's not a locative'. Subsequently, the students solve the problem together with the teacher. After two clarifying answers (lines 23–24) and the teacher's ratification (line 25), Gaëlle acknowledges the information. The use of the lengthened *o:::h* (line 27) at this point of sequence closure also suggests that the information was unexpected (Bert et al. 2008: 689). Moreover, Gaëlle takes a personal stance (ibid: 689) in her display of disappointment, a reaction that is taken up by the others with amusement and consolation. Hélène then ascribes the emotional stance of being upset to Gaëlle (line 30) and compares her own state of mind to that of Gaëlle (line 35).

The analysis of the examples provides evidence of the speaker's awareness of expectations regarding questions and the distribution of rights as well as an awareness concerning responsibilities to respond and to display knowledge. When students discover a detail that is surprising, unexpected, or even contrasting, they have the option of bringing it into the interaction. One means is to request clarification. Clarissa's (extract 2, line 07) and Gaëlle's (extract 3, 01–02) turns reveal that students expect that the information given by the teacher will be coherent and unambiguous. This implies that the teacher should not contradict herself. This is valid for language rules as well.

Meanwhile, questions should relate to matters that are new and to which students do not have access. In extract (3), Gaëlle accounts for her question (line 02) by claiming a lack of comprehension, which she connects to an incoherent grammatical detail. Her reaction to the solution (line 27) and Hélène's supportive turns (lines 30, 32) support the importance of access to a knowledge domain. The detail was in the range of Gaëlle's knowledge (she reacted to it with a display of exaggerated disappointment) and she is assisted by peers and the teacher in dealing with the situation of having forgotten or not seen something.

In general, requests for clarification that detect an unclear linguistic detail involve students seeking reliable information through them. Participants use requests as tools to ascertain the reliability of information and the trustworthiness of generalizations. When students initiate these types of sequences, they are seeking confirmation of their prior knowledge and assumptions, and their aim is to establish reliable rules. Requests for clarification therefore reveal the *students' understanding* of the grammatical problem at hand, so that these requests can be interpreted as stating and requesting information at the same time. Additionally, the turn design can reveal assumptions about appropriateness and correctness, so that speakers can evaluate through the activity of asking questions.

The student can express the unexpectedness or incoherence of a linguistic detail to the teacher as the person "responsible" for the matter. The above excerpts show that (reliable) knowledge and group-specific norms concerning knowledge territories are established simultaneously and that they are created during and linked to previous Finnish lessons. This means that students first interpret grammatical phenomena and new lexemes turn-by-turn in connection to their background knowledge, and second, they then state what cannot be taken for granted yet, and what they can or cannot be expected to know.

As is evident in these excerpts, an interactional dynamics is created by normative expectations pertaining to knowledge in this classroom. Firstly, the teacher needs to state rules correctly and to not contradict herself. Secondly, language rules should also not be contradictory. The language classroom is a place where these expectations of regularity in language and language learning are spelled out and put into action. Let us now turn to the relationship of specific turn designs to action formation and their relation to the expression of epistemic stance and moral challenge in an institutional context.

Negation and contrast as means for introducing a conflicting viewpoint

A sequence-initiating request for clarification characterizes something as being unknown, unclear, or unexpected, which is how it will be treated in the following interaction. Requests for clarification may express expectations of regularity in grammar or coherence of information and they do this by pointing out an irregularity. A turn design with negation can be used to spell out the item or representation of a state of affairs that does not correspond to the expected one. The negatively valenced turn presents the irregularity as a conflicting or divergent piece of information. Negation can be found in quotatives that introduce reported speech (2a) and in accounts that follow the question and claim non-understanding (3a), in causal question-word interrogatives (4), and in polar questions formulated as declaratives (5).

(2a) vous avez pas dit que c'était pour (>poivre-et-sel<)
      didn't you say it was for (greyish)

(3a) je comprends pas l'usage des cas locatifs ici
      I don't understand the use of local cases here

(4)   et pourquoi on a pas auto-n pour la première (-)
      and why don't we have   car-ACC for the first one

(5)   cent et cinquante là dedans il y a pas un mot qui veut dire billet ou
      hundred and fifty in there isn't there a word which means note or

Violation of coherence can also be expressed through contrast. Contrasts can be expressed by placing adversative markers at the beginning of the turn (6), by referring to a competing state of affairs (7) or by juxtaposing two elements either that run counter to the rules, or evoke otherwise a conflicting state of affairs (3b).

(6)   mais les lieux qui sont déjà ouverts comme la gare ça restera ouvert
      but the places which are already open like the station they stay open

(7)   mais quand il y avait X (…) vous avez dit que c'était Y
      but when there was X (…) you said that it was Y

(3b) pourquoi c'est inessif et et et illatif les deux.
      why is there inessive and and and illative both

These turn designs evoke a comparison between two contrasting states of affairs that cannot simultaneously be true, indicating that the actual fact is not in line with expectations and therefore requires clarification. This is intrinsically expressed by negation, because it encodes the non-existence of a state of affairs and implies the existence of a corresponding positive. Adversative turns, by contrast, introduce a competing state of affairs. The conflicting viewpoints are framed by the adverbial *déjà* 'already' (6) or the temporal subordination *quand il y avait* 'when there was' (7) in these 'but'-initiated turns. Quotations (2a & 7) constitute a special case, because they refer to incoherence in the participant's talk. Here, it is not the violation of a grammatical rule that is subjected to scrutiny, but rather the recipient's prior explanation. In the next section I will demonstrate that requests for clarification evoking a conflicting or divergent viewpoint can implicate evaluative and moral issues.

The case of negation

Speakers use turns with negation to comment on diverse aspects of the on-going talk. Negation can likewise be used either to redirect talk or to correct false implications in the preceding sequence (Haakana & Visapää

2014). Negative turns that claim divergent or disaffiliative viewpoints are frequently followed by subsequent elaboration (Ford 2000).

As the negation in the sequences at hand is embedded in the sequences' first position, it is the recipient who is assigned the position of elaborating. This can potentially become a moral issue. According to Sacks (1992: 49–56), negative causal questions in particular put the recipient in a position of being expected to justify a previous claim. The following analysis aims to show how claiming knowledge becomes a moral issue and that recipients design their responses to anticipate possible moral implications in the upcoming sequence.

Extract (8a) is an example of a negative why-question that compares two states of affairs. It also activates the issues of 'right' and 'wrong'. These issues may relate to prescriptive conceptions of grammatical rules. The question sequences examined here, however, imply issues that concern the right to claim knowledge and express criticism.

The topic of the lesson in extract (8a) is the Finnish possessive construction, e.g., 'Leena has a car'. In Finnish possessives, the possessor is an oblique, so the construction could be paraphrased as 'With Leena is a car'. Prior to this, the participants have been discussing a sentence on the blackboard, *Leena-lla on kaksi auto-a* 'Leena has two cars', in which 'car' is marked with a partitive singular case ending (*-a*). The use of the partitive singular form has caused confusion, so the teacher has reminded the students that numbers are always followed by nouns with a partitive singular case ending. At this point, Gaëlle is intrigued by the first sentence on the blackboard (*Maijalla on auto* 'Maija has a car') in which the possessed (and hence object-like) noun *auto* 'car' is not marked as a grammatical object (with an accusative ending *-n*) but appears instead in the nominative case.

(8a) Why not the accusative

```
01 Gaë:  et pourquoi on a pas au↑to-n (.) pour la première (phrase),
         and why don't we have   car-ACC      for the first one

02       ((teacher turns to the blackboard))

03 Gaë:  pourquoi on a pas l´accusatif [comme c´est dénombrable que,]
         why don't we have the accusative as it's countable

04 Cla:                                [>comme c´est le sujet<      ]
                                        >because it's the subject<

05 Hél?: [((groaning))                 ]

06 Cla:  [parce que c´est le su<u>jet</u> (.) c´est] le sujet ça°
         because it's the subject that's the subject

07 Luc:  parce que c´est [toujours le nomina↑tif]
         because it's always the nominative

08 Tea:                  [oui ça c´est une::    ]
                          yes that's a::
```

115

```
09        une (.) une PArticularité de ↑cette structure. .hh
          a (.) a particularity of this structure .hh

10        (.)

11 Gaë:   °oké°

12        (.)

13 Tea:   de: la, la structure de posses↑sion si euh-
          of the, the possessive structure if uh-
```

Gaëlle's negative why-question implies that her expectations are not met. The *et* 'and' conjunction in the beginning of the turn indicates that Gaëlle pursues the on-going discussion with her observation. The turn design also shows what types of expectations have not been met and hints at an accountable action that has occurred previously (Sacks 1992: 4). In this particular context, this could be paraphrased as "the object-like noun *car* is not marked with any grammatical object case ending". In this particular situation, Gaëlle expected an accusative instead of a nominative, and the grounds for her hypothesis is that *auto* 'car' is a countable noun. Her assumption is strengthened by the fact that in possessive constructions that contain uncountable nouns and nouns preceded by numbers, these types of nouns are always marked with a grammatical object case ending, the partitive.

The first to respond are Gaëlle's peer-students. They both start in overlap with Gaëlle as well as with each other. Clarissa and Lucie orient to explicit reason-giving, as they begin their turns with the causal conjunction *parce que, comme* 'because'. The immediateness of their responses suggests that Gaëlle's question concerns commonly known matters.

The causal question design challenges the grounds on which a prior claim has been made, but at the same time, the questioner becomes accountable for launching a challenging move. The reason for this comment may be that Gaëlle requests an account but bases her criticism on false assumptions. The groaning (line 05) suggests that for some reason her question is judged to be misplaced. In fact, the possessive construction never allows the use of a *n*-marked accusative case. Even though the students had studied this rule in detail, it is information that is easily forgotten.

The analysis of extract (8a) demonstrated that negative why-questions can indicate upcoming moral issues concerning both knowledge claims and the correctness of assumptions. In these cases peer students respond even before the teacher. In their responses, students claim to be knowledgeable, which creates a distribution of knowledge that is different from what is normally the case.

The teacher remains the main recipient of the question and in her first move she acknowledges the request for clarification before responding. Let us examine extract (8b) more closely. The teacher is in overlap with Lucie and Clarissa, stating the following:

(8b) Why not the accusative, continued

```
08 Tea: oui ça c´est une::
        yes that's a::

09      une (.) une PArticularité de ↑cette structure. .hh
        a particularity of this structure .hh

10      (.)

11 Gaë: °oké°

12      (.)

13 Tea: de: la, la structure de posses↑sion si euh-
        of the, the possessive structure if uh

14      ↑est-ce que vous vous souvenez de la ↑phrase
        existentielle.
        ↑do you remember the existential phrase

15      des règles pour la phrase existentielle.
        the rules for the existential phrase
```

The teacher first acknowledges the question (line 08). This turn also reestablishes a common focus after two other students have responded in overlap and competed with explanations. But the teacher does not use a causal marker to link her response to the question, and this means that her response is not framed as an explicit explanation. Instead, she states that something is specific to the syntactic (possessive) construction. She uses the anaphoric pronoun ça 'this' to refer to the phenomenon. Yet, the turn does not specify *what* the particular phenomenon is. Her response is formulated as an assertion and it implies that the surprising grammatical element (the use of the nominative) is in accordance with the rules. The syntactic structure of the teacher's turn includes a left dislocation, ça c'est. This suggests that the teacher pursues a direction that is divergent from what has occurred previously on both the interactional and the topical levels (Pekarek Doehler 2001: 190). Even if the first part of the teacher's response (lines 08 and 09) does not include an explanation, Gaëlle accepts the teacher's response in the third position by stating *oké* (line 11).

It is important to note that the teacher neither topicalizes nor sanctions Gaëlle's false assumption. Instead, the teacher reacts with a change of direction. Her response is not type-conforming (Raymond 2003) and is minimally projectable in that her response does not build on the explanandum suggested in Gaëlle's turn. Firstly, no causal markers (*parce que, comme* 'because') mark her turn as an explicit explanation. Secondly, as her turn does not address the concrete problem, it does not offer an explanation as to why the accusative *auto-n* is unsuitable. Nevertheless, the teacher aligns with the inquiry about an unexpected detail and initiates an explanation sequence. She proceeds to activate the students' memory as language learners: *est-ce que vous vous souvenez* 'do you remember' (line 14), which is the first part of a subsequent explanation.

Consequently, Gaëlle is not the only addressee of the instruction, but the whole group is addressed. From this it follows that neither the potentially challenging issue (there is something wrong here) initiated by Gaëlle, nor an obligation to know matters is attributed to a single recipient. Instead, they are directed to the whole group.

The case of contrast

Negatively formatted declaratives or question-word interrogatives are only one type of turn design pointing to a violation of expectations. Another recurrent turn design is the adversative declarative, which begins with a contrastive marker *mais* 'but'. In contrast to negatively formatted declaratives, adversative declaratives make a stronger epistemic claim and may signify in this institutional setting an advance into the teacher's territory of knowledge.

In extract (9), the group is studying the abstract use of local cases in combination with verbs such as 'lend', 'borrow', 'call' and their animate or inanimate complements. After a teaching IRE-sequence, the teacher makes a generalization regarding the distribution of inner and outer local cases and at this point, Gaëlle requests a clarification of the rules for concrete locations (line 06).

(9) Open places

```
01 Tea:    et avec des:: >disons des *lieux::? des institutions?<
           and with     >let's say    *places institutions?<
   Gaë                                *((rises gaze))

02 Tea:    ou même un objet comme une ↑lettre. répondre ↑à ↑une ↑lettre or
           even an object like a ↑letter answer ↑to ↑a ↑letter

03         (.) vous pouvez plus longtemps utiliser (.) le alla↑tif
           (.) you cannot take any longer (.) the allative

04         mais il faut changer (.) faut prendre le le cop<u>ain</u> (0.5)
           but you have to change you have to take the the fri<u>e</u>nd (0.5)

05         parmi les cas int<u>é</u>rieurs oui (.)↑l'illatif.
           among the int<u>e</u>rior cases right the ↑illative.

06 => Gae: mais les li<u>eu</u>x qui sont déjà ouve<u>rts</u> comme la g<u>a</u>re ça
           but the pl<u>a</u>ces which are already <u>o</u>pen like the st<u>a</u>tion they

07         restera, (.) ouvert?
           stay (.) open ?

08         (.)

09 Gaë:    (enfin) °dans la phrase°
           (I mean) °in the sentence°
```

```
10              (.)

11 Tea:    o::ui >si tu vas dire< vie-n    paketi-n   asema-lle   si.
                                  take-1SG parcel-ACC station-ALL
           y::es >if you say< I take the parcel to the station yes

12 Gaë:    °hmhm?°
           °uhu?°

13 Tea:    si. vien paketin asemalle# mais ça c'est. (.) oui.
           yes. I take the parcel to the station but this is. (.) yes.

14         (0.5) vraiment l'lieu (1.0) oui ça c'est le lieu (.)
           (0.5) really the place (1.0) yes that's the place

15         ici je pense on pense plus tôt à à ↑l'institution.
           here I think they have rather an an ↑institution in mind.

16 Gaë:    oké

17 Tea:    oui la la ↑poste ou la banque °comme institution.°
           yes the the ↑post or the bank °as institution.°
```

During her turn (line 06), Gaëlle claims knowledge about the use of the local cases related to concrete locations. The contrastive construction of her turn implies that the new information is not coherent with her previous knowledge. Her turn is a request for clarification, which she formulates as a declarative, projecting a response with the same polarity. However, no immediate uptake occurs, neither from her peers, nor from the teacher. Gaëlle continues and uses a turn expansion (line 09) to back down from her claim about "open" places in general and reduces her claim to open places on the "sentence" level. Her expansion may modify the epistemic stance of her prior claim in that she becomes less accountable for doubting the general trustworthiness of rules (cf. the practice of retracting overstatements, Couper-Kuhlen & Thompson 2005).

The teacher's delayed response and hesitation indicate that she finds Gaëlle's request to be a problem. This may be because it is "outside" the agenda and is therefore unexpected. Nevertheless, the teacher confirms Gaëlle's assumption; she does this once at the beginning of her turn: *oui* 'yes', and a second time at the end with *si* 'yes' (line 11). The teacher first gives an example for the concrete use of local cases. Her turn could be interpreted as a symbiont (Auer 2014: 534) hosted by Gaëlle's turn; the turn-final *si* 'yes' implicitly takes up Gaëlle's assumption about places that are already open and that remain open. The teacher subsequently continues to resolve the ambiguity by explaining in detail the difference between *lieu* 'place' and *institution* 'institution'.

Even though it is delayed, the teacher's response in line 11 is both type-conforming and a symbiont aligning with respect to Gaëlle's inquiry. This response reacts to the polarity of the declarative and confirms Gaëlle's analysis on the use of external local cases and "open" places. In admitting that the student is right, the teacher accepts the contesting move and accepts it as adhering to the norms (cf. Koshik 2002: 1855 on *epistemic stance*).

Gaëlle's turn design (*mais* 'but' with resumption marker quality + left dislocation) reveals that she is initiating an ancillary sequence rather than introducing a new topic (Mazeland & Huiskes 2001; Merke, forthcoming). This suggests that the request is legitimate in terms of content, design, and sequential position (cf. Deppermann 2009: 52–53 on the German modal marker *denn* in retrospective questions).

The previous analysis has demonstrated that challenging turns and even criticism are introduced in interaction through diverse linguistic means. Students display their expectations for grammatical coherence and the types of expectations that have not been met. One possible moral aspect is inherent in the entitlement to claim that something is "wrong" or "behaves" incoherently. Students can also be held responsible for the knowledge they already have access to. In other words, certain details are treated as already belonging to the students' epistemic domain. This leads to the issue of responsibility and the morality of knowledge.

The teacher as recipient can recognize the previous turn as launching criticism, but she does not necessarily need to acknowledge herself as someone who is morally responsible. Thus, the recipient of criticism can distance herself from the criticized feature, acknowledging it, but declining responsibility for it (for example, by responding with *oui* 'yes' to a why-question). In this case, the recipient rejects identification as the author of the criticized matter (see Günthner 1999 on reproach activities). The criticized matter may be a surprising grammatical detail without being related to participants' behavior. Even so, the teacher can still be held responsible for (not) presenting language rules in a coherent way.

Extracts (8ab and 9) are evidence that when a moralizing issue has been made relevant in the FPPs, the second pair parts (SPPs) indicate whether or not the participants consider the FPP a problem. The teacher as expert and "referee" expresses in her response to what degree, if any, the critical move can be classified as legitimate. In (8ab) she confirms the question as being justified but at the same time, she sequentially deletes the students' responses with overlapping talk. In (9) she confirms Gaëlle's analysis twice. In extract (3), it is evident that when students have sufficient access to knowledge, they can also do "legitimizing" work (Peräkylä 2014).

The term "legitimate" is defined here as 1) "the student is entitled to interrupt with a question", 2) "the student is entitled to be confused, disappointed", or 3) "the student is right to point out incoherence". As I have already stated, identifying incoherence or stating a divergent viewpoint is in itself a moral move. Peer students tend to react more immediately than the teacher. They are especially sensitive to knowledge claims that compete with their own understanding of the facts. Let us now turn to one final example of an aspect of the initiated question being treated as illegitimate.

Resisting potential moralizing
Not all requests for clarification that implicate expectations for regularity in grammar rules and that include strong claims are considered to be

legitimate. There may be divergent viewpoints regarding the justification of the challenging move. For example, the teacher may disalign with one aspect of the criticism presented, even if the disagreement is not explicitly apparent (contesting turns are rarely sanctioned). In this context, instead of acknowledging the request for clarification, the teacher moves directly to information-giving. The informing sequence is not explicitly marked as an "explanation" as usually occurs after positively valenced why-questions with *parce que* 'because' (Merke 2012). When the teacher is overtly "accused" or held responsible (see extract 2), she introduces a side sequence or initiates repair.[2]

The next example contains a request for clarification and the reactions of a peer student reveal that something controversial has occurred. In extract (10), the group is translating Finnish dialogues into French. The student question (line 14) concerns the morphological components of *sata-nen* and *viisikymppi-nen*. Both lexemes are derived (diminutive *-nen* ending) from numbers (*sata* 'hundred', *kymppi,* colloquial form for 'ten'). They both are used to refer to objects (such as bank notes, bus numbers) and even human beings (a person in her fifties). The translatable item in the exercise, *satasta* 'one-hundred-note', is in the partitive case and consequently difficult to identify as belonging to the same paradigm as *satanen*.

In line (01), the teacher initiates the exercise. The target line is (14). The negative form that occurs in the question shows that Gaëlle finds something unexpected. Subsequently, a peer student, Lucie, reacts (line 20) to an aspect of Gaëlle's turn.

(10) One hundred note

```
01 Tea:   minu-lla    ei     ole       satas-ta.
          1SG-ADE     NEG    be.NEG    hundred-PAR
          I don't have a one hundred note.

02 Luc:   °je n'ai pas de [billet de cent°
          I don't have a one hundred note

03 Hél:                   [°je n'ai pas de billet de cent°

04 Tea:   oui
          yes

05 Tea:   je n'ai pas de billet de cent <satas-ta,>

06 Tea:   vous reconnaissez le partitif oui? c'est en fait
          you recognize the partitive yeah? it's in fact

07 Tea:   c'est un mot avec ↑n e n ↓à la fin,
          it's a noun type with ↑n e n ↓in the end

08 Tea:   donc ça fait un parti↑tif comme ça,
          so it builds a partitive like that,
```

2   In contrast to the teacher, who passes over the contesting implication, peer students readily display disagreement, as in examples (3), (8a) and (10).

121

```
09 Tea:      j'ai pas de billet de cent,
             I don't have a one hundred note,

10           minu-lla   on      va↑in viisikymppinen
             1SG-ADE    be.3SG  only  fifty marks note
             I have on ↑only a fifty marks note

11 ?         j'ai seulement un billet de cinquante
             I have on ↑only a fifty marks note

12 Luc:      j'ai se[ulement (x)

13 Tea:             [j'ai seulement un billet de cinquante oui
                     I have only a fifty marks note yes

14 => Gaë:   °et pourquoi ça se construit pas sur le même
              and why isn't that constructed in the same

15           euh >des↑sin enfin.<°cent et cinquante là dedans
             uh design hundred and fifty (in there)

16           il y a pas un mot qui veut dire bil↑let ↓ou°,
             isn't there a word which means ↑note ↓or,

17 Tea:      hh. *[äm ää        ]
   Tea          *turns to the blackboard and starts writing
                                              'viisikymppinen'

18 Luc:           [c'est (-)ça]
                   it's (-)

19           ((teacher writes on the blackboard))

20 Luc:      si ça se construit sur [le même (principe)
             PRT it's constructed in the same principle

21 Tea:                              [si c'est un peu par↑eil
                                      PRT it's still a little bit the ↑same

22           >quand même< non?
             isn't it

23           (0.5)

24 Gaë:      (°je sais pas°)
             (°I don't know°)

25 Tea:      ((writes 'kymppi' on the blackboard))

26 Tea:      *parce ↑que eum kymppi
             *because  uhm ten
   Tea       *continues writing
```

As in example (8a) Gaëlle initiates her turn with the conjunction *et* 'and', which combined with the anaphoric pronoun *ça* 'that', indicates that the referent of her question should be known from the previous talk and easily recognized by everyone. The why-question also indicates that the accountable matter lies in the incoherence of the lexemes. Immediately after the request for clarification Gaëlle continues and explicates what she would have expected: *satanen* and *viisikymppinen* should be compounds with the word 'note' in them.

The teacher begins to respond (line 17), although the main part of her response is communicated non-verbally: She turns and begins writing the lexeme *viisikymppinen* 'fifty' on the blackboard. Lucie launches a response but discontinues it right after the teacher begins writing (line 18), but as the teacher does not reply with a spoken turn, Lucie begins responding (line 20). Lucie's turn disagrees with the presupposition of the why-question and she claims to know more about the matter.

The teacher initiates her proper spoken response (line 26) only after she has written *kymppi* 'ten' on the blackboard. Before that, she seconds Lucie's claim about the similarity of the two lexemes (line 21). Furthermore, her causal marker *parce que* 'because' (line 26) is linked to her previous claim (line 21) regarding the similarity of the items. This claim becomes trustworthy because it was made by the teacher. At the same time, she sequentially deletes both Gaëlle's false assumption that there is no analogy between the two lexemes, and Lucie's competing epistemic stance. Gaëlle is honestly requesting information. Her disclaimer (line 24) indicates that she cannot detect any structural analogy between the two items. Her turn (line 14) is "moralizing", as Gaëlle "reproaches" the grammar for behaving incoherently. The teacher ignores the false assumption. She neither acknowledges the question as being legitimate with *oui* 'yes', nor does she adopt a clear position. Instead, she merely delivers the information needed to recognize the analogical elements in the lexemes *sata+nen* 'hundred+noun' and *viisikymppi+nen* 'fifty+noun'.

The conflicting viewpoint in all the previous examples was expressed in the first position of a sequence through a request for clarification. The analysis demonstrated that the recipients in all examples orient to the classroom expectations that questions will be answered and problems explained. On the other hand, one finding in this analysis was that even in this institutional setting, speakers are aware of the underlying moral issues related to the obligation and morality of knowledge. The turns could therefore be considered challenging and criticizing. The analysis also revealed that questions are responded to differently according to how strongly they imply the existence of "wrong" or accountable information. The initiating turns themselves implied the teacher's obligations toward her students (things have to be explained) and the students' expectations towards language and language studies.

Summary: Epistemic gradient and action ambiguity of challenging questions

Requests for clarification initiate epistemic search sequences. Specific clausal formats in relationship to the sequential position offer a hint as to the degree of the speaker's epistemic access and epistemic primacy. The requests can be formulated as negatively formatted declaratives, adversative declaratives, or question-word interrogatives. English interrogatives and declaratives index differently the speaker's epistemic stance towards the matter questioned. In initial position, interrogatives make a weak epistemic claim and index the recipient as someone who is accountable for knowing. Nonetheless, declaratives in sequence-initial position index a higher knowledgeability. They formulate a state of affairs for confirmation or agreement (Raymond & Heritage 2013). As the study illustrates, it is also possible in French to observe a distribution between question-word interrogatives and adversative declaratives.

Additionally, recipients' interpretation of sequence-initiating turns is highly context-specific. Questions make a response relevant and when a question has been triggered by a preceding norm violation, the appropriate interpretation of it is charged to the recipient. The recipient's turn indicates whether the recipient interprets the question as being an "innocent" request for clarification or instead as containing a challenge (Günthner 2000: 112). For example, Koshik (2005: 18) notes that grammatically negative yes/no questions produced by interviewers are heard as accusations, whereas in ordinary talk, these questions convey the meaning of assertions of reversed polarity.

Another source of potential action ambiguity is the causal question. Why-questions in everyday conversation are likely to be interpreted as seeking justification, whereas why-questions in a classroom context can be used and interpreted as genuine requests for clarification.

The moral dimension of challenging turns in classroom interaction

A precondition for the emergence of contrasting viewpoints and for criticism arising in the classroom context is that the participants have common knowledge of the established norms and rules. The students in the data share knowledge of the earlier lessons and the topics that have been discussed. Students also have both knowledge and expectations regarding classroom practices, including expectations for the lesson's agenda and other participants' behavior. In short, speakers harbor presuppositions about how their social environment is organized. As Garfinkel (1967) observes, our expectations are influenced by our inner moral reality, and speakers' actions and accounts for actions reveal their conception of "right" and "wrong" regarding their own actions and those of others. However, inner moral reality cannot be directly observed in the data. As moral issues are only inferred from participants' actions and reactions (for example, humorous reception), it is more appropriate to speak in terms of *moral communication* rather than of moral phenomena per se (Bergmann & Luckmann 1999: 22).

For the present analysis, this means that first-position challenges can be regarded as initiating moral communication in that they tackle issues of "right" and "wrong". This is put into action in the form of *interactional repertoires* based on pragmatic projection (Ford 2001: 59). By this, I refer to turn formats with contrast or negation that project an orientation to solution-seeking, explanation, or elaboration (Ford ibid; Kern 2009: 287). I have described these interactional repertoires as requests for clarification, which include negation or contrast markers and hence claim a divergent viewpoint.

In general, phenomena related to moral communication are characterized by agency, values, and the possibility and capacity to choose between right and wrong. This also entails the issue of responsibility (Bergmann & Luckmann 1999: 25–27). In epistemic search sequences, the student can step out of the student collective and assume the moral position of a criticizer. But at the same time the student becomes vulnerable to social sanctions by other participants (Bergmann & Luckmann 1999: 31). This is one reason for speakers exerting caution when they attack the moral integrity of a third. In my data, students use diverse fine-grained realizations of turn design to communicate their epistemic stance and primacy. At the same time, (peer) student reactions to untoward criticism (extracts 3, 8 & 10) clearly indicate that claims of knowledge constitute a morally sensitive matter (Stivers et al. 2011).

By making strong claims of possessing knowledge students are doing "being good" students, as this behavior conveys that they are informed and active participants (extract 2). An additional normative aspect related to student turns is that the classroom context limits the types of emotions that can be expressed (extract 3), how strongly they can be communicated, and by whom. However, challenging and criticizing turns must be reasonable and justified and not merely based on an emotional stance.

In a multi-party institutional context, social norms and rules may cover very diverse aspects of knowledge territories and demands for regularity and coherence. I suggest that a foreign language is locally part of the interactional setting; it is comparable to a personified interactional participant with moral responsibilities. The learner's inner moral reality is sensitive to incoherent or illogical "behavior" based on language rules. The representative of the foreign language is the teacher, and students address their complaints, challenges, and criticism to the teacher. When students detect aspects of grammar that are illogical, incoherent, or ambiguous or inconsistencies in the teacher's prior explanations, they express this through contest, criticism, or reproach embedded in a request for clarification.

By posing a question, speakers can claim knowledge, present facts, and contest information, which are all activities that require extra interactional work in everyday conversation. Classroom interaction likewise involves students who use concrete practical ways to express their criticism by putting it into an appropriate form (Lehtimaja 2011: 354). Nevertheless, classroom interaction seems to be an environment that inherently consists of moral communication and this is normative. For example, it is noteworthy that *pre-delicates* (such as the pre-sequence 'Can I ask something') that would project a dispreferred FPP (Schegloff 1980) are rare in the data.

I argue that specific epistemic search sequences in classroom interaction can represent one genre of moral communication. These sequences should be considered a normative part of classroom interaction practices, as participants do not account for them. These sequences are part of legitimate classroom actions and reflect one aspect of the learning activity. During the activity of 'questioning', norms of "right" and "wrong" can be challenged so as to defend old norms and construct new ones.

Conclusions

This analysis has focused on student-initiated question sequences involving students who either challenge a grammatical phenomenon, or disagree with a previous state of affairs. The students' challenges and disagreements are motivated by their expectations, all stemming from their epistemic access and epistemic primacy. As expectations are built on an inner morality and on a normative conception of how the world is organized, violated expectations can lead to moralizing communication in which speakers search for explanations and accounts concerning the violated norms. The present analysis has shown how language learners explore the foreign language, how they try to deduce reliable rules and obtain trustworthy information, and how these activities are connected to expectations and morally sensitive matters.

The turns analyzed were designed as negatively formatted declaratives, adversative declaratives, or causal question-word interrogatives implying a contrast. These are turn formats that in the present study evoke a competing or conflicting state of affairs and therefore could be interpreted as displaying a challenge. The turn designs were tilted to get further elaboration, which was understood to be expected of the teacher due to the institutional setting and the question-sequence format. Challenges project a positioning of the recipient's responsibility towards the contested matter. In ordinary talk, where the criticism normally is directed to another participant, the challenge can be interpreted as a reproach or complaint without leading to any corrective action. The responses can vary between a complete rejection of "didn't do it" to an acknowledging "not at fault" (Dersley & Wootton 2000) or they can also be a counter reproach (Günthner 1999).

However, the classroom cases analyzed are naturally organized in three-part question sequences. Requests for clarification contest a grammatical point and tend to criticize unexpected and irregular "behavior" by the language. In this respect I compared the foreign language to an interactional participant who is held accountable for his or her behavior or whose irregular behavior should at least be clarified. At any rate, the teacher's expected response to the challenge is to offer an explanation – not a justification or an excuse. The reception of potentially moralizing moves depends on whether or not the interactants classify them as legitimate. To distinguish between legitimate and illegitimate moves, I suggested three points that need the teacher's alignment: 1) the student has to be entitled to interrupt with a question, 2) the student's confusion must be based on justifiable grounds; 3) the student has correctly pointed to an incoherent presentation of a grammatical detail.

The legitimacy of a turn at talk in this study is acknowledged through the response design. Thus, negative causal questions are acknowledged by the dialogue particle *oui* 'yes' and 'accepted'. Nonetheless, the teacher does not continue with an explicit reason-giving marker *parce que* 'because', which occurs with positively valenced why-questions (Merke 2012).

The response type is dependent upon whether the student's claim is based on correct assumptions and whether the student's confusion is justified. False assumptions are never acknowledged, nor are they explicitly corrected. Instead they are followed by concrete evidence-giving, which sequentially deletes the implied false claim. As mentioned previously, when the confusion is classified as legitimate, the teacher acknowledges the request for clarification. The acknowledgement token is then followed by an assertion (or even explanation) that states that the unexpected grammar element is actually based on coherent grammatical grounds. In these situations, the teacher legitimates the contesting viewpoint, but rejects her own moral responsibility. As in everyday conversations, the recipient accepts the moralizing move without identifying with the criticism (Günthner 1999).

Adversative declaratives present a different case. Students normally use them to make strong claims concerning their access to knowledge. In this context, adversatives are used to introduce ancillary sequences that highlight conflicting or contrasting information. A response that aligns with the challenging move confirms the correctness of the highlighted detail. The teacher clarifies a possible ambiguous detail only as a second step.

Most of the responses are followed in the third position of a sequence by an agreement token (*d'accord, oké*) and this closes the sequence and signals that the student has received a satisfactory answer. Exceptions are instances of protest: when students disagree with a teacher's prior explanation. However, these have not been analyzed in this study.

Students are the first experiencers of surprising or perplexing information, which means that they are "experts" concerning their own surprise, disappointment, or frustration. They are also experts regarding their own learning process. The problems of comprehension that they confront belong to their territory of knowledge. In any case, situations arise where the emotional experience and the experience of factual expertise are interwoven. This occurs when speakers challenge representations of states of affairs. The tension between 'old' knowledge and competing 'new' knowledge is achieved through questioning and criticizing.

In conclusion, the analysis showed that epistemic search sequences permit students to take the floor. The sequences serve as environments for the tackling of norms and the adaptation of expectations. At the same time, students can incorporate an epistemic stance in them and raise morally loaded issues. Uptakes of morally sensitive turns are constructed through verbal linkages that profit from projection and from symbiont/host relationships to take on the moral aspect made relevant in the previous turn (see Auer 2014). The teacher uses these devices to signal (non-)alignment according to whether she accepts or rejects the challenge. The questioning activity connects knowledge of the study content and normativity concerning actions on a common basis so that collective learning is inherently embedded in social relations. In this sense, challenging epistemic search sequences create learning opportunities and contribute to the learning process. I conclude from my analysis that the process of language learning is interwoven with social rules and expectations. The perception and thus the acquisition of grammar rules is connected to morality and emotions and this is comparable to what occurs in other types of social interaction.

References

Auer, Peter. 2005. Projection in interaction and projection in grammar. *Text* 25(1): 7–36.
Auer, Peter. 2014. Syntactic structures and their symbiotic guests. Notes on analepsis from the perspective of on-line syntax. *Pragmatics* 24(3): 533–560.
Bergmann, Jörg & Thomas Luckmann (eds.). 1999. *Kommunikative Konstruktion von Moral*. Mannheim: Verlag für Gesprächsforschung.
Bert, Michel, Sylvie Bruxelles, Carole Etienne, Lorenza Mondada, Sandra Teston & Véronique Traverso. 2008. "Oh::, oh là là, oh ben…", les usages du marqueur "oh" en français parlé en interaction. In Jacques Durand, Benoît Habert & Bernard Laks (eds.), *Actes du Congrès Mondial de Linguistique Française (CMLF08)*. 685-701. Paris: Institut de Linguistique Française. [www.linguistiquefrançaise.org]
Couper-Kuhlen, Elizabeth & Sandra Thompson. 2005. A linguistic practice for retracting overstatements: Concessive repair. In Auli Hakulinen & Margret Selting (eds.), *Syntax and lexis in conversation. Studies on the use of linguistic resources in talk-in-interaction*. 257–288. Amsterdam/Philadelphia: John Benjamins.
Deppermann, Arnulf. 2009. Verstehensdefizit als Antwortverpflichtung: Interaktionale Eigenschaften der Modalpartikel *denn* in Fragen. In Susanne Günthner & Jörg Bücker (eds.), *Grammatik im Gespräch. Konstruktionen der Selbst- und Fremdpositionierung*. 23–56. Berlin, New York: Walter de Gruyter.
Dersley, Ian & Anthony Wootton. 2000. Complaint sequences within antagonistic argument. *Research on Language and Social Interaction* 33(4): 375–406.
Drew, Paul. 2013. Self-repair and action construction. Lecture given at the CoE/University of Helsinki, 21.1.2013.
Drew, Paul & John Heritage. 1992. *Talk at work. Interaction in institutional settings*. Cambridge: Cambridge University Press.
Enfield, Nick. 2011. Sources of asymmetry in human interaction: Enchrony, status, knowledge and agency. In Tanya Stivers, Lorenza Mondada & Jakob Steensig (eds.), *The morality of knowledge in conversation*. 285–332. Cambridge: Cambridge University Press.
Ford, Cecilia. 2000. The treatment of contrast in interaction. In Elizabeth Couper-Kuhlen & Bernd Kortmann (eds.), *Cause – Condition – Concession – Contrast. Cognitive and discourse perspectives*. 283–311. Berlin: Mouton de Gruyter.
Ford, Cecilia. 2001. At the intersection of turn and sequence: Negation and what comes next. In Elizabeth Couper-Kuhlen & Margret Selting (eds.), *Studies in interactional linguistics*. 51–79. Amsterdam: John Benjamins.
Garfinkel, Harold. 1967. *Studies in ethnomethodology*. Cambridge: Polity Press.
Günthner, Susanne. 1999. Vorwürfe in der Alltagskommunikation. In Jörg Bergmann & Thomas Luckmann (eds.) *Kommunikative Konstruktion von Moral*. 206–241. Mannheim: Verlag für Gesprächsforschung.
Günthner, Susanne. 2000. *Vorwurfsaktivitäten in der Alltagsinteraktion. Grammatische, prosodische, rhetorisch-stilistische und interaktive Verfahren bei der Konstitution kommunikativer Muster und Gattungen*. Tübingen: Niemeyer.
Haakana, Markku & Laura Visapää. 2014. Eiku – korjauksen partikkeli. *Virittäjä* 1: 41–70.
Hayashi, Makoto. 2004. Projection and grammar: Notes on the 'action-projecting' use of the distal demonstrative are in Japanese. *Journal of Pragmatics* 36(8): 1337–1374.
Jakonen, Teppo & Tom Morton. 2015. Epistemic search sequences in peer interaction in a content-based language classroom. *Applied Linguistics*. 36(1): 73–94
Jefferson, Gail. 1972. Side sequences. In David N. Sudnow (ed.), *Studies in social interaction*. 294-333. New York: Free Press.

Kasper, Gabriele & Johannes Wagner. 2011. A conversation-analytic approach to second language acquisition. In D. Atkinson (ed.), *Alternative approaches to second language acquisition.* 117–142. New York: Routledge.

Kerbrat-Orecchioni, Catherine. 2001. Oui, Non, Si : un trio célèbre et méconnu. *Marges Linguistiques* 2: 95–119.

Kern, Friederike. 2009. Positionieren im Kontrast: Zum Gebrauch einer Konstruktion im Türkendeutschen. In Susanne Günthner & Jörg Bücker (eds.), *Grammatik im Gespräch. Konstruktionen der Selbst- und Fremdpositionierung.* 283–305. Berlin, New York: Walter de Gruyter.

Koole, Tom. 2003. The interactive construction of heterogeneity in the classroom. *Linguistics and Education* 14(1): 3–26.

Koole, Tom. 2007. Parallel activities in the classroom. *Language and Education* 21(6): 487–500.

Koshik, Irene. 2002. A conversation analytic study of yes/no questions which convey reversed polarity assertions. *Journal of Pragmatics* 34(12): 1851–1877.

Koshik, Irene. 2005. *Beyond rhetorical questions. Assertive questions in everyday interaction.* Amsterdam/Philadelphia: John Benjamins.

Lehtimaja, Inkeri. 2011. Teacher-oriented address terms in students' reproach turns. *Linguistics and Education* 22: 248–363.

Lehtimaja, Inkeri. 2012. *Puheen suuntia luokkahuoneessa. Oppilaat osallistujina yläkoulun suomi toisena kielenä -tunnilla.* Ph.D. dissertation. University of Helsinki, Department of Finnish, Finno-Ugrian and Scandinavian Studies.

Majlesi, Ali & Mathias Broth. 2012. Emergent learnables in second language classroom interaction. *Learning, Culture and Social Interaction* 1: 193–207.

Mazeland, Harrie & Mike Huiskes. 2001. Dutch "but" as a sequential conjunction: Its use as a resumption marker. In Margret Selting & Elizabeth Couper-Kuhlen (eds.), *Studies in interactional linguistics.* 141–169. Amsterdam: John Benjamins.

Mazeland, Harrie. 2013. Grammar in conversation. In Jack Sidnell & Tanya Stivers (eds.), *The handbook of conversation analysis.* 475–491. Chichester, West Sussex, UK: Wiley-Blackwell.

Mehan, Hugh. 1979. *Learning lessons. Social organization of turns at formal talk in the classroom.* Cambridge, MA: Harvard University Press.

Merke, Saija. 2012. Kielen opiskelu ja tunteet: Affekti jäsentämässä opiskelijoiden aloittamia kysymyssekvenssejä vieraan kielen oppitunneilla. *Virittäjä* 2: 198–230.

Merke, Saija. Forthcoming. Exprimer et gérer des désaccords à l'aide de relations contrastives en cours de langue: la question causale et la question déclarative adversative. *Cahiers de Praxématique.*

Pekarek Doehler, Simona. 2001. Dislocation à gauche et organisation interactionnelle. *Marges Linguistiques* 2: 177–194.

Pekarek Doehler, Simona. 2011. Clause-combining and the sequencing of actions. Projection constructions in French talk-in-interaction. In Ritva Laury & Ryoko Suzuki (eds.), *Subordination in conversation.* 103–148. Amsterdam: John Benjamins.

Pekarek Doehler, Simona. 2013. Social-interactional approaches to SLA: A state of art and some future perspectives. *LIA, Language, Interaction and Acquisition* 4(2): 134–160.

Peräkylä, Anssi & Sanna Vehviläinen. 2003. Conversation analysis and the professional stocks of interactional knowledge. *Discourse & Society* 14(6): 727–750.

Peräkylä, Anssi. 2014. The intersubjective contexts of emotion: Co-presence, joint action, and shared referential world. Lecture given at the CoE seminar *Intersubjectivity of emotions*, 19.6.2014.

Raymond, Geoffrey. 2003. Grammar and social organization: Yes/no interrogatives and the structure of responding. *American Sociological Review* 68: 939–967.

Raymond, Geoffrey & John Heritage. 2013. One question after another: Same-turn repair in the formation of yes/no type initiating actions. In Makoto Hayashi, Geoffrey Raymond & Jack Sidnell (eds.), *Conversational repair and human conversation*. 135–171. Cambridge: Cambridge University Press.

Sacks, Harvey. 1992. *Lectures on conversation*, Volume I. Oxford: Blackwell.

Sacks, Harvey, Emanuel A. Schegloff & Gail Jefferson. 1974. A simplest systematics for the organization of turn-taking for conversation. *Language* 50: 696–735.

Schegloff, Emanuel A. 1980. Preliminaries to preliminaries: "Can I ask you a question?" *Sociological Inquiry* 50(3–4): 104–152.

Schegloff, Emanuel A. 2007. *Sequence organization in interaction: A primer in conversation analysis*. Cambridge: Cambridge University Press.

Scott, Marvin B. & Stanford M. Lyman. 1968. Accounts. *American Sociological Review* 33(1): 46–62.

Sinclair, John & Malcolm Coulthard. 1975. *Towards an analysis of discourse: The English used by teachers and pupils*. London: Oxford University Press.

Spranz-Fogasy, Thomas. 2005. Argumentation als alltagsweltliche Kommunikationsideologie. *Deutsche Sprache* 33(2): 141–156.

Steensig, Jakob & Paul Drew. 2008. Introduction: questioning and affiliation/disaffiliation in interaction. *Discourse Studies* 10(1): 5–15.

Stivers, Tanya. 2008. Stance, alignment, and affiliation during storytelling: When nodding is a token of affiliation. *Research on Language and Social Interaction* 41(1): 31–57.

Stivers, Tanya, Lorenza Mondada & Jakob Steensig. 2011. Knowledge, morality and affiliation in social interaction. In Tanya Stivers, Lorenza Mondada & Jakob Steensig (eds.), *The morality of knowledge in conversation*. 3–24. Cambridge: Cambridge University Press.

Aino Koivisto
http://orcid.org/0000-0002-9380-5953

5. On-line emergence of alternative questions in Finnish with the conjunction/particle *vai* 'or'

Introduction: vai *as a conjunction and a question particle*

This article discusses the on-line emergence of alternative questions in Finnish conversations. The focus is on the role of the conjunction/particle *vai* ('or') and its capability to retrospectively transform the interpretation of a prior, already completed question or assertion. This article builds on the previous finding that in conversation, *vai* is multifunctional: it can be used as a coordinating **conjunction** in alternative questions, linking syntactically and semantically equivalent alternatives, and as a turn-final question **particle** (see Hakulinen et al. 2004: § 1698–1704).[1] In this respect it behaves roughly like alternative conjunctive elements in other languages that have been studied previously: Swedish *eller* (Lindström 1999), English *or* (Drake 2013; 2015), and also Icelandic *eða* (Blöndal 2008). This article will suggest, however, that the distinction between a conjunction and a turn-final particle is not clear-cut. That is, the interpretation of an occurrence of the word *vai* itself can change over the moment-by-moment unfolding of action, as a reaction to interactional contingencies. Furthermore, the article will show that *vai* can also be used turn-initially. In that case *vai* does not always introduce a syntactically and semantically symmetrical alternative within a question but it can be used to initiate revised versions of the prior, already completed question (or sometimes an assertion) in order to pursue an agreeing response.

Some of the uses of Finnish *vai* in spoken language have been previously described in *Iso suomen kielioppi* (The Comprehensive Grammar of Finnish, Hakulinen et al. 2004). As a coordinating **conjunction**, *vai* can connect both polar interrogatives and phrases. In example (1), *vai* connects two polar questions.

1 The capability to function both as a linking element between syntactic units and turns-at-talk and as a turn-final particle is not restricted to *vai* alone. Other conjunctions in Finnish behave similarly (see Koivisto, Laury & Seppänen 2011 on Finnish *että*; Koivisto 2012 on *mutta* and *ja*). However, *vai* has a turn-final use that is more grammaticalized, that is, it is used as a question particle in some fixed contexts (such as in checking questions), where it does not leave the second alternative implicit (cf. Mulder & Thompson 2008 and Thompson & Suzuki 2012 on the criteria for grammaticalization of final particles).

(1) [Hakulinen et al. 2004: § 1698]

A: On**ks** hänkin opiskelija **vai** on**ks** hän töissä.
    be-Q 3SG-CLI student   PRT be-Q 3SG work-PL-INE
    Is he a student as well or is he working.

B: Töissä.
    work-PL-INE
    Working. ((lit. 'at work'))

Phrases connected with *vai* can be incorporated in a clause (example 2), but they can also occur without a clausal frame (example 3) (see Hakulinen et al. 2004: § 1698).

(2) [Hakulinen et al. 2004: § 1698]

Haluutsä pitkän version **vai** lyhyen.
want-Q-2SG long-GEN version PRT short-GEN
Do you want the long version **or** the short one.

(3) [Hakulinen et al. 2004: § 1698]

A: Turussa   **vai** Helsingissä.
    NAME.OF.A.CITY-INE PRT NAME.OF.A.CITY-INE
    In Turku **or** in Helsinki.

B: Turussa.
    NAME.OF.A.CITY-INE
    In Turku.

Alternative questions make relevant a response that chooses one of the alternatives, which highlights the fact that as a coordinating conjunction, *vai* is exclusive (Hakulinen et al. 2004: § 1098; see also Penttilä 1957: 558–559). That is, "it excludes the possibility that both conjoins are true, or are to be fulfilled" (Quirk et al. 1985: 932; Drake 2013: 20 on English *or*). In examples (1) and (3), where also the response is provided, the recipient orients to the exclusivity of *vai* by picking one of the alternatives offered.

Each of the examples presented above represents a "clean" alternative question with two syntactically and semantically symmetrical parts. *Vai* thus functions as a coordinating conjunction proper. However, Hakulinen et al. (2004: § 1698) also point out that the second alternative can emerge as an increment-like, grammatically loose addition to an already completed polar question[2]:

2 This use is mentioned already in Penttilä's (1957: 559) grammar. He says that *vai* can be used at the beginning of an "unconnected" question, but in this use as well, the *vai*-question has to be thought of as a continuation of a prior question. The example he gives is the following: *Tämä on korjattava. Vai onko työ tehtävä kokonaan uudestaan?* ('This needs to be fixed. Or does the work need to be done all over again?') What is noteworthy is that Penttilä draws his examples from written language. Adding a *vai*-increment to a completed question indeed occurs in written language as well (at least in newspapers and fiction).

(4) [Hakulinen et al. 2004: § 1698]

```
Mut oisko      se sinusta sopiva         tänä iltana pisttee?
but be-COND-Q DEM 2SG-ELA good/suitable  tonight     put-INF
```
But do you think it would be good to do it tonight?

Vai, mieluummin huomenna.
PRT rather   tomorrow.
Or, rather tomorrow.

In example (4), the second alternative is a syntactically and semantically fitted phrasal addition: the phrase 'tonight' gets an alternative 'tomorrow'. However, increment-like *vai*-additions do not necessarily need to be grammatically fitted to the prior, first alternative. Different kinds of combinations may occur: declarative + polar question, *WH*-interrogative + polar question, and polar question + *WH*-interrogative (Hakulinen et al. 2004: § 1699). The following case is an example of *vai* connecting a polar question (*onks* 'be-Q') and a *WH*-interrogative (*miten* 'how'):

(5) [Hakulinen et al. 2004: § 1699]

```
Onks teillä    ihan täyttä   vai miten se  on.
be-Q 2PL-ADE   PRT  full-PAR PRT how   DEM be
```
Are you fully booked or how is it.

In cases like this, the following *vai*-prefaced interrogative may be addressing or expressing doubts about something that has been assumed in the prior declarative/interrogative clause, or acknowledging that there are other possible answers (see Hakulinen et al. § 1699, 1700).

Besides its use as a coordinating conjunction and at the beginning of a grammatically loose addition, *vai* also occurs as a **particle** in turn-final position, that is, without the presence of an (explicit) alternative (see Hakulinen et al. 2004: § 1700–1701; see also Halonen 2002: 60–69; Korpela 2007: 129–131). In this case, according to Hakulinen et al., turn-final *vai* behaves differently depending on the grammatical form of the turn it is attached to. When turn-final *vai* occurs with **interrogatives**, it implies that there are other (albeit unspoken) alternatives. According to Korpela (2007: 130–131) *vai* can also operate as an element that opens up the question to more elaborate answers than just confirmation or disconfirmation. Consider the following example:

(6) [Hakulinen et al. 2004: § 1699]

```
S: Onks Seija   lähteny jo      kirjastoon opiskelemaan vai,
   be-Q 1name-F leave-PPC already library-ILL study-INF  PRT
```
   Has Seija already left for the library to study or,

```
V: Ei, ku soon,    tuolla,  pääsykokeit         valvomassa.
   PRT PRT DEM be  DEM.ADV  entrance.exam-PL-PAR supervise-INF
```
   No, she is there supervising an entrance exam.

133

In example (6) *vai* ends a polar question that seeks confirmation for the suggested state of affairs. What does *vai* add to it besides making the question "open"? According to Drake (2013: 169–172; 2015), a turn-final *or* functions as an epistemic downgrade, indexing a lack of certainty with respect to the proposition encoded in the *or*-turn by weakening the speaker's commitment to it. Another point made with respect to the interactional functions of turn-final 'or' (in English and in Swedish) is that it relaxes the preference for a positive, confirming response by facilitating a 'no'-type response so that the latter can be produced without any markers of dispreference (see Lindström 1999: 55 on Swedish *eller*; Drake 2013: 38 on English *or*). These ideas seem to apply to cases such as example (6) as well.

When *vai* conveys that there are unstated alternative(s), it seems to retain some of its connective flavor (cf. Mulder & Thompson 2008: 197 on English *but*). However, according to Hakulinen et al. (2004: § 1699; see also Raevaara 1993: 48–49, 60), when attached to a **declarative clause** or to a **single phrase** or a word, *vai* functions as a question particle, which marks the utterance as a question without setting up a contrast between two imaginable states of affairs. The format phrase/word + *vai* is used to form checking questions or repair initiations targeting some detail in the prior turn. These types of turns may also function as newsmarks or markers of ritualized disbelief (cf. Heritage 1984: 339–440). See (7a) below. The format declarative + *vai* is used in inferences made from the prior talk that are offered for confirmation. See (7b) below.

(7a) [Hakulinen et al. 2004: § 1699]

```
V: Minä tulen      huomenna Helsinkiin.
   1SG  come-1SG   tomorrow Helsinki-ILL
   I'm coming to Helsinki tomorrow.

S: Tuut       vai.
   come-2SG   PRT
   (Oh) you are (coming).
```

(7b) [Hakulinen et al. 2004: § 1699]

```
S: Millos    se   on.
   when-CLI  DEM  be
   When is it.

V: No  se  ois       itse asiassa nyt aika   kiirekki jo.     Jos,
   PRT DEM be-COND   in fact      now pretty hurry-CLI already if
   Well in fact it's kind of urgent already. If,

S: Nii että olis    pitäny      jo       ilmottaa vai.
   PRT PRT Ø be-COND have.to-PPC already  inform-INF PRT
   So we should have already informed you or.
```

In example (7a) S's turn *Tuut vai* ('(Oh) you are (coming)') addresses the newsworthiness of V's prior informing rather than indicating uncertainty by implying the existence of an alternative. In example (7b) S's turn ending in *vai* offers a candidate understanding of what was implied in V's prior turn.

The examples presented above have shown that *vai* is multifunctional: it can occur as a coordinating conjunction (linking two symmetrical alternatives), as a turn- or utterance-initial particle (adding an alternative to an already completed question), and in turn-final position (implying the existence of an alternative, or just marking the turn as a question). In what follows, I will show that the multifunctionality of *vai* can also be made use of in expanding, adjusting, and reformulating a question or an assertion when the questioner is facing problems in receiving an answer. My analyses will also illustrate and confirm the more general point presented in previous research, namely that syntactic structures (in this case, clause combinations) in conversation are emergent and contingent (Ford 2004) processes. That is, they are constructed temporally and their boundaries and functions are negotiated and constantly reassessed in the interaction (see, e.g., Goodwin 1979 for an early demonstration of this). More specifically, the focus of this article will be on "loose", incrementally produced *vai*-constructions. In terms of their syntax, the parts connected with *vai* are not necessarily symmetrical "alternatives", representing the same category, nor do they present equally "preferred" alternatives. Temporally, they do not form one coherent prosodic unit. In terms of their function, I will show that *vai*-prefaced increments are a way of transforming the prior question or assertion (or assessment) and its interpretation *on-line*, monitoring recipient reactions and reacting to incipient disagreement or disaffiliation.

Data and method

The data for the study come from two sources, the data archive housed at the Department of Finnish, Finno-Ugrian and Scandinavian Studies (University of Helsinki) and the data archive housed at the Institute for the Languages of Finland. The first corpus includes conversations between friends, family members, and acquaintances, whereas the latter consists of service encounters in low-key settings such as convenience stores and hair salons.

Theoretically and methodologically, this study draws on Conversation Analysis and Interactional Linguistics. This means that I am interested in how the multifunctionality and flexibility of *vai* is made use of as an interactional resource and how grammatical structures emerge in temporally unfolding interaction (cf., e.g., Ford 1993; Ford, Fox & Thompson 2002; Ford 2004; Barth-Weingarten & Couper-Kuhlen 2011). The core collection for the study was formed of occurrences of *vai* that seem to involve departures from the standard alternative questions involving two symmetrical parts produced within one coherent prosodic unit (as in examples 2 and 3). However, instead of focusing on the occurrences of turn-final *vai* that are responded to upon their completion (which is the focus of Lindström 1999 and Drake 2013; 2015 in their work on Swedish *eller* and English *or*, respectively), I will be examining cases where a possibly complete question or assertion is expanded by adding an alternative which emerges after a pause or recipient reaction. In addition, I have included cases where a stand-alone *vai* is attached to an already completed prosodic unit and turn. The following schemas illustrate the different possibilities I will deal with here:

```
1) A:   ………VAI
        (pause)
   A:   ………VAI
        (pause)
   A:   ………… (VAI)

2) A:   ……VAI……
        (pause or B's reaction)
   A:   VAI……… (VAI)

3) A:   …………VAI
        (pause or B's reaction)
   A:   VAI…………

4) A:   ………………
        (pause or B's reaction)
   A:   VAI……………

5) A:   ……………
        (pause)
   A:   VAI
```

The analysis: Transforming questions and assertions with vai

This section will discuss different uses of *vai* in question formation from a temporal perspective and the different properties of *vai* that can be deployed to transform the interpretation of the turn *on-line*.[3] In these cases *vai* occurs at the juncture of two TCUs, which entails both utterance-initial and utterance-final uses. First, I will analyze the use of *vai* as a listing device in questions (connecting more than two alternatives) and the negotiable completion of such lists (see possibilities 1–2 above). Second, I will show that *vai*-prefaced additions can be used to reopen a possibly complete alternative or polar question (see possibilities 2–4 above). Finally, I will analyze an instance of the particle *vai* added to a possibly complete assertion (see possibility 5 above). In all of these cases, *vai* is used to transform the interpretation of the first question or assertion retrospectively.

---

3   I will use the term "question" to cover utterance-types that make an informative response relevant in the next turn. These thus include not only interrogatives but also declarative clauses as well as phrases used to elicit an informative response.

UTTERANCE-FINAL *VAI* AS A LISTING DEVICE

As a coordinating conjunction, *vai* has the capacity to connect more than two equally standing alternatives. Moreover, when *vai* occurs as the last item in a list of alternatives, it implies that the speaker could go on listing similar alternatives even if he/she does not do so. This creates the impression of an inexhaustible list of alternatives (cf. Koivisto 2011; 2012 on turn-final *ja*; cf. Jefferson 1990). The next example is from a service encounter recorded at a convenience store.

(8) [T363, Kotus, R-kioski, S=salesperson, C=client]

```
01  S:      hei.
            hello.

02  C:      he:i. (0.4) onkos tuota ni; (0.6) sulla poru:koita.
            hello. (0.4) do you uhm; (0.6) have groups.

03          (0.6) ((C IS LOOKING AT THE COUPON STAND, S MOVES BEHIND THE STAND))

04  S:->    monivetoo            vai; viikinkiä           vai;
            name.of.a.lottery-PAR PRT  name.of.a.lottery-PAR PRT
            Multibet or;              Viking or;

05          (0.4)

06          lottoa               vai;
            name.of.a.lottery-PAR PRT
            Lotto or;

07          (1.0) ((C IS LOOKING AT THE COUPON STAND,
                   S IS BEHIND THE STAND BUT NOT VISIBLE))

08  S:      [moniveossa tämä on:; vii- kolmaskymmenes päivä
            elikkä
            in Multibet this is; the thirtieth day so
            [((S GRABS A COUPON FROM THE STAND))

09          se on; onks se; (0.2) <huominen vai>; (0.4) joo.
            huomiselle
            that is; is it; (0.2) tomorrow or; (0.4) yes. that one

10          päivälle on tuo:;
            is for tomorrow
```

In line 2, the client presents his reason for the visit. He wants to join a lottery that has a "group" option (which means that the client can buy a share of the group ticket). The seller's *vai*-ended list in line 4 is a reaction to the client's inquiry. In her list, the seller details the different types of lotteries that have the group option. By doing so, she seems to be accomplishing two intertwined things. For one, the list functions as an appendor question

137

seeking clarification ('which one do you want') (see Schegloff 1997; Stivers 2010: 2776). This is a way of treating the client's initial inquiry as being underspecified. The implication is that the seller cannot grant the request before the client has specified the type of lottery he wants to join. At the same time, however, the list lays out options to choose from, thus functioning as an offer. Either way, the seller's turn makes relevant a response that picks one of the options offered.

Each of the three alternatives in the list forms a prosodic unit of its own, ending in *vai*. The second and the third part are also separated by a clear (0.4 second) pause. The existence of multiple, prosodically separated *vai*-items makes the list easily expandable with similar items, while also providing the opportunity for the client to pick an item once it has been mentioned. This creates a negotiable turn-ending where each *vai* forms a point of possible completion. The fact that the last item of the whole list is also *vai* creates an impression of inexhaustibility. That is, it makes the question open-ended by implying that the list (and the offer) is not restricted to the items that are mentioned explicitly. This example then shows that the combination NP + *vai* does not necessarily function as a pure checking question but may project/enable list construction with multiple alternatives. Here, the prosodic features seem to matter: an NP + *vai* that has a non-final intonation may be interpreted also as an item in a list that can be expanded beyond the current item if needed.

A list construction can also be created retrospectively. For example, an alternative question with two parts connected with *vai* can be expanded after its completion, resulting in a multi-part list. This happens in the next example, where a designedly complete, "closed" alternative question with two alternatives is *reopened* with a *vai*-prefaced list including two more list items. Furthermore, as in the previous example, the turn and the list are left open-ended with a turn-final *vai*. Juha and Ari are discussing sweatpants that Juha is supposed to get for the two of them.

(9) [Vai32 Sg080 A01]

```
01 Juha: =tai jotaki semmosta.  (0.3) .h >tosin kyllä suattas sua
          or something like that.              actually one might get them

02        halavalaki jos kahtos Urheilusopistah.
          at a cheap price as well if one checks Urheilusoppi ((name of a shop))

03 Ari:   niin nii.
          right.

04 Juha: .hh mutk#u:,# (0.2)   minkäs väriset ne pitäs ollahh,
          but uhm              what colour should they be

05        (0.4)

06 Ari:   no e:ihän sillä mittääv väliä o.
          well that doesn't make any difference whatsoever
```

```
07 Juha: mm(h)y.  (mut)  vaaleanpunasetk(h)o  v(h)ai    kukal[liset.
          PRT             pink-PL-Q             PRT     flowery-PL
                    (but) pink or flowery

08 Ari:                                                 [no e:i
                                                        PRT NEG
                                                        well not

09        [nyt sentään mu [t°ta°,
          now at.least but
          those but

10 Juha: [.hh            [vai mustat:ko >mieluummin vai< siniset #vai#,
                         PRT  black-PL-Q  rather    PRT  blue-PL  PRT
                         or black rather or blue or

11        (.)

12 Ari:  no e:i nyt ehkä  mustatkaa.
         PRT NEG  now maybe black-PL-CLI
         well maybe not black either

13        (0.6)

14 Ari:  kyllä joku: semmonem muu väri
                     some other colour
```

Juha's first question in this extract is a *WH*-question that makes relevant an answer that would suggest a color for the sweatpants (line 4). After receiving a non-answer by Ari ('well that doesn't make any difference whatsoever', line 6), Juha produces an alternative question consisting of two symmetrical parts, laying out two (jokey) options to choose form ('pink or flowery', line 7).[4] Structurally, this second try makes relevant an answer that picks either of the alternatives. Content-wise, of course, pink and flowery are not serious alternatives. This addition is arguably produced as a reaction to Ari's answer in line 6, where he refused to take a stand on the color. In overlap with the final syllables of the question, Ari provides an answer (lines 8-9). As expected, he does not pick either of the alternatives but rejects them both. However, he does not suggest any colors himself either. This means that the question about the color remains unsolved. As a solution, Juha extends his question with a *vai*-initial extension that presents two more colors (line 10). By continuing the list (and not reacting straightforwardly to Ari's answer) Juha treats the sequence (the question-answer pair) as being still unfinished. It is important to note that even though Juha's turn sequentially deletes Ari's answer, it can still be seen to be motivated by that answer. That is, the continuation of the list is not a projected, anticipated part of the question but rather an attempt to get a straightforward answer to Juha's original

---

4   In fact, the first alternative contains the question clitic -ko that also occurs in the first element in the second set of alternatives (line 10) (see Hakulinen et al. 2004: § 1698 on this phenomenon). While the occurrence of the clitic in the first element but not in the second one makes them less symmetrical structurally, the alternatives offered are still symmetrical in terms of their category.

question after two failures to get one. By initiating the addition with *vai*, Juha transforms his prior, already completed two-part question into the beginning of a list with multiple elements connected with *vai*. Interestingly, in terms of content, the *vai*-addition also transforms the question into a more serious one, now offering alternatives that are more realistic (black and blue). Turn-final *vai* implies that there are still more alternatives to choose from.

Examples (8) and (9) demonstrated the use of incremental *vai*-lists as a resource for offering more alternatives in a context where the recipient does not choose one of the first two options right away. In these extracts the questioner needs specific information from the recipient in order to proceed to some pending activity, such as granting a request (ex. 8) or fulfilling a plan that concerns the recipient (ex. 9). A *vai*-list is used to offer a set of candidate answers to choose from, which functions to facilitate the production of a response. Simultaneously, however, the operation of producing a list of alternatives is a way of treating the prior turn by the recipient as insufficient or underspecified.

TRANSFORMABILITY OF THE STATUS OF *VAI*
As already mentioned, the word *vai* can be used as a forward-projecting conjunction, turn/utterance-initial particle, and as a turn-final question particle. Furthermore, its status is transformable. That is, something that was initially produced as a turn-final particle can be subsequently transformed into a conjunction by repeating the word and adding an element that fits to the prior as an alternative. In the next example, two women are talking on the phone. In lines 1–2 U produces an invitation, which is receipted with a counter-invitation by M in line 3.

(10) [Vai20_Sg142_A03]

```
01 U:   ↓selevä. .hh ↑mitä se, olisi, jos te: lähtisitte meillä
        okay. how would it be if you guys would come to

02      käymään >nytt [e me<=.hh]
        visit us now.

03 M:                [↑e:ikum mä]ä aattelisi et:tä, kävelkää te tänne.
                     PRT         1SG  think-COND-1SG PRT  walk-2PL-IMP 2PL DEM.ADV
                     no I was thinking that, why don't you guys walk here.

04 U:   jaa:< (.) oikein kaikki    °vai°.hh
        PRT            really everybody   PRT
        oh (.) (you mean) everybody or.

05 M:   ↑no vaikka.
        PRT PRT
        well if you like.

06 U:   vai tarkottiks te  yhtä     he[nkee. h]
        PRT mean-2PL-Q  2PL one-PAR person-PAR
        or did you mean one person.
```

```
07   M:                    [iha:n  ]         kaikkiki
                                             everybody

08        sa [a tulla.]
          can come.

09   U:      [.h hh   ] ha ha .h jos me käveltäs
                                  what if we would walk

10        rivissä teille.
          in a line to your place.
```

Instead of responding to M's invitation, U begins an insertion sequence by checking her understanding (line 4). The turn is composed of an NP *oikein kaikki* ('(you mean) everybody') and the particle *vai*, which is typical of checking questions. It also carries prosodic features typical of a turn-ending: decrease in volume and audible outbreath (see Ogden 2004). The turn is treated as complete by M, who answers the question in line 5. After that, a response to the invitation in line 3 is due. Instead of providing one, U extends her checking question by adding a *vai*-initial increment to it. This is a way of transforming the *vai*-ended checking question into an alternative question with two alternatives to choose from. That is, the interpretation of the final *vai* in line 4 is retrospectively interpretable as (or masked as) a conjunction that was projecting continuation with an alternative. What results is a syntactically asymmetrical coordination, a full clause linked to an NP. Semantically, however, the two alternatives are symmetrical in the sense that they represent the same category, number of invitees: everybody or just one person.

The motivation for the expansion can be attributed to the nature of M's answer in line 5. The formulation *no vaikka* ('well if you like') treats U's inquiry as a suggestion that she is willing to accept rather than as something that she had been planning all along. The *vai*-addition serves to retract the original question by addressing the assumptions behind it. U does this very explicitly by referring to the recipient's intention ('did you mean'). Here, as in line 10 of example (9), the *vai*-increment can be treated as a reaction to the prior turn, which was not the projected answer (in example (9), the answerer did not pick one of the offered alternatives, and in example (10), the answerer did not produce a clear yes-response). In what follows, I will discuss in more detail how *vai*-prefaced increments that offer a contrasting alternative to be confirmed are used to deal with the possibility of getting a dispreferred or disconfirming response and to facilitate its production (see also Couper-Kuhlen 2012: 133).

TRANSFORMING A POLAR QUESTION INTO AN ALTERNATIVE QUESTION

A *vai*-prefaced increment does not need to be attached to an utterance that is an alternative question (as in example 9) or a question that ends in *vai* (as in example 10). It can also be attached to other kinds of interrogatives. In the following, I will show that even though the *vai*-continuation does not stand as a proper alternative, it can be used to deal with hesitant or insufficient answers as in examples (9) and (10). It does this by reopening the question and transforming its interpretation retrospectively. The following schema illustrates the sequential pattern produced when these *vai*-additions emerge.

> A: polar Q preferring an affirmative answer
> B: silence or other signs of a dispreferred turn
> A: *vai*-prefaced "alternative" that re-opens the question

In these cases, *vai* is not adding alternatives *per se* but rather addressing the assumptions behind the first question. It is designed to enable a grammatically preferred "yes" answer. A point of comparison is multiple questions as discussed by Sacks (1987). According to Sacks (1987: 60), a "second question in a series will commonly be a candidate answer to the first". The second question is then designed to get an agreeing response after an initial failure to get one. The way to do this is to revise the question to exhibit reversed preference (ibid. 64; see also Schegloff 2007: 70–71), as in the following example:

(11) [Sacks 1987: 64]

```
A: They have a good cook there?
   ((pause))
A: nothing special?
B: No, everybody takes their turns.
```

In this example the first declaratively formatted question remains without an immediate confirming answer. The questioner resolves this situation by offering a candidate answer (*nothing special*) that reverses the preference so that the answerer can now confirm the opposite option instead of having to disconfirm the first one. (Sacks 1987: 64.)

The following examples will illustrate that *vai*-additions may be produced just for this purpose. That is, they provide a candidate answer for a question that does not get an immediate preferred answer. As in Sacks' example, the added questions are formulated so that they enable a grammatically preferred answer even though it would be socially dispreferred from the perspective of the initial question. Consider the following example where two young women, S and V, are discussing the date when V (and her spouse) could visit S.

(12) [Sg401 liisa2]

```
01 S:  mun piti sen takii soittaa et ku toi:  Tuiskun se
       the reason I had to call is because that Tuisku's that

02     pikkuserkku se Totti ni se on tulos huomen?
       second cousin that Totti (s)he is coming tomorrow?
```

```
03       (0.8)

04  S:   k[ylää ] sen tyttöystävän kaa,
         to visit with his/her girlfriend,

05  V:   [okei?]
          okay?

06       (0.5)

07  S:   nii: käviskö    teille  sunnuntaina?
         PRT  suit-COND-Q 2PL-ALL sunday-ESS
         so would Sunday work for you guys?

08       (0.5)

09  V:   .hh ööö:  [     ku tota tai kävi]skö
                         well uhm or would ((it)) work

10  S:->          [vai onks teil   muuta.]
                   PRT BE-Q you-ADE else
                   or do you have something else.

11  V:   ↑maanantai-iltana mul on maanantaiki vapaa mul on
         on Monday evening ((for you)) I have Monday free as well I have

12       tälläne kolmipäiväne viikolloppu.=
         this kind of three-day weekend.

13  S:   =mm.

14       (0.4)

15  S:   okei: eli hetkinen,
         okay so wait a minute
```

S's question in line 7 forms a syntactically complete utterance that implements a recognizable first action, a proposal or an invitation. Thus, it makes relevant a second pair part, an agreement that implies a commitment to the future action (see Couper-Kuhlen 2014: 629) or a rejection. In line 8 then, a response is noticeably absent. The pause in line 8 as well as the hesitation sounds in the beginning of line 9 project a dispreferred answer, in this case a rejection of the invitation (see Davidson 1984). In a situation like this, the inviter "may subsequently display an attempt to deal with the inadequacies of the initial formulation or offer and thereby to deal with the possibility of rejection", as Davidson (1984: 104) puts it. The *vai*-addition is doing precisely this. That is, even though it is grammatically linked to the prior question (resulting in two polar questions linked by *vai*), it can be analyzed as a reactive action. The *vai*-continuation reopens the question by addressing the candidate reason behind the projected dispreferred answer. That is, it is a pre-emptive move that is designed to enable a 'yes'-type answer (see Schegloff 2007: 70–71). However, by initiating the second question with *vai*, the first question (the first "alternative") still holds as a possibility: V could, in principle, choose to respond to either of them. However, she does not respond to either question but continues her ongoing turn by making a counter-proposal.

Consider another example of this practice. This is from a face-to-face conversation between three teenage girls. Apparently, Susa has borrowed some money from a mutual friend, Jenni. In lines 1–2 Milla asks whether Susa has the money now. In the same turn, Milla offers to take the money to Jenni.

(13) [Sg151]

```
01 Milla:  .hh hei muute. onks siul    sitä     seitkytneljää
                PRT PRT    be-Q 2SG-ADE DEM-PAR  seventy.four-PAR
           hey by the way. do you have that seventy four

02         mie voisin       viiä     sen       Jennille.
           1SG can-COND-1SG take-INF DEM-GEN   1nameF-ALL
           I could take that to Jenni.

03              (2.0)  ((MILLA DRINKS COFFEE, SUSA LOOKS AT MILLA AND CHEWS FOOD))

04 Susa:   MM: pitää    >käydä< [pankissa.]
               have.to   go-INF  bank-INE
           Ø have to go to the bank.

05 Milla:                      [vai< vai] haluuk sie tota:
                                PRT  PRT  want-Q 2SG PRT
                                or or do you want uhm

06         Jennin<  (mie voin)    tilinumeron.
           1name-GEN (1SG can-1SG) account.number-GEN
           Jenni's (I can) account number.

07              (0.4)
08 Susa :  joo. anna Jennin tilinumero ni mie maksan
           yes. give me Jenni's account number and I'll pay

09         [sen (kyl).]
            it

10 Milla:  [miul ois  ] kalenterissa mie voin antaa sen.
           I have it in my calendar I can give it (to you).
```

As in the previous example, *vai* connects two polar questions. However, the first interrogative ('do you have that seventy four', line 1) is followed by an offer that serves as an account for making the request. This turn is clearly brought to its completion, as witnessed by the fact that the questioner, Milla, takes a sip of her coffee immediately upon the completion of her question (see line 3). This first question is followed by a long pause (line 3) and an answer that is clearly problem-indicative. In her delayed answer, Susa provides a report ('have to go to the bank') that indicates that she cannot fulfill the request immediately. The *vai*-addition is then clearly formulated as a reaction to this: it presents an alternative way of handling the money issue – even though it is connected to Milla's own question and not to Susa's response. By initiating the continuation with *vai*, Milla implies that the two ways of handling the issue linked with *vai* both hold as alternatives. However, the two options are not equal alternatives. That is, the *vai*-addition addresses the presupposition of the first inquiry, Susa's ability to pay in cash. The operation that the *vai*-addition accomplishes is to transform the original request into an offer that is more likely to receive a preferred answer. This also happens in line 8.

The previous three examples have shown that *vai*-prefaced continuations to an already completed question are not best characterized as just providing an alternative. Instead, they unpack the presupposition of the first questions in order to deal with the possible obstacles to getting a preferred answer. In other words, the *vai*-addition addresses the underlying assumption behind the question. In practice, this is a way of enabling a grammatically preferred answer (cf. Sacks 1987: 64; Raymond 2003) after an ambiguous answer or signs of a dispreferred answer. This means that the two questions connected with *vai* are not equally preferred alternatives. Furthermore, the one that comes last is the one that has greater salience and is thus likely to be responded to (cf. Sacks 1987: 60).

What is the contribution of the turn-initial *vai* then? I would like to suggest that the main motivation is similar to increments in general, that is, adding something retrospectively as a part of what was already completed serves to deal with the lack of an appropriate reaction (on increments, see, e.g., Schegloff 1996; Ford, Fox & Thompson 2002; Couper-Kuhlen & Ono (eds.) 2007). This is done by masking the second question as a part of the prior question, which suggests that the first question was actually incomplete. It should also be noted that by prefacing the second question with *vai* the speaker does not mark her turn as overtly reacting to the dispreferred turn but as connected to her own, previous question. *Vai* thus not only masks the turn as a continuation of the first question but also as non-reactive to the prior answer. Furthermore, it does not erase the first question and replace it with a new one but rather suggests that they both still stand as alternatives.

STAND-ALONE *VAI*: A WAY OF ADJUSTING ONE'S EPISTEMIC POSITIONING

There is at least one more way of expanding a possibly complete turn with *vai*. The core observation here is that *vai* can also occur alone, meaning that it is not prosodically integrated with the prior turn but is produced after its possible completion, at the "post-possible completion point" (Schegloff 1996: 90). This type of *vai* seems to retrospectively increase the level of uncertainty of the just-completed turn (cf. Drake 2013 on turn-final *or*) by making a confirming response relevant. What is noteworthy is that the prior turn is not necessarily a (clear) question but it can also be a statement. In other words, the speaker does not necessarily first position him/herself in an unknowing position but it is only the occurrence of the post-completion *vai* that does this. *Vai* is then used to transform the prior turn into something that is in search of a confirmation. In the following example from a hair salon, the client makes a remark about the hairdresser's hair color (line 1). This engenders the client's self-evaluation about the condition of her own hair color (lines 8–10), which is our target turn:

(14) [Vai64_T473_a]

```
01 C:     [(oo) ↑TSÄÄ pannut ittelles tummaa.
           have you put yourself dark (hair color).

02        (0.8)

03 H:     no n:ii:hän se minunkip pittää joskus ko#:#;
          well yes I have to do that sometimes as well cause;

04        (0.2)

05 C:     [eh heh

06 H:     [tässä muita värjäilee ja ka- a- ihfhailee
          you dye other people and admire

07        toisten väriä ni; .nffff
          others' color so;

08 C: ->  mää en      kyllä pistä [<nyt väriä      tähän>.et siinä
          1SG NEG-1SG PRT         put  now   color-PAR DEM-ILL    PRT DEM-INE
          I'm not going to put any color in this now. there's
                                   [((H GLANCES AT C THROUGH THE MIRROR))
09        om  mum      mielest  vie#lä#< (0.4)    #riittävästi#.
          be  1SG-GEN mind-ELA  still              enough
          in my opinion still< (0.4) enough.

10        vai?
          PRT?

11        (0.6)

12 H:     j:oo ja kesäaikanahan se [vaalenee <nii]
          yeah and in summertime it'll become lighter so
13 C:                               [joo; joo-o;  ]
                                    right; right;

14 H:     et:>tä [(ka↑totaan)    ] sitte [jatkossa?
          that we will look at that in the future then?

15 C:            [>mut kyllähän<,]       [nii; joo.
                 but surely              yes; right.

16 C:     kyllä mää; (.) ha- haluun pi[tää sen vaaleena;
          I do (.) want to keep it blond;
```

More specifically, the client's turn in lines 8–10 consists of an announcement about her plans regarding her hair and an assessment that functions as an account for the announcement. In this case, it is important to consider what kind of response – if any – this turn makes relevant. As the second part of the turn is an assessment or an evaluation, it makes relevant a second assessment, that is, an agreement or a disagreement (Pomerantz 1984). In terms of epistemics, the client can be considered as the person who has the primary epistemic rights to evaluate her own hair (Heritage & Raymond 2005). However, the situation and the institutional roles of the participants make the distribution of epistemic rights more complicated. That is, as a professional, the hairdresser also has the epistemic right to evaluate the condition of his client's hair. Even though formed as an announcement, the client seems to be orienting to this already in the design of her turn, prior to *vai*: the expression *mun mielestä* ('in my opinion') functions as an epistemic downgrade by conveying an implication that there might also be other opinions (see Rauniomaa 2007: 233). This marking can be seen as an invitation for the hairdresser to validate the client's viewpoint. The prosodically independent *vai* does this work even more overtly due to its nature as a question particle (see Hakulinen et al. 2004: § 1701). It makes a confirming response relevant – not just an agreeing second assessment. Through the use of the final *vai*, the client then transfers the epistemic rights to evaluate the hair to the hairdresser.

In contrast to the previous examples, the *vai*-addition is attached to the prior turn without a pause. The falling intonation in line 9, however, creates a transition relevance place. Despite this, it is difficult to tell whether *vai* is added as a reaction to incipient disagreement. The only detectable thing is the hairdresser's brief glance at the client in the mirror in the midst of the client's statement (line 8). However, nothing definite can be said about how the glance affects the client's behavior. It is still probable that the client is monitoring the hairdresser's reactions and formulates her turn in response to what is possibly perceived as hesitation. The formulation of the hairdresser's response in line 12 (pause and lengthening of the initial sound in *joo* and an addition shifting the perspective into the future) suggests that he does not whole-heartedly agree.

Conclusion

This article has discussed the on-line temporal emergence of alternative questions in Finnish, and the usage potential that the conjunction/particle *vai* has in the service of question formation. I have demonstrated that even though *vai* can be used to combine phrases and interrogative clauses to form fixed packages without an intervening pause, alternative questions can also emerge as solutions to interactional needs, so that the second part of a question is delivered as a reaction to something that the co-participant has done or has failed to do. As Couper-Kuhlen (2012: 134) puts it, "[alternative] questions are produced in conversation as parts of courses of action carried out in real time and in this sense are interactional achievements".

The word *vai* is especially suitable for adjusting the interpretation of an emerging question. First, I have shown that *vai* can link more than two alternatives, which allows its use as a listing device. A list of objects linked by *vai* can be expanded in response to interactional needs, e.g., due to lack of uptake, providing more similar alternatives seamlessly, without actually starting anything new. Furthermore, by ending a list-so-far with *vai* the speaker conveys an implication that the list of alternatives is not exhaustive (cf. Koivisto 2011; 2012 on turn-final *ja* 'and'). Second, I have suggested that the capability of the word *vai* to function as a coordinating conjunction, turn-initial particle, or a turn-final question particle can be made use of in the formation of an emergent alternative question. That is, a turn ending in the question particle *vai* can be retrospectively transformed into the beginning of an alternative question by repeating the word at the beginning of a post-pausal continuation of the turn. Third, I have shown that other kinds of questions can also be expanded with a *vai*-initial increment after a pause or signs of a dispreferred response. They reverse the preference of the first alternative and thereby facilitate the production of a (grammatically) preferred answer. Finally, I have demonstrated that *vai* can also occur at a point of post-possible completion, i.e., it can stand alone. In this position it does not function as a linking element but rather performs an epistemic adjustment and solicits confirmation in retrospect.

This study has provided yet another demonstration of the emergent nature of syntactic structures in spoken interaction in general and of clause combinations in particular, as well as the multifunctionality of conjunctions in conversation (see Laury 2008; Suzuki & Laury 2011). Moreover, I have shown that *vai*-constructions can be used in the on-line negotiation of questions (and sometimes assertions) and their responses. More specifically, they are a questioner's resource for dealing with preference issues, that is, the threat of receiving a dispreferred or an otherwise inadequate response. *Vai*-additions respond to this need in a specific way: they do not redo the question or replace it with a new question. Instead, they extend the possibly completed question by providing a candidate answer that is marked as an alternative. By extending the original question with a *vai*-prefaced question the questioner does not overtly react to the (signs of a) dispreferred answer but marks or masks the second question as a part of the previous one, something that was "on its way" all along. This is a way of adjusting the interpretation of a question that has been treated as problematic.

References

Barth-Weingarten, Dagmar & Elizabeth Couper-Kuhlen. 2011. Action, prosody and emergent construction: The case of *and*. In Peter Auer & Stefan Pfänder (eds.), *Constructions: Emerging and emergent*. 262–292. Berlin: De Gruyter.

Blöndal, Þórunn. 2008. Turn-final eða ('or') in spoken Icelandic. In Jan Lindström (ed.), *Språk och interaction 1*. 151–168. Institutionen för nordiska språk och nordisk litteratus vid Helsingfors universitet.

Couper-Kuhlen, Elizabeth. 2012. Some truths and untruths about final intonation in conversational questions. In Jan P. de Ruiter (ed.) *Questions. Formal, functional and interactional perspectives.* 123–145. Cambridge: Cambridge University Press.

Couper-Kuhlen, Elizabeth. 2014. What does grammar tell us about action? *Pragmatics* 24(3): 623–647.

Couper-Kuhlen, Elizabeth & Tsuyoshi Ono (eds.). 2007. Turn continuation in crosslinguistic perspective. *Pragmatics* 17. Special issue.

Davidson, Judy. 1984. Subsequent versions of invitations, offers, requests, and proposals dealing with potential or actual rejection. In J. Maxwell Atkinson & John Heritage (eds.), *Structures of social action. Studies in conversation analysis.* 102–128. Cambridge: Cambridge University Press.

Drake, Veronika. 2013. *Turn-final or in English: A conversation analytic perspective.* An unpublished dissertation. University of Wisconsin-Madison.

Drake, Veronika. 2015. Indexing uncertainty: The case of turn-final *or*. *Research on Language and Social Interaction* 48(3): 301–318.

Ford, Cecilia. 1993. *Grammar in interaction. Adverbial clauses in American English conversation.* Cambridge: Cambridge University Press.

Ford, Cecilia. 2004. Contingency and units in interaction. *Discourse Studies* 6(1): 27–52.

Ford, Cecilia, Barbara Fox & Sandra A. Thompson. 2002. Constituency and the grammar of turn increments. In Cecilia Ford, Barbara Fox & Sandra Thompson (eds.), *The language of turn and sequence.* 14–38. Oxford: Oxford University Press.

Goodwin, Charles. 1979. The interactive construction of a sentence in natural conversation. In George Psathas (ed.), *Everyday language: Studies in ethnomethodology.* 97–121. New York: Erlbaum.

Hakulinen, Auli, Maria Vilkuna, Riitta Korhonen, Vesa Koivisto, Tarja Riitta Heinonen & Irja Alho. 2004. *Iso suomen kielioppi.* Helsinki: Finnish Literature Society.

Halonen, Mia. 2002. *Kertominen terapian välineenä. Tutkimus vuorovaikutuksesta myllyhoidon ryhmäterapiassa.* Helsinki: Finnish Literature Society.

Heritage, John. 1984. A change-of-state token and aspects of its sequential placement. In J. Maxwell Atkinson & John Heritage (eds.), *Structures of social action. Studies in conversation analysis.* 299–345. Cambridge: Cambridge University Press.

Heritage, John & Geoffrey Raymond. 2005. The terms of agreement: Indexing epistemic authority and subordination in assessment sequences. *Social Psychology Quarterly* 68: 15–38.

Jefferson, Gail. 1990. List-construction as a task and resource. In George Psathas (ed.), *Interactional Competence.* 63–92. New York, NY: Irvington Publishers.

Koivisto, Aino. 2011. *Sanomattakin selvää? Ja, että ja mutta puheenvuoron lopussa.* Ph.D. dissertation. University of Helsinki, Department of Finnish, Finno-Ugrian and Scandinavian Studies.

Koivisto, Aino. 2012. Discourse patterns for turn-final conjunctions. *Journal of Pragmatics* 44: 1254–1272.

Koivisto, Aino, Ritva Laury & Eeva-Leena Seppänen. 2011. Syntactic and actional characteristics of Finnish *että*-clauses. In Ritva Laury & Ryoko Suzuki (eds.), *Subordination in conversation. A crosslinguistic perspective.* 69-101. Amsterdam: John Benjamins.

Korpela, Eveliina. 2007. *Oireista puhuminen lääkärin vastaanotolla. Keskustelunanalyyttinen tutkimus lääkärin kysymyksistä.* [Talking about symptoms during medical consultation. – A conversation analytical study of doctor's questions.] Helsinki: Finnish Literature Society.

Laury, Ritva (ed.). 2008. *Crosslinguistic studies of clause combining. The multifunctionality of conjunctions.* Amsterdam: John Benjamins.

Laury, Ritva & Ryoko Suzuki (eds.). 2011. *Subordination in conversation: A crosslinguistic perspective.* Amsterdam: John Benjamins.

Lindström, Anna. 1999. *Language as social action. Grammar, prosody, and interaction in Swedish conversation.* Institutionen för nordiska språk vid Uppsala universitet.

Mulder, Jean & Sandra A. Thompson. 2008. The grammaticization of *but* as a final particle in English conversation. In Ritva Laury (ed.), *Crosslinguistic studies of clause combining: The multifunctionality of conjunctions.* 179-204. Amsterdam: John Benjamins.

Ogden, Richard. 2004. Non-modal voice quality and turn-taking in Finnish. In Elizabeth Couper-Kuhlen & Cecilia E. Ford (eds.), *Sound patterns in interaction.* 29–62. Amsterdam: John Benjamins.

Penttilä, Aarni. 1957. *Suomen kielioppi.* [Finnish grammar.] Porvoo: WSOY.

Pomerantz, Anita. 1984. Agreeing and disagreeing with assessments: Some features of preferred/dispreferred turn shapes. In J.M. Atkinson & John Heritage (eds.), *Structures of social action. Studies in conversation analysis.* 57–101. Cambridge: Cambridge University Press.

Quirk, Randolf, Sidney Greenbaum, Geoffrey Leech & Jan Svartvik. 1985. *A comprehensive grammar of the English language.* London: Longman.

Raevaara, Liisa. 1993. *Kysyminen toimintana. Kysymys–vastaus-vieruspareista arkikeskustelussa.* Lisensiaatintyö. University of Helsinki, Department of Finnish language.

Rauniomaa, Mirka. 2007. Stance markers in spoken Finnish: *Minun mielestä* and *minusta* in assessments. In Robert Englebretson (ed.), *Stancetaking in discourse: Subjectivity, evaluation, interaction.* 221-252. Amsterdam: John Benjamins.

Raymond, Geoffrey. 2003. Grammar and social organization: Yes/no interrogatives and the structure of responding. *American Sociological Review* 68: 939–967.

Sacks, Harvey. 1987. On the preferences for agreement and contiguity in sequences in conversation. In Graham Button & John R. Lee (eds.), *Talk and social organisation.* 54-69. Clevedon, UK: Multilingual Matters.

Schegloff, Emanuel A. 1996. Turn organization: one intersection of grammar and interaction. In Elinor Ochs, Emanuel A. Schegloff & Sandra A. Thompson (eds.), *Interaction and grammar.* 52-133. Cambridge: Cambridge University Press.

Schegloff, Emanuel A. 1997. Practices and actions: Boundary cases of other-initiated repair. *Discourse Processes* 23: 499–545.

Schegloff, Emanuel A. 2007. *Sequence organization in interaction: A primer in conversation analysis.* Cambridge: Cambridge University Press.

Stivers, Tanya. 2010. An overview of the question–response system in American English conversation. *Journal of Pragmatics* 42: 2772–2781.

Thompson, Sandra A. & Ryoko Suzuki. 2012. The grammaticalization of final particles. In Heiko Narrog & Bernd Heine (eds.), *The Oxford handbook of grammaticalization.* 668–680. London: Oxford University Press.

Linking of grammatical structures III

Anna Vatanen
http://orcid.org/0000-0002-8236-657X

6. Delayed completions of unfinished turns: On the phenomenon and its boundaries[1]

Introduction

It has been claimed in Conversation Analysis that turn transition is coordinated around the possible completion points of turn-constructional units (Sacks et al. 1974: 703). It has also been argued that unfinished turns or fragments of turn-constructional units do not usually lead to a response from the recipient (Selting 2001: 250), even if the recipient recognizes what kind of response will be relevant next (Lerner 2004a: 152). However, several scholars have discovered that this may not always be the case. For instance, Chevalier and Clift (2008; see also Chevalier 2008) found that unfinished turns in French conversation are regularly followed by appropriate responses, and Vatanen (2014) showed that in Finnish and Estonian talk-in-interaction, speakers who start up a response to the ongoing turn at a place where the turn is not yet transition-ready (i.e., not at a transition-relevance place (TRP)) appear to have recognized the gist of the turn and respond appropriately, and that they even use the non-TRP onset for specific purposes in interaction. In Chevalier and Clift's (2008) data, the initiating speakers typically cut off their turn once the response has set in, while in Vatanen's (2014) data, the overlapped speakers typically continue to produce their turn despite the response onset, which results in rather extended simultaneous talk. Another trajectory attested is one where the initiating speaker cuts off, and after hearing some parts of the response, continues and completes his/her turn. The last mentioned phenomenon is the focus of this article.

The interactional practice to be investigated here has been termed *delayed completion* by Lerner (1989, see also 2004b).[2] The current article builds on Lerner's work and sheds further light on the phenomenon in several respects – for instance, by exploring the boundaries of the phenomenon,

---

1   I would like to express my gratitude to Marja Etelämäki, Ritva Laury, Elizabeth Couper-Kuhlen, Florence Oloff, and the anonymous reviewers for their detailed comments on earlier versions of this paper. All remaining shortcomings are mine.
2   The phenomenon was, however, already identified in Sacks' lectures (1992a: 647ff., 1992b: 348ff.).

by investigating it in two non-Indo-European languages, and by showing that the interactional work accomplished in these sequences is patterned. This study is based on a collection of cases where the delayed completion is positioned in overlap with a turn that is responsive to the not-yet-completed turn, i.e., the host.[3] The onset of the responsive turn occurs at a place other than a TRP: the turn that is later completed is not yet possibly complete at the point when the response sets in.[4] This makes delayed completions different from increments – continuations of already completed turns (see Ford et al. 2002; Couper-Kuhlen & Ono 2007; cf. also Jefferson 1981). The practice investigated here is schematized in Figure 1. The arrows on the left will be used in the transcripts to mark the corresponding items:

Figure 1. Overlapping delayed completions

```
1  >  A: talk that does not reach its completion        ← host
2  -> B: talk responding [to talk in line 1             ← response to the host
3  => A:                 [continuation of talk in line 1] ← delayed completion of the host
```

The current article investigates this phenomenon using the methodology of conversation analysis (see, e.g., Sidnell & Stivers 2013) and interactional linguistics (see, e.g., Couper-Kuhlen & Selting 2001). The data come from 7 hours of videotaped naturally occurring Estonian and Finnish everyday conversation, 3.5 hours from each language.[5] The core collection, 20 instances, has been selected from a larger collection of turn continuations in the data. It will be shown that the practice is similar in both languages.

In his pioneering work on the phenomenon, Lerner (1989, 2004b) focused mainly on the syntactic relationship between the incomplete host and its delayed completion. Later work on delayed completions has been carried out by Oloff (2008, 2009, 2014a, 2014b), who focuses mostly on the embodied practices the participants exploit in these situations (especially 2014a, 2014b), but also on other means used for achieving coherence between the host and its delayed completion. Oloff's collections from French and German data consist of cases where the intervening turn, although often constructed as responsive, most often either begins a new sequence or completes the host in a collaborative manner (for more on this practice, see, e.g., Lerner 1996, 2004b). Most of the cases examined by Oloff fall into one of these two types, while in the cases examined here, the intervening turn typically is more clearly designed to be a response to the not-yet-completed host. However, some of the instances in the current collection also seem to be used to do more than purely responsive work. Furthermore, all the delayed completions examined here are positioned in overlap at a non-TRP in the intervening response. The current study thus sets its focus on a specific

---

3   Lerner, on the other hand, does not specify the type of intervening talk.
4   In these cases, the syntactically incomplete turn is not completed in an embodied way; for embodied completions, see, e.g., Ford et al. 2012, Keevallik 2013, Keevallik 2015, Li 2014, and Mondada 2015.
5   The language of each extract is marked after the name of the example.

type of delayed completion, both regarding its temporal positioning (it is in overlap) and the nature of the intervening turn (which is a responding turn).

In the following sections, I will analyze my examples not only with respect to grammar but also with respect to the prosodic[6] and embodied resources[7] the speakers use to achieve the linkage between the host and the delayed completion (on prosodic properties of continuing talk, see Local 1992, and on turn continuation in general, see Couper-Kuhlen 2012). It will be demonstrated that the interactional work initiated in the hosts is similar across the cases, and that the course of the sequences is rather uniform. Furthermore, it will be shown that speakers use delayed completions for insisting on their own viewpoint and on their rights to complete a turn. That is, in my data, the use of delayed completions in interaction is patterned and situated in specific types of action sequences. We will now start with simple cases of delayed completions and then move towards exploring the boundaries of the phenomenon.

Illustrating the core phenomenon

Let us begin with a rather simple example. Prior to this fragment, speaker A has brought up the claim that cats are not gregarious animals. She then counters this claim by telling about a documentary on wild cats she has seen, and based on this, she concludes:

(1) Laumaeläimiä / Gregarious animals (Finnish)
Sg 377, 22:07

```
01  A:     et niil on aika tarkkaki sitte
           that they nevertheless have a quite strict

02         kuitenki semmonen
           such a

03         sosi[aalinen järjeste]lmä(1) #niillä:#,
           soc [ial      group     ] ing they (have)
               [                    ]
04  B:         [on       niillä;    ]
               [they do  (have)     ]
```

---

6 As the delayed completions are produced in overlap and as the recordings are made with one microphone only, it is unfortunately not possible to provide acoustic analyses of the prosodic phenomena, e.g., with the program Praat. The prosodic analyses are based on auditory observation (i.e., listening) only.
7 Gaze behavior has also been analyzed but for the most part it was found not to account for the turn-taking behavior in these cases and for this reason – with the exception of example (3) – is not shown in the transcriptions. For more on embodiment in delayed completions, see Oloff (2014a, 2014b).

```
05  A:  >    et   ne       on  [kuitenkin            #niinku#,
             COMP DEM3:PL   be:3SG however           PRT
             so that they   neverthe[less are like
                                     [
06  B:                              [°nii,°
                                    [yeah


07           (.)


08  B:  ->   .h ja siis osa kis[soistahan  o]n      sosiaalisempia
             and PRT   part cat:PL:ELA:CLI be:3SG   sociable:CMP:PL:PAR
             .h and I mean some   ca[ts you know    ar]e more sociable
                                    [               ]
09  A:  =>                         [laumaeläimiä?]
                                   gregarious.animal:PL:PAR
                                   [gregarious  animals]


10  B:       ku osa et [niis on sellasii tolla- (.)
             than others (so that) [there are that ki- (.)
                        [
11  A:                 [jaa;
                       [okay


        B            |TURNS RAPIDLY TOWARDS HER CAT AND POINTS TO IT
12  B:       niinku tollasii, (.) y- yksinäisii £körmyjä£?
             that kind of (.) lo- lonesome trolls among them


13           hehhh .hh ja s(h)it £niis on niit
             hehh .hh and th(h)en there are those


14           sellasii laumatyyppejä£?
             gregarious characters among them
```

Lines 1–3 contain a summarizing utterance by speaker A, beginning with the complementizer/particle *et* (see Koivisto et al. 2011). B agrees with A in her response (line 4), yet by using a specific word order [verb + subject[8]] (see Hakulinen & Sorjonen 2009) she implies some epistemic authority on the matter in question.[9] After B's response, A starts up another *et*-prefaced, paraphrasing utterance (line 5; Seppänen & Laury 2007, Laury & Seppänen 2008). With this summary-like assertion turn, she starts to make the point of her telling even more explicit: *et ne on kuitenkin niinku - -* 'so that they nevertheless are like - -'. Speaker B first places a very softly produced response particle *nii* in overlap with A's utterance (line 6) and then starts up a more extensive turn reacting to A's talk (line 8) at a point where A's ongoing utterance is not yet complete: the clause lacks the projected predicate

---

[8] Strictly speaking, *niillä* is not a subject in this clause but a habitive adverbial. The clause is a possessive clause, and in Finnish possessive clauses, the possessor is expressed with a habitive adverbial that occurs in the place of the subject (Hakulinen et al. 2004: 852-855).

[9] For this and other similar responses, see Vatanen 2014.

nominal, and the level pitch contour at the end is not clearly turn-final in Finnish (see Tiittula 1985). The so-far-last element of A's turn is the particle *niinku*, which can be heard as signaling a word search or planning of talk (Kunelius 1998), and after that there is also a micro pause, indicating some hesitation. The summary-like characteristic of the not-yet-complete host, which is typical in the current collection, is among the properties which facilitate the launching of the response in spite of the fact that the host is not yet complete: the main points of the talk have already been made, and so the responding speaker can start his/her turn even before the previous turn has been fully completed (see also Oloff 2009: 484ff.).

B's turn (line 8) is constructed as an addition to A's prior talk (it begins with the additive conjunction *ja*, 'and'; see Kalliokoski 1989) and is as such a seemingly aligning utterance. However, the particle *siis* implicates an explanatory turn, often drawn from the speaker's personal knowledge (Hakulinen & Couper-Kuhlen 2015), which suggests its speaker constructs herself as a knowing participant. The stressed noun *osa* 'part/some' may also be heard as foreshadowing a contrast to or at least a refinement of A's talk. Upon hearing this item, A produces a delayed completion of her prior talk: *laumaeläimiä* 'gregarious animals'. It is typical for the whole collection that the responding turn contains some non-aligning and/or non-affiliative elements in relation to the prior utterance, which seems to trigger the production of the delayed completion.

The delayed completion in example (1) is both grammatically and prosodically fitted to the host. Grammatically, it is a classifying predicate nominal in plural partitive (which is what was projected); its number matches the number of the subject of the copular clause (*ne*) and its partitive case reflects its classifying function. Prosodically the delayed completion is designed to fit the host in that the pitch, loudness, and tempo in it are similar to those in the host (or at the end of it) (cf. Local 1992). Furthermore, the delayed completion completes the social action begun in the host: it concludes A's telling of her understanding of the nature of cats. Here the intervening turn (line 8), responding to talk in lines 1–3 and 5, comes right after the host, with no gap and no overlap. However, although this temporal positioning is recurrent in my collection, it is not the only one, as some of the following examples will illustrate.

In sum, example (1) demonstrates several features typical for delayed completions in the current collection. The host begins an assertion turn – a description-like declarative statement in which the speaker claims something rather generic about the world from his/her own perspective, typically also including some type of stance or attitudinal expression (evaluation) (on "assertion turns", see Vatanen 2014, section 8.1). The assertion here begins to summarize the point of the prior telling, and it ends with slight markers of hesitation (on hesitation and delayed completions, see Oloff 2014a; cf. also Chevalier 2008; Chevalier & Clift 2008). The intervening response comes right after the host and is not totally in alignment with the host, as it goes slightly beyond just-responding (cf. Oloff 2014b). The delayed completion, begun at a non-TRP in the responsive turn, is fitted to its host via grammatical and prosodic means. The delayed-completion speaker appears to defend her right to produce a full, complete turn-at-talk, and thus she displays an orientation to the turn-taking rules as proposed by Sacks et al. (1974), especially to the right to talk until the TRP (for a similar conclusion, see Oloff 2008, 2009). In other words, the delayed completion displays insistence on speakership. By producing the delayed completion the speaker also insists on her own viewpoint and its sequential/interactional relevance. It is also typical that it is the response-speaker, and not the delayed-completion-speaker, who continues to hold the floor after these turns; the delayed completion does not, however, succeed in inviting a separate reaction from the co-participant.

The next example includes misalignment as well, and in addition, there is even more explicit competition for turn space. In this fragment, the participants are talking about formulaic liturgies in church services. Maia and Jaan are a couple, and Tõnu (not talking here) and Angela are visiting them. There are two instances of delayed completion here, the first one in line 15 and the second one in line 17. From line 1 on, Maia responds to a prior turn by Tõnu in which he has claimed that in the present-day context, it is like a sign of retardation when an adult, as a child of God, always turns to God using the same formula (e.g., reciting ready-made prayers):

(2) Liturgia / Liturgy (Estonian)
PI1, 10:50

```
01 Maia:     nojah? a:ga aga samas .h samas võib-olla
             yeah, but but at the same time .h at the same time maybe

02           see vormel, (.) `teatud vormel on pär-
             the formula, (.) a certain formula is still qui-

03           päris ea `ka.
             quite good too.

04           (0.4)

05 Maia:     ↓°teenistusel° et see on nagu, (.)
             for the ((church)) service so that it is like (.)

06           niisukese, (.) `korraarmastuse;¹⁰
             DEM.ADJ:GEN           order.loving:GEN
             of such, (.) (of) order loving

07           (0.4)

08 Angela:   °mm.°

09           (0.4)
```

---

10 This structure is left grammatically incomplete.

```
10  Maia:   >    ↑ega  vanas    Iisraelis    ne[il olid    ↑`ka omad,
                 PRT   OLD:INE  NAME:INE     3PL:ADE BE:3PL  ALSO  OWN:PL
                      indeed in old Israel  the[y also had their own,
                                                 [
11  Jaan:                                    [°no?°
                                              PRT
                                             [well

12  Maia:   >    omad ee [ee
                 own:PL
                 their own uhm [uhm
                               [
13  Jaan:   ->              [>no-  olid      neil      oli<    `siis
                             (PRT) be:3PL:PST 3PL:ADE  be:3SG:PST then
                            [(well?) (they) were they had at that time

14         ->    oli         see   nii   `LEvinud  et[=ä-
                 be:3SG:PST  DEM1  PRT   spread:PPC COMP
                 it was so widespread             tha[t
                                                     [
15  Maia:   =>                               [kindlad
                                              certain:PL
                                             [specific

16         ->    asj[ad.    oli       ↑`ka   niöelda  li`turgia. ]
                 matter:PL be:3SG:PST also   so.called liturgy
                 thin[gs. (there) was also a so-called liturgy.    ]
                    [                                              ]
17  Jaan:   =>      [palvetasidki      `valmis sõnadega.          ]
                    pray:3PL:PST:CLI   ready   word:PL:COM
                    [they actually prayed with ready-made words.   ]

18  Jaan:        .h inimkond oli sellega rohkem harjund ja
                 .h humankind was more accustomed to it and

19               `oskas võbolla ka seda oma tunnet sinna
                 was maybe able to include their own feelings in there

20               `sisse panna.  .h aga präägu meile tundub
                 as well.  .h but nowadays we feel

21               see-  .h ni=et-  [tundub nagu veidi-]
                 it-  .h so- (it) [feels a bit-       ]
                                  [                   ]
22  Maia:                         [noo `sina oled    ] lihtsalt
                                  [well you have     ] simply

23               nii kasvanud.
                 grown up like that.

24  Jaan:        £noh eks se muidugi on jah?£
                 well that of course is (the case) yeah
```

Maia is the primary speaker in the beginning of this extract. Her assertion (lines 1–3), an assessment of formulaic church services as something good, gets no response, and her continuation (lines 5–6) meets only with a weak acknowledgement token *mm* from Angela (line 8). Maia continues talking and shifts the focus to the history of church services in line 10, bringing in past liturgies as support for her positive view about liturgies in the present: *ega vanas Iisraelis neil olid ka omad - -* 'indeed in old Israel they also had their own - -'. In Estonian, the word *omad*, 'own' cannot stand alone, thus Maia's turn is clearly incomplete. However, by repeating the word *omad*, 'own' and producing the sound *ee*, she displays hesitation, whereupon her husband Jaan comes in. Jaan's response (from line 13 on) is at first sight quite in line with Maia's talk – he agrees on the historical fact of liturgies. However, because Jaan did not explicitly agree with Maia's assessment before, and also in part because of the particle *no* (line 11; cf. Schegloff & Lerner 2009 on the English *well*) as well as the prosodic formatting used, his turn sounds somewhat contrastive from the beginning. As it turns out, Jaan's view about the present-day church services is different from Maia's.

In this fragment, the overlapped host (lines 10, 12) is not conclusion-like, since this is the first time Maia has mentioned 'old Israel', which makes this example different from most of the delayed completions in the current collection. However, it still supports the speaker's prior claim and thus is in line with it. Jaan reformulates his turn beginning several times, and at a point where he has fully uttered the first clause (*siis oli see nii levinud* 'at that time it was so widespread') and projected continuation with the complementizer *et*, Maia comes in and completes her own turn, albeit with a generalized item: *kindlad asjad* 'specific things' (lines 15–16). In line 17, Jaan, having interrupted his turn immediately upon Maia's delayed completion onset (see the abrupt end in his *et=ä-*, line 14), comes in and in turn completes his prior utterance: *palvetasidki valmis sõnadega* 'they actually prayed with ready-made words' (line 17). Maia, however, does not stop talking this time but continues beyond a possible TRP, adding one more argument to her assertive talk (line 16: *oli ka niöelda liturgia* '(there) was also a so-called liturgy'); this is simultaneous with Jaan's talk. Jaan's turn in lines 13–14 functions thus both as (the beginning of) a response to Maia's turn and at the same time as a host to his own delayed completion in line 17.

Both delayed completions in this extract (lines 15 and 17) are linked to their hosts by several means, not only grammatical but also prosodic: they begin at the same pitch level as the end of the host and they are uttered with the same tempo as well. Grammatically they provide the elements that were projected at the end of the host: Maia provides the last elements of the phrase expressing the possessed item in the possessive clause, and Jaan provides the explanatory clause projected by the complementizer *et* (for this type of construction in Finnish, see Seppänen & Herlin 2009).

In this extract both the fact that currently participating speakers produce delayed completions as well as the fairly extended overlap in lines 16–17 suggest that there is rather substantial competition over turn space. As is the case in both examples (1) and (2), the delayed completions in the current collection tend to be used in non-aligning and even disagreeing contexts.

This makes sense: if the response were totally aligning and agreeing with the not-yet-completed turn, there would not be so much of a need to insist on producing one's own turn and bringing it to full completion (see also Oloff 2008, 2009, 2014a). Providing a delayed completion to a not-yet-completed turn, even though the response-speaker has appropriately understood the gist of the turn, appears thus to be a practice to insist on one's own viewpoint in conversation.

We will now move on to some more complex cases that are at or near the boundaries of the phenomenon of delayed completion and differ more or less from the cases investigated above.

Exploring the boundaries of delayed completions

Each of the examples to be examined in this section will illustrate an aspect of the complexity around delayed completions. All these cases are, in one sense or another, at the boundaries of the phenomenon. In example (3), one difference compared to the cases discussed above is that the intervening response is positioned in very early overlap with the not-yet-complete host. In this case, the not-yet-complete turn speaker cuts off right after the response is initiated but produces a delayed completion after only a few syllables of the response have been produced. This makes the turn completion only slightly delayed, and raises the question of how long a distance is needed to call a turn completion *delayed*. In the following example (3), Margit starts to talk about a couple who have gone together on a trip (*sinna* 'there', line 3) and the state of their relationship. Both participants know the people talked about.

(3) Päris hea olla / Doing quite well (Estonian)
AN3, 05:30

```
01 M:      et see on, `ikkagi vastab see `tõele mis
           so it is, it nevertheless is true what

02         ma ju sulle ju nagu `ütlesin ennem et noh,
           I you know said to you previously that um,

03         nad läksid ikkagi vaata `eraldi sinna
           they went anyway y'see separately there

04         on[ju.  ]
           rig[ht.  ]
              [    ]
05 K:      [jaa,]apso`luutselt.
           [yeah,] absolutely.

06 M: >    see     `mõjub              et    tal     on
           DEM1    have.influence:3SG  COMP  3SG:ADE be:3SG
           it/that has the effect that she is
```

```
07        >      `tege [lt-   ]
                 actually
                    actu[ally-  ]
                        [       ]
08  K:    ->     [apso] `luutselt  [mõjub.       ta    on     ju   `t]ema:ga:
                 absolutely         have.influence:3SG 3SG be:3SG PRT    3SG:COM
                 [it abso]lutely   [has.  she is you know              w]ith him/her
                                   [                                              ]
09  M:    =>                       [päris `ea   olla.                             ]
                                    quite  good be:INF
                                   [feeling quite good.                           ]

10  K:           .hhh äää=ener`geetiliselt `ka väga lähedases kontaktis.
                 .hhh uhm in so close contact also energetically.

11               (1.0)

12  K:           kuna ta=on nii=öelda `eraldi.
                 as she is so called separately.


13               (2.4)
```

Margit's assertion turn in lines 6–7 has not yet reached a TRP when it is slightly overlapped by Katrin (line 8). In her response Katrin confirms Margit's assertion – that something has an effect on the person talked about –, as if already anticipating the content of the rest of the turn. She also implies some prior knowledge on the issue (*apsoluutselt mõjub* 'it absolutely has').[11] Having done this, she now initiates something new with *ta on - -*, 'she is - -'. Katrin starts up her response when the possessive clause that Margit is constructing still lacks its complement, *tal on tegelt **päris hea olla***.[12] In contrast to more typical hosts, which initiate summary-like generalizations of the previous talk (as, e.g., in example (1)), the host here is positioned rather early in talk that seems to be launched as a more extensive informing or telling. The host is thus positioned close to the very beginning of the talk on this topic – even though the speaker refers to some earlier talk in lines 1–2.[13]

In overlap with Katrin's response, Margit, having previously cut off her not-yet-completed turn (lines 6–7), now completes it by providing the complement (line 9), continuing at the same pitch level she used before. However, her delayed completion is slightly louder in volume compared to the host, which may indicate some competition for turn space – indeed, Katrin's response is positioned very early both with regard to the ongoing turn and the sequence. The loudness of the delayed completion may be reactive to the fact that the response comes both in early overlap and also

---

11 For a fuller analysis of this response, see Vatanen 2014: 74ff.
12 The English translation is in a different form, not a possessive clause: *she is actually feeling quite good*.
13 The earlier talk is not captured in the video recording. Right before this fragment, however, the participants have talked about an SMS message exchange between Margit and one member of the couple they discuss here; the identity of *ta* 'she' here is not stated explicitly but seems clear to both participants.

early in the sequence (see also Oloff 2009). The delayed completion-speaker thus appears to orient to the positioning of the co-participant's response as premature. However, Margit's delayed completion is not responded to in the subsequent talk, as Katrin, after the clearly responsive part in her turn (line 8), continues her own assertions regarding the people they are talking about. That the response-speaker continues is typical for these kinds of sequences.

Thus far we have seen cases in which the response has come very close to the not-yet-completed host: in the first delayed completion case (1), there was a micro pause, and in examples (2) and (3), there was overlap. The next case differs from the preceding ones: the response is preceded by a long pause and the delayed completion appears to accomplish multiple kinds of work, which adds to the boundary-like character of this instance. Prior to this fragment, Eve has been telling Mari about an essay she is writing at the moment (both of them are university students). The assignment includes reading specific magazines to find certain items. Eve has read paper magazines, and Mari now wonders whether Eve could not read the magazines in electronic form, implying that it would facilitate her work (lines 1–3):

(4) Virtuaalsel kujul / In a virtual form (Estonian)
TÄ1, 14:00

```
01 Mari:     aga kas: ee neil põ- `üldse ei ole neid netis
             but uhm do they (-) at all not have them in the internet,

02           olem- või tähendab mitte `netis vaid (.) `arvutis
             or I mean not in the internet but, (.) in a

03           `olemas;=kas sa ei saa `küsida nagu vä.
             computer. can't you ask.

04           (.)

05 Mari:     kellegi käest mingeid `faile. .hh
             someone for some files. .hh

06 Eve:      .mhhh ma ei kujuta `ette sellepärast et:,
             .mhhh I can't imagine because

07           mhh mai `tea. ((SHRUGS SHOULDERS))
             mhh I don't know.

08 Eve:      [(-)]
09 Mari:     [(- ]-) ke- noh kes neil see `toimetaja `on[:.
                     wh- um who is their editor              the[re.
                                                             [
10 Eve:                                                      [jaa,
                                                             [yeah

11 Mari:   > m'arvan      ju neil peaks   `olema ikkagi
             1SG think:1SG PRT 3PL:ADE should  be:INF anyway
             I think they should anyway you know have them
```

```
12      >       ju:   need  `olemas     ikkagi   ju:#:# noh mingi:,  .hh
                PRT   DEM.PL be:INF     anyway   PRT    PRT some
                you know anyway um (in) a/some .hh

13              (2.5) ((M GAZES FIRST ELSEWHERE AND THEN TO E, E GAZES DOWN UNTIL
                      LINE 19))

14  Eve: ->  >j[aa  aga  ma  e]i  kujuta   ette
              PRT   but  1SG NEG  imagine
              y[es but I       ca]n't imagine
              [               ]
15  Mari:   [°ee#::#°    ]
            [ uhm        ]

16  Eve: ->  mis  `kujul     na [d (-)<  ]
             what form:ADE   3PL
             in which form   the [y (-)  ]
                                 [       ]
17  Mari: =>                   [£virtu  ]`aalsel  kujulf.  mhhe
                                virtual:ADE        form:ADE
                                [in a vir ]tual form. mhhe

18              (2.0)

19  Eve:   mh võimalik.
           mh (that's) possible.
```

In lines 11–12 Mari presents an opinion, i.e., asserts a state of affairs she thinks is the case, prefacing it with *ma arvan* 'I think'.[14] The assertion explicates what Mari has already been hinting at in her previous turns (lines 1–5), which makes this case similar to the one we saw in extract (1), where the host summarizes something from before. In the extract above, Eve has not yet aligned with Mari and her ideas at this point. Towards the end(-so-far) of her utterance (lines 11–12), Mari repeats the elements *ikkagi ju* 'anyway you know', prolongs some sounds (those at the end of both instances of *ju* and at the end of *mingi*), uses the particle *noh* and the particle-ized determiner *mingi* 'some' (characterizable as a hesitation marker; see Pajusalu 2000: 99–100), and breathes in audibly, all of which indicate that she is searching for words (see, e.g., Goodwin & Goodwin 1986; Kurhila 2006) and that she is still going to produce something in this utterance. A longish pause ensues (line 13) before either of them continues. During the pause Mari first gazes elsewhere and then shifts her gaze to Eve, who gazes down throughout. Mari's gaze to Eve may be working towards pursuing a response from her (see Stivers & Rossano 2010); on the other hand, also Mari seems to be oriented to continuing her not-yet-completed turn via the hesitation sound °ee#::#°

---

[14] The fused item *m'arvan* is not followed by the complementizer *et*, and this fact, together with the integrated prosodic formatting of the item, suggests that the phrase is used here as an epistemic certainty marker rather than as a clause (Keevallik 2010).

(line 15). The pause ends when Eve starts up a response to Mari's talk-so-far, indicating that she understands its point already (lines 14, 16). She uses an agree-disagree-format (*jaa aga* 'yeah but').[15] But at a point where she has not yet completed her utterance (*ma ei kujuta ette mis kujul nad - -*, 'I can't imagine in which form they - -'), Mari overlaps by producing what seems to function as a delayed completion to her own prior utterance: *virtuaalsel kujul* 'in a virtual form' (line 17). The phrase fits and completes the structure of the prior talk even though the just-prior pronominal element, *mingi*, is not inflected in the same case, adessive (which is what normally happens in Estonian noun phrases): *mingi* can also be used as a particle-ized element, in which case it is not grammatically related to the surrounding sentence (Pajusalu 2000: 99).

However, Mari's contribution not only completes her prior utterance but also seems to function as an answer to the indirect question in Eve's turn: *ma ei kujuta ette mis kujul* 'I can't imagine in which form', in which the problematic matter seems to be what format the magazines might have (for instance, a .pdf or a .doc). The prosodic characteristics of Mari's contribution (*virtuaalsel kujul*, line 17), however, make it sound like a completion of her prior utterance: its pitch and loudness fit those in the talk at the end of line 12. Unambiguously new turns, such as an answer to Eve's question here, are typically started at a higher pitch (Wichmann 2000; cf. also Couper-Kuhlen 2004). Moreover, the participants' embodied behavior adds to the interpretation of line 17 as a delayed completion: from line 13 until the end of the fragment, the participants' body postures and gaze behavior remain stable (Eve gazes down continually, while Mari gazes at Eve), as if they were carrying on with their prior activities.

Eve's subsequent turn in line 19 (*võimalik* '(that's) possible') fits either interpretation of Mari's contribution. It could be regarded as an acknowledgement in second position after a suggestion, in which case line 17 would be analyzed as a delayed completion of lines 11–12; or it could be analyzed as a third-position acknowledgement token in a question-answer sequence, in which case line 17 would be analyzed as an answer to the indirect question in lines 14 and 16. In any case, Eve does not accept Mari's idea but acknowledges it only as a possibility. In other words, Eve takes up Mari's delayed completion in her subsequent turn. Hence this case is different from most cases in the collection, where the delayed completion rarely gets responded to in the subsequent turns by the other participant (cf. the cases discussed by Oloff 2009).

In the previous examples, the host is not-yet-complete either grammatically or prosodically, and the delayed completion provides the missing elements projected. However, similar delayed completions are produced also after hosts that are grammatically and prosodically possibly complete but pragmatically/actionally possibly not-yet-complete. The next example will illustrate this point and bring in the question of multi-unit turns: a whole turn-constructional unit can also be regarded as a delayed completion when it has been projected to occur as a part of a multi-unit

---

15   On such formats in other languages, see, e.g., Niemi 2014 on Finnish.

turn. The extract will also suggest that even if the host could be regarded as complete, the speaker's next contribution can be designed and constructed as only now completing it, thus retrospectively making the previous turn as yet incomplete (cf. Tanaka 2001). In the following fragment (5), three young adults (C is off camera) are discussing the life of city rabbits. Prior to this example, B has reported that she has seen many rabbits in a certain area of the city and that she is worried about how they will manage now that winter is approaching. Speaker A responds to her by saying that probably many of them will die. At this point, C comes in.

(5) Traagista / Tragic (Finnish)
Sg 377, 42:18

```
01 C:      mut e↑lääks ne ees kauheen <kauan>.
           but do they live so long anyway.

02         (.)

03 C:      >en tiedä kyl[hän< (-)
           I don't know    real[ly (-)
                              [
04 B:                     [↑kylhän [ne
                          [they (do) [really
                                     [
05 A:                                [mut ne
                                     [but they

06         lisääntyy kun kaniinit.
           reproduce like rabbits.

07         (0.3)

08 B:      ehhh heh n(h)ii
           ehh heh r(h)ight

09 C: >    niim mut ↑mieti- ne s- ne elää sen
           yeah but consider they (s-) they live through the

10 >       ihanan kesän ja, (0.5) se riitt#ää#.
           lovely summer and, (0.5) it is enough.

11         (0.5)

12 C: >    ajat>tele<;
           think.IMP.2SG
           think

13         (0.2)

14 A: ->   niim mut on   se   aika t- (.)
           PRT  but be:3SG DEM3 quite
           yeah but it is quite t-
```

```
15  A:     [traagista ku   ne    k-  kituu       siel      ] talvella- (.)
            tragic:PAR when DEM3:PL  suffer:3SG DEM3:LOC     winter:ADE
           [tragic when they s- suffer there              ]  in the winter-
           [                                              ]
16  C: =>  [↑sit  ku   ne     kuolee silleen, (-) ]
            then when DEM3:PL die:3SG PRT
           [then when they die like, (-)                  ]

17  A:     kylmä[ssä ja?
           in the co[ld and
                [
18  B:          [nii:ei se [nyt oo kauheen hienoo; ]
                [yeah  it  is real[ly not so great         ]
                                 [
19  C:                           [↑miten hienon elämän o]len elänyt;
                                 [how great a life I     ha]ve had

20  ?:     mm

21  B:     nii kesäkissat ajattelee varmaan (kans) #noi(n)#.
           yeah summer cats¹⁶ probably think like that as well.

22  C:     n(h)ii;
           ye(h)ah
```

In line 1, speaker C starts to talk about the length of city rabbits' lives in general. In lines 9–10, she implies that a life so short (living a summer and dying in the winter) might be enough for the rabbits, at the same time explicitly inviting the other participant(s) to think about this (*mieti*, 'consider. IMP.2SG'). Both the grammar and the prosody (falling final intonation and creaky voice; Ogden 2004) at the end of line 10 (*se riitt#ää#.* 'it is enough') suggest that she might have finished her contribution. However, after a pause (line 11) she continues by producing the imperatively formatted verb *ajat>tele<;* 'think.IMP.2SG' (line 12), the end of which is prosodically somewhat truncated. The prosodic production of this word appears to be projecting more to come. The verb itself can be seen as inviting a response to a completed story as well as a story-internal prompt that does not invite a full response from a recipient. It is, however, responded to by speaker A (line 14) with a turn that begins with an agree-disagree format *niim mut* 'yeah but'. This format suggests that while A recognizes C's point and follows her line of action, she does not totally align with her but has a wider perspective on the matter (Niemi 2014). At a point where A's turn is not yet completed (*on se aika t-* 'it is quite t-'), C comes in again and continues her talk (line 16) – perhaps reacting to the disagreement-implicating *niim mut* turn, insisting on her own line of talk.

C's talk until line 12 is somewhat ambiguous as to whether it projects more to come or not. If we analyze line 12 (*ajat>tele<;* 'think') as not yet complete – an interpretation which is supported by the prosodic design

---

16 This refers to cats that are taken as pets before or during the summer and abandoned in the fall.

of the item –, the continuation from line 16 on is a delayed completion of a multi-unit turn that is designed to be such. On the other hand, if we analyze line 12 as a complete unit (focusing on its grammatical structure), the added contribution is one more TCU in a turn that only retrospectively emerges as a multi-unit turn (cf. increments, turn continuations that are grammatically fitted to the prior, already complete turn: e.g., Ford et al. 2002; Couper-Kuhlen & Ono 2007). The target utterance here is not a grammatical completion of the prior turn (the host), as it forms a separate clause. However, it can be analyzed as a new TCU that continues a multi-unit turn (Couper-Kuhlen & Ono 2007; Couper-Kuhlen 2012), produced under the real-time interactional contingencies of the current situation (see Ford 2004).

C's talk in line 16 is grammatically designed to be connecting to and continuing the prior talk, beginning with the conventionalized particle chain *sit ku* 'then when' (cf. Oloff 2008 on the French *donc* in delayed completions) by which the speaker starts up a new turn-unit but nevertheless ties it to the prior talk: *sit ku* is not a "recognizable beginning" (Schegloff 1996: 74) but it rather begins a "post-completion increment" (Schegloff 1996: 121, fn. 35). The *sit ku* 'then when' clause (where the clause beginning with *ku* 'when' modifies the adverb *sit* 'then') seems to function as a temporal marker for what follows, with the whole construction being loosely connected to the preceding predicate *ajattele* 'think'. The word *ajattele* here is best understood as a particle-like element that does not need grammatical complements connected to it with an explicit complementizer (*että*). Prosodically speaker C's turn (line 16) begins with higher pitch and louder volume compared to her previous utterances *se riittää, ajattele*, and so, regarding prosody, she sounds as if she is doing something specific, perhaps related to the intervening, non-aligning response. The specific work might also be that her utterance creates a contrast and hence conveys affect: first there is the 'lovely summer' and then a death in the winter. Action-wise, she continues the social action of constructing an opinion and accounting for it, which she was implementing in her prior talk already.

The verb *ajattele* 'think.IMP.2SG' in line 12 thus appears to be connected not only to C's preceding talk (*ne elää sen ihanan kesän ja, se riittää, ajattele* 'they live through the lovely summer and, it is enough, think') but also to her talk in line 16 (*ajattele, sit ku ne kuolee - -* 'think, then when they die - -'). Hence, the *ajattele* in line 12 seems to be pivotal (see Linell 1981; Schegloff 1996; Walker 2004) in that it can belong to both the preceding and the following talk, forming a multi-unit turn with one and/or the other. Retrospectively, it combines all the three TCUs into one multi-unit turn.

This example demonstrates that further talk by the same speaker can be constructed as a continuation of prior talk. In this case, the connection between the host and the completion is constructed in retrospect, exploiting the grammatical properties of the host; the pragmatic connection between the two parts is strong anyway. Concerning delayed completions after several types of intervening turns in French and German, Oloff (2008, 2009) has come to the conclusion that delayed completions can be added to both "complete" and "incomplete" turns. As she argues, the preceding turn (the host) can be retrospectively treated as (having been) incomplete, and the completion of a turn is negotiated turn by turn by the participants (2008: 776). The example above also shows that judging pragmatic completeness can be ambiguous.

As in example (4), and unlike in many of the other examples in the current collection, in this example (5) the delayed completion (or, the continuation) is explicitly responded to, as both A and B disagree with C's ideas at various points in her talk: A responds already from line 14 on, and B joins in in line 18. In overlap with B's turn, C still continues her line of talk (line 19), and B responds to this with an ironic agreement (i.e., disagreement) in line 21. There is some tension in this situation, as A and B team up to disagree with C. This example includes thus some misalignment between the participants, as is common in sequences with delayed completions.

To sum up the features of the cases discussed in this section, there are several ways in which an actual instance may be at or near the boundaries of the phenomenon of delayed completions. Extract (3) shows how the time that elapses between the host and the completion can be quite short, and thus the completion is at the boundary of whether it is *delayed*. Still, in that case a crucial element of the intervening response has been produced in between the host and the completion, and the completion appears to react to the premature and not-fully-aligning nature of the response. In extract (4), in turn, the delayed completion seems to accomplish multiple kinds of work: it works not only as a delayed completion of the host but also as a response to the turn that is produced after the host. Finally, extract (5) brings in the question of multi-unit turns and the many resources for both completing a turn and projecting more to come: not only grammar and prosody but also pragmatics/action play a role, and these features do not always coincide. This also introduces the somewhat fuzzy boundary between delayed completions and increments in the context of multi-unit turns. The extract illustrates the conversation-analytic understanding that unit completion can be stretched for the purposes of the speaker's interactional goals.

Summary and discussion

This article provides several additions to the research on delayed completions, a phenomenon initially investigated by Lerner (1989). The article examines cases in Estonian and Finnish conversations where a not-yet-completed turn (the host) is followed by a responsive turn, after which there is a delayed completion of the host that starts up in overlap at a non-TRP in the response. The examples demonstrate several points. First, the delayed completion speakers (may) use several resources to connect the completion to the host: grammar, embodied practices, and prosody – pitch, tempo, and loudness (for somewhat similar results, see Oloff 2008, 2009, 2014b; cf. Local 1992 on the prosodic properties of "continuations" and Walker 2004 on increments). In addition, the action begun in the host is continued in the delayed completion, and in some of the cases it is brought to closure in it.

Second, my data show that the unfinished nature of the host can be either grammatical (see examples 1–4) and/or pragmatic (see example 5) – in the latter case the turn is grammatically (possibly) complete but the larger social action is not yet complete (cf. Schegloff 2002: 302–304); delayed completions are used for similar purposes in both situations. Also Oloff (2008, 2009) shows that delayed completions can be used after both syntactically "complete" and "incomplete" hosts. Both these results indicate that the boundaries between delayed completions and other kinds of turn continuations are fuzzy and negotiable.

Third, the turns in these sequences are typically assertion turns (see Vatanen 2014: section 8.1), such as expressions of understandings, opinions, and experiences. Somewhat similarly, in Oloff's (2009) collections, the sequences with delayed completions involve activities such as explications and negotiations over expertise, and the turns preceding the interventions and the completions are rather complex, which is not unusual in my cases either. Furthermore, and in contrast to what Oloff (ibid.) has observed, my collection reveals that in most cases the host to some extent concludes or summarizes the previous talk, which facilitates turn initiation by the responding speaker even before the host has reached its projected completion.

Fourth, the intervening response in my collection is typically somewhat non-aligning or even disagreeing with the host, and the delayed completion positioned in overlap with it may be occasioned by this very fact. In one of her studies, Oloff (2008) examined delayed completions in all temporal positions and found that when the intervening turn was more problematic, the delayed completion started up further away from the TRP, whereas after the more collaborative interventions, the onset of the delayed completion was more close to the TRP. My findings are thus in line with and corroborate these results by Oloff, and they also provide further insight on delayed completions at the more non-aligning end of the continuum.

Although the intervening turns in my collection begin before the previous turns have been completed, they are nevertheless "appropriate" in the sense that they most often carry out the responding action that was invited in the host, although they are not in (full) agreement with it (cf. the appropriate responses after unfinished turns in Chevalier 2008 and Chevalier & Clift 2008).[17] The practice of completing a turn in a delayed fashion after an intervening response thus typically occurs in argumentative talk, even in disagreements. It is interesting that both Schegloff (2001) and Walker (2004) have found that regarding different types of increments – continuations of already completed turns –, it is the ones positioned after a gap that orient to

---

17 A phenomenon related to the one examined here is that of collaborative completions (see Lerner 1996, 2004b, also Vatanen 2014: 151ff. and, e.g., Kim 1999). In these, the recipient completes a turn-at-talk by another speaker and thus pre-empts completion by the original speaker. In the cases investigated here, instead, the intervening speaker responds to the initiating turn from his/her own point of view. For delayed completions occurring after collaborative completions, see also Oloff 2008, 2009, and 2014a.

a possible non-alignment between the participants; increments coming after talk by another are typically used for other purposes. We can thus draw the conclusion that in the cases of delayed completions and increments, non-alignment occurs in different kinds of sequential positions: in the case of increments, non-alignment is related to situations where the co-participant has not responded, whereas delayed completions are found when the co-participant provides a non-aligning response to a turn before it is completed.

Further issues demonstrated in the analyses include the following: Typically there is no gap between the not-yet-complete(d) host and the intervening response, and the response may even overlap the host. It is rather common that the host includes some signs of hesitation prior to the response onset. In most of the cases, the delayed completion is not responded to but it is the response-speaker who carries on his/her own line of talk. In other words, the delayed completion gets sequentially deleted. Delayed completions thus occur in contexts where the speakers compete for turn space and speaking rights, and, crucially, also negotiate if and how they agree with one another. The phenomenon of delayed completions, according to both my own and Oloff's studies, seem to corroborate the idea that participants, or at least the delayed-completion speakers, orient to the fundamental turn-taking principle proposed by Sacks et al. (1974): a speaker is initially entitled to talk until the TRP. As already described by Lerner (1989), delayed completions appear to be a device to claim the right to produce a turn-at-talk until its first possible completion.

Prior to the current study, delayed completions and other closely related phenomena have been studied mostly in Indo-European languages: in addition to studies on English (e.g., Lerner 1989, 2004b), research has been carried out based on data from German (Ahrens 1997; Oloff 2009, 2014a) and French encounters (Oloff 2008, 2009, 2014a, 2014b) (see, however, related analyses on Korean data in Kim 1999). This paper has demonstrated that even though previous studies have concentrated on Indo-European languages, delayed completions are not limited to that language family only: they exist also in conversations carried out in non-Indo-European languages, at least in the Finno-Ugric languages Estonian and Finnish. Delayed completions are thus a practice that occurs in typologically different languages.

A final issue is the action accomplished via delayed completions. In the delayed completion, the speaker continues and completes the action begun in the host, but s/he may be doing something else as well: indicating that the response perhaps started up too early, and/or, especially, reacting to the non-aligning nature of the response. Delayed completions indeed seem to be coupled with non-aligning responses – they occur together. If the response had been in full alignment with the host, it would be less necessary to complete one's turn, because it was agreed with and its point was shared between the participants. Completing a turn after the response has set in may thus be regarded as a practice to insist on one's own viewpoint and to indicate that one is sticking to it, regardless of the co-participant's divergent view. In this way, producing a delayed completion treats the response as an intervention, not as an interruption (cf., e.g., Ahrens 1997; Kim 1999; Lerner

2004b; also Schegloff 2002: 302). By producing the delayed completion the speaker gets to complete his/her turn. The host and the completion are not separate from each other, as they are connected to each other with specific resources. On the other hand, they do not unambiguously combine into one action either – the delayed completion accomplishes additional work as well.

References

Ahrens, Ulrike. 1997. The interplay between interruptions and preference organization in conversation. New perspectives on a classic topic of gender research. In Helga Kotthoff & Ruth Wodak (eds.), *Communicating gender in context*. 79–106. Amsterdam: John Benjamins.

Chevalier, Fabienne H. G. 2008. Unfinished turns in French conversation: How context matters. *Research on Language and Social Interaction* 41(1): 1–30.

Chevalier, Fabienne H. G. & Rebecca Clift. 2008. Unfinished turns in French conversation: Projectability, syntax and action. *Journal of Pragmatics* 40(10): 1731–1752.

Couper-Kuhlen, Elizabeth. 2004. Prosody and sequence organization: The case of new beginnings. In Elizabeth Couper-Kuhlen & Cecilia E. Ford (eds.), *Sound patterns in interaction: Cross-linguistic studies from conversation*. 335–376. Amsterdam: John Benjamins.

Couper-Kuhlen, Elizabeth. 2012. Turn continuation and clause combinations. *Discourse Processes* 49(3/4): 273–299.

Couper-Kuhlen, Elizabeth & Tsuyoshi Ono. 2007. 'Incrementing' in conversation. A comparison of practices in English, German and Japanese. *Pragmatics* 17: 513–552.

Couper-Kuhlen, Elizabeth & Margret Selting. 2001. Introducing interactional linguistics. In Margret Selting & Elizabeth Couper-Kuhlen (eds.), *Studies in interactional linguistics*. 1–23. Amsterdam: John Benjamins.

Ford, Cecilia. 2004. Contingency and units in interaction. *Discourse Studies* 6(1): 27–52.

Ford, Cecilia, Barbara A. Fox & Sandra A. Thompson. 2002. Constituency and the grammar of turn increments. In Cecilia E. Ford, Barbara A. Fox & Sandra A. Thompson (eds.), *The language of turn and sequence*. 14–38. Oxford: Oxford University Press.

Ford, Cecilia, Sandra A. Thompson & Veronika Drake. 2012. Bodily-visual practices and turn continuation. *Discourse Processes* 49(3/4): 192–212.

Goodwin, Marjorie Harness & Charles Goodwin. 1986. Gesture and coparticipation in the activity of searching a word. *Semiotica* 62(1/2): 51–75.

Hakulinen, Auli & Elizabeth Couper-Kuhlen. 2015. Insisting on 'my side': *Siis*-prefaced utterances in Finnish. *Journal of Pragmatics* 75: 111–130.

Hakulinen, Auli & Marja-Leena Sorjonen. 2009. Designing utterances for action: Verb repeat responses to assessments. In Markku Haakana, Minna Laakso & Jan Lindström (eds.), *Talk in interaction: Comparative dimensions*. 124–151. Helsinki: Finnish Literature Society.

Hakulinen, Auli, Maria Vilkuna, Riitta Korhonen, Vesa Koivisto, Tarja Riitta Heinonen & Irja Alho. 2004. *Iso suomen kielioppi [Finnish Descriptive Grammar]*. Helsinki: Finnish Literature Society.

Jefferson, Gail. 1981. The abominable 'ne?' An exploration of post-response pursuit of response. *Sprache der Gegenwart. Jahrbuch 1980 des Instituts für deutsche Sprache*. 53–88. Düsseldorf: Pädagogischer Verlag Schwann.

Kalliokoski, Jyrki. 1989. *Ja: rinnastus ja rinnastuskonjunktion käyttö*. Suomalaisen Kirjallisuuden Seuran toimituksia 497. Helsinki: Finnish Literature Society.

Keevallik, Leelo. 2010. Clauses emerging as epistemic adverbs in Estonian conversation. *Linguistica Uralica* 46(2): 81–100.

Keevallik, Leelo. 2013. The interdependence of bodily demonstrations and clausal syntax. *Research on Language and Social Interaction* 46: 1–21.

Keevallik, Leelo. 2015. Coordinating the temporalities of talk and dance. In Arnulf Deppermann & Susanne Günthner (eds.), *Temporality in interaction*. 309–336. Amsterdam: John Benjamins.

Kim, Kyu-Hyun. 1999. Phrasal unit boundaries and organization of turns and sequences in Korean conversation. *Human Studies* 22: 425–446.

Koivisto, Aino, Ritva Laury & Eeva-Leena Seppänen. 2011. Syntactic and actional characteristics of Finnish *että*-clauses. In Ritva Laury & Ryoko Suzuki (eds.), *Subordination in conversation: A cross-linguistic perspective*. 69–102. Amsterdam: John Benjamins.

Kunelius, Sirja. 1998. *Niinku*-partikkeli keskustelussa. MA thesis. University of Helsinki, Department of Finnish language.

Kurhila, Salla. 2006. *Second language interaction*. Amsterdam: John Benjamins.

Laury, Ritva & Eeva-Leena Seppänen. 2008. Clause combining, interaction, evidentiality, participation structure, and the conjunction-particle continuum: the Finnish *että*. In Ritva Laury (ed.), *Crosslinguistic studies of clause combining*. 153–178. Amsterdam: John Benjamins.

Lerner, Gene. 1989. Notes on overlap management in conversation: The case of delayed completion. *Western Journal of Speech Communication* 53: 167–177.

Lerner, Gene. 1996. On the "semi-permeable" character of grammatical units in conversation: Conditional entry into the turn space of another speaker. In Elinor Ochs, Emanuel A. Schegloff & Sandra A. Thompson (eds.), *Interaction and grammar*. 238–276. Cambridge: Cambridge University Press.

Lerner, Gene. 2004a. On the place of linguistic resources in the organization of talk-in-Interaction: Grammar as action in prompting a speaker to elaborate. *Research on Language and Social Interaction* 37: 151–184.

Lerner, Gene. 2004b. Collaborative turn sequences. In Gene Lerner (ed.), *Conversation analysis: Studies from the first generation*. 225–256. Amsterdam: John Benjamins.

Li, Xiaoting. 2014. Multimodal construction of syntactically incomplete turns in Mandarin conversation. Paper given at 4th International Conference on Conversation Analysis (ICCA-14). University of California, Los Angeles. June 25–29.

Linell, Per. 1981. Svenska anakoluter. In Sigurd Fries & Claes-Christian Elert (eds.), *Svenskans Beskrivning 12*. Umeå Studies in the Humanities. 173–184.

Local, John K. 1992. Continuing and restarting. In Peter Auer & Aldo di Luzio (eds.), *The contextualization of language*. 272–296. Amsterdam: John Benjamins.

Mondada, Lorenza. 2015. Multimodal completions. In Arnulf Deppermann & Susanne Günthner (eds.), *Temporality in interaction*. 267–307. Amsterdam: John Benjamins.

Niemi, Jarkko. 2014. Two 'yeah but' formats in Finnish: The prior action engaging *nii mut* and the disengaging *joo mut* utterances. *Journal of Pragmatics* 60: 54–74.

Ogden, Richard. 2004. Non-modal voice quality and turn-taking in Finnish. In Elizabeth Couper-Kuhlen & Cecilia E. Ford (eds.), *Sound patterns in interaction: Cross-linguistic studies from conversation*. 29–62. Amsterdam: John Benjamins.

Oloff, Florence. 2008. La complétude négociée des unités de construction de tour: les complétions différées comme ressource en français parlé. In J. Durand, B. Habert & B. Laks (eds.), *Congrès Mondial de Linguistique Française - CMLF'08*. 773–788. Paris: Institut de Linguistique Française.

Oloff, Florence. 2009. Contribution à l'étude systématique de l'organisation des tours de parole: Les chevauchements en français et en allemand. Thèse de doctorat / Dissertation, Ecole normale supérieure Lettres et Sciences humaines, Lyon &

Universität Mannheim. Mannheim: Universität Mannheim.

Oloff, Florence. 2014a. Analyse multimodale de complétions différées suite à des interventions collaboratives. In Lorenza Mondada (ed.), *Corps en interaction: Participation, spatialité, mobilité.* 107–143. Lyon: ENS Editions.

Oloff, Florence. 2014b. Skipping other-speaker talk after disaligned responses: A multimodal perspective on delayed completions. Paper given at 4th International Conference on Conversation Analysis (ICCA-14). University of California, Los Angeles. June 25–29.

Pajusalu, Renate. 2000. Indefinite determiners *mingi* and *üks* in Estonian. In Mati Erelt (ed.), *Estonian: Typological studies IV.* 87–117. Publications of the Department of Estonian of the University of Tartu 14. Tartu: Tartu University Press.

Sacks, Harvey. 1992a, b. *Lectures on conversation*, Volumes I & II. Oxford: Blackwell.

Sacks, Harvey, Emanuel Schegloff & Gail Jefferson. 1974. A simplest systematics for the organization of turn-taking for conversation. *Language* 50: 696–735.

Schegloff, Emanuel A. 1996. Turn organization: One intersection of grammar and interaction. In Elinor Ochs, Emanuel A. Schegloff & Sandra A. Thompson (eds.), *Interaction and grammar.* 52–133. Cambridge: Cambridge University Press.

Schegloff, Emanuel A. 2001. Conversation analysis: A project in process - "Increments". Forum lecture delivered at the *LSA Linguistic Institute*, University of California, Santa Barbara.

Schegloff, Emanuel A. 2002. Accounts of conduct in interaction: Interruption, overlap, and turn-taking. In Jonathan H. Turner (ed.), *Handbook of sociological theory.* 287–321. New York: Kluwer Academic / Plenum Publishers.

Schegloff, Emanuel A. & Gene H. Lerner. 2009. Beginning to respond: *Well*-prefaced responses to wh-questions. *Research on Language and Social Interaction* 42(2): 91–115.

Selting, Margret. 2001. Fragments of units as deviant cases of unit production in conversational talk. In Margret Selting & Elizabeth Couper-Kuhlen (eds.), *Studies in interactional linguistics.* 229–258. Amsterdam: John Benjamins.

Seppänen, Eeva-Leena & Ilona Herlin. 2009. Kuvauksista seurauksiin: kaksiuloitteinen konstruktio *niin A että*. *Virittäjä* 113(2): 213–245.

Seppänen, Eeva-Leena & Ritva Laury. 2007. Complement clauses as turn continuations: The Finnish *et(tä)*-clause. *Pragmatics* 17: 553–572.

Sidnell, Jack & Tanya Stivers. 2013. *The handbook of conversation analysis.* Chichester: Wiley-Blackwell.

Stivers, Tanya & Federico Rossano. 2010. Mobilizing response. *Research on Language and Social Interaction* 43(1): 3–31.

Tanaka, Hiroko. 2001. The implementation of possible cognitive shifts in Japanese conversation: Complementizers as pivotal devices. In Margret Selting & Elizabeth Couper-Kuhlen (eds), *Studies in interactional linguistics.* 81–109. Amsterdam: John Benjamins.

Tiittula, Liisa. 1985. Puheenvuorojen vaihtuminen keskustelussa. *Virittäjä* 89: 319–336.

Vatanen, Anna. 2014. Responding in overlap. Agency, epistemicity and social action in conversation. PhD thesis. University of Helsinki, Department of Finnish, Finno-Ugrian and Scandinavian Studies.

Walker, Gareth. 2004. On some interactional and phonetic properties of increments to turns in talk-in-interaction. In Elizabeth Couper-Kuhlen & Cecilia Ford (eds.), *Sound patterns in interaction: Cross-linguistic studies from conversation.* 147–170. Amsterdam: John Benjamins.

Wichmann, Anne. 2000. *Intonation in text and discourse. Beginnings, middles and ends.* Harlow: Pearson Education.

Elizabeth Couper-Kuhlen
http://orcid.org/0000-0003-2030-6018

Marja Etelämäki
http:// orcid.org/0000-0002-3896-7159

7. Linking clauses for linking actions: Transforming requests and offers into joint ventures

A 'joint venture' is commonly understood to be a business agreement in which two parties come together to take on a new project, making more or less equal investments in terms of money, time, and effort. Since the cost of starting new projects is generally high, a joint venture allows the parties to share the burden of the project as well as the resulting profits (and losses). Not surprisingly, there are also moments in the social world when a new project is 'costly' and when accordingly it could be advantageous for parties to share in the work of carrying it out. It is in moments like these that participants find themselves combining efforts (or actions) in the service of a common goal. And as we will show, in combining efforts and actions they may quite naturally find themselves combining clauses as well.

In this paper we will investigate a specific clause combination found in everyday naturally occurring talk-in-interaction which, we will argue, is used for bringing off joint ventures: we call it the *division-of-labor* pattern. We explore empirically its social interactional functions as well as its general schematic structure in English and Finnish conversations. At the same time we compare its specific structural variants in the two languages. In conclusion, we work out the characteristics of this clause and action combination as compared to other action combinations documented in language and described by, e.g., Ford (2001), Kärkkäinen and Keisanen (2012), Rauniomaa and Keisanen (2012), and Steensig and Heinemann (2013).

The division-of-labor phenomenon

Our attention was first drawn to divisions of labor in talk-in-interaction by the following episode from a telephone conversation between Emma and her grown daughter Barbara. Emma's husband Bud has recently left her after a quarrel. Emma is now calling Barbara to enlist her help in persuading Bud to come down to their beach house for the Thanksgiving dinner she has planned for later that week. When we join the conversation, Emma has already asked Barbara twice to call her father but Barbara has avoided making a commitment. Now the following transpires:

(1) "Barbara" (nb025-3)

```
1   Emm:   [nyeah, .t.h W [ILL YOU HELP M]E OU:T OF [THI:S:,]
2 → Bar:                  [o k a y .     ]              [yeah ↑I]'ll call
3 →              him to↓ni:ght,hh
4                (0.2)
5 ⇒ Bar:   [en you can] call] [me]
6   Emm:   [A:LRIGHT    ] DEA:]R [.h] [h.hh]
7 ⇒ Bar:                                 [↑you] call me at n:ine tomorrow
8 ⇒              ↓mo[rning.
9   Emm:         [.t alright darling I APPRECIATE *I [T.
10  Bar:   :                                         [oka:y,
```

When Emma, in a pleading voice, once again asks Barbara to help her out (line 1), Barbara finally agrees: she commits to calling Bud that evening (lines 2–3) but goes on to ask Emma, in return, to call her the next morning to find out what he said (lines 5 and 7–8). At the time of the recording, these were long-distance calls; in fact, earlier in the conversation, Emma has suggested that Barbara should call her collect. In other words, there are grounds for concluding that from the participants' perspective the last-minute endeavor of persuading Bud to join the family for Thanksgiving is costly. What Barbara is doing is thus proposing that she and Emma divide the labor and in a rather literal sense not only share the work but also the costs of the endeavor.

The division of labor that Barbara proposes is accomplished through a combination of clauses: the first clause is marked with → and the second with ⇒ in ex. (1). Table 1 represents this division-of-labor structure:

Table 1. Division of labor in example (1)

Ex.	Clause 1	Combining element	Clause 2
(1)	↑I'll call him to↓ni:ght, hh	en	you can] call] [me] [↑you] call me at n:ine tomorrow ↓mo[rning.

In clause 1 Barbara commits to calling Bud and in clause 2 she asks her mother to call her the next morning.[1] The two clauses are combined with the conjunction *and*.

Something rather similar can happen in Finnish, as can be seen from the following excerpt from a telephone conversation between Irja and her grown daughter Sini. Irja wants her daughter to buy a long overcoat and has agreed to finance it.

---

1   Because Barbara's first attempt *En you can call me* (line 5) is fully overlapped by Emma's *Alright dear* (line 6), she breaks off and re-does it in the clear as *You call me at nine tomorrow morning* (lines 7–8).

(2) "Tukun rahaa" 'Pile of money' (Sg124_A03 Jess2)

```
01 Irja:   [ja ] tota<, (.) @ja  a↑siahan on      kyllä niin että
            PRT  PRT         PRT  thing-CLI be.3SG PRT   so   COMP
           and so and the thing is actually that

02         ↑mie en  lähe siun     kans  kauppoihin mihkää
            1SG  NEG go   2SG-GEN  with  shop-PL-ILL anywhere
           I won't go browsing through any shops

03→        ↑kiertelemää,= mie  tuon        sinulle  tukun       rahaa
            browse-INF-ILL 1SG  bring-1SG   2SG-ALL  stack-GEN   money-PAR
           with you = I'll bring you a pile of money

04⇒        [ni  sie  saat       mennä  ostamaan    sen
            PRT  2SG  get to-2SG go-INF buy-INF-ILL DEM3-GEN
           and you can go buy the

05 Sini:   [£nsh hh h hi hi£

06⇒Irja:   takin.@
           coat-GEN
           coat
```

This example comes from a return call by Sini: prior to this call, Irja has called Sini while Sini was taking a bath. It turns out that Irja had several reasons for her original call. The two previous and extended sequences dealing with these have been closed, and in lines 1–4 Irja introduces yet a third issue, namely her daughter's overcoat. Although purchasing a new overcoat is introduced to this call for the first time, the way it is presented implies that the topic has been discussed earlier. The turn includes elements such as the clitic particle *-han* (*asia-han* 'the thing' line 1) and the demonstrative *se* (*sen takin* 'the coat' lines 4, 6) that index shared knowledge of the matter (see Hakulinen et al. 2004) and knownness of the referent (Laury 1997). Furthermore, the turn begins with a negative announcement (lines 1–2), and negative announcements imply that there is an expectation of a positive alternative (cf. Schegloff 1988), here that Irja and Sini will go shopping together. This is supported by the particle *kyllä* (line 1), which is used for countering positive presuppositions (see Hakulinen & Keevallik, forthc.). Moreover, in negatively formulated utterances, the word *mihkää* (*kauppoihin mihkää* 'to any shops', line 2) indexes negative affect (Kotilainen 2007). Browsing through the shops is thus formulated as a strenuous job that Irja will not attend to. Instead, she proposes a division of labor: she will bring the money and Sini will look for and actually buy the coat.

Table 2 represents the division-of-labor structure in this exchange:

Table 2. Division of labor in example (2)

Ex.	Clause 1	Combining element	Clause 2
(2)	mie tuon sinulle tukun rahaa I'll bring you a pile of money	[ni and	sie saat mennä ostamaan sen [takin.@] and you can go buy the coat

In clause 1 Irja commits to bringing the money for the coat, and in clause 2 she tells Sini to go and buy the coat. The clauses are combined by the particle *ni(in)*. Although the Finnish particle *ni(in)* is the equivalent of 'so' in English, in translating example (2) we have opted for 'and' in the interest of idiomaticity. The two actions of (Irja) bringing the money and (Sini) buying the coat will lead to the successful achievement of a common goal, ensuring that Sini has warm outdoor clothing for the winter.

In both these cases, (1) and (2), the speakers first promise to do something themselves and then ask their interlocutor to do something complementary in order to achieve a common goal. Together the two actions lead to the establishment of a joint venture. Yet interestingly, the order of the actions proposed in a division of labor structure can be reversed. That is, in both English and Finnish we also encounter cases in which speakers first ask the other to do something and then promise to do something complementary themselves. Here is a case in English:

(3) "Deliver another day" (Holt 1:3)
Lesley is a replacement teacher and has agreed at the last minute to substitute for a sick colleague on Thursday. She is now calling her grocer Mr Bathwick to reschedule the order and home delivery of groceries she had originally planned for Thursday.

```
11 Les:   =.hh and (.) I'm coming in tomorrow:
12        or I could pop in quickly on Wednesday,
13        I wonder .hhh
14        a:re you able to do: (.) deliver another da:y (.)
15        o:r: w-what d'you think.
16        (0.4)
17 Bat:   it would be very difficult t'deliver another da::y,
18 Les:   yes.
19 Bat:   uh:m
20 Les:   .hh well if I could (0.2) is it possible for me
21        to leave an order with you.=
22→Bat:  =that's perfectly alright.=leave the order with us,
23⇒      we'll make it up'n deliver it on Thursday.
24 Les:   .hh Yes.
```

Because Lesley will be unavailable for shopping on Thursday, she is ostensibly hoping that she can select her green groceries on Tuesday or Wednesday of that week and have them delivered the same day (lines 11–14). However, Mr Bathwick maintains that he cannot deliver on any day but Thursday (line 17), whereupon Lesley now asks if she can place her order early, i.e., on Tuesday or Wednesday (lines 20–21), implying that Mr Bathwick would then put it together and deliver it on Thursday. It is this implicit proposal for a division of labor that Mr Bathwick ratifies and explicitly confirms in lines 22–23. He does so by first instructing Lesley to leave the order with him and then promising to put it together and deliver it on Thursday. Together, their two actions will lead to the realization of a common goal, getting fresh green groceries to Lesley that week.

Like in (1) and (2), here too the proposal for a division of labor is accomplished via a combination of clauses, as shown in Table 3:

Table 3. Division of labor in example (3)

Ex.	Clause 1	Combining element	Clause 2
(3)	leave the order with us,		we'll make it up'n deliver it on Thursday.

In contrast to (1) and (2), the speaker here first directs his interlocutor to do something and then commits to doing something complementary himself in order to realize a common goal. Unlike (1), there is no overt combining element *and* in (3): this is a case of asyndetic clausal linkage (Quirk et al. 1985).[2]

The same order of actions is also documented in Finnish for a division of labor. In the following telephone conversation, Sepe has called his friend Simppa's house in order to check whether he (Sepe) and his partner can come over for coffee, but it turns out that Simppa is not at home. This is what now transpires between Sepe and Simppa's partner Vera:

(4) "Kahvi" 'Coffee' (Sg94_B01)

```
1  Sepe:  =me   'ltiin        tulos         kahville
           1PL  be-PST-PAS-4  coming-INE    coffee-ALL
           we were coming for coffee

2         sinnepäin      mut  tota noin  ni   (.)
           DEM3.LOC.about PRT  PRT  PRT   PRT
           there but
```

---

2 The two clauses are hearable as being in construction with one another on prosodic grounds: the first has slightly rising final pitch (continuing intonation) and the second picks up the prior pitch contour where it left off in order to complete it (see below).

```
3              täytyy     nyt ootttaa  ku   se  Simp:pa
               ∅ have.to-3 PRT wait-INF when DEM3 Simppa
               ∅ must wait now until Simppa

4              tulee   sieltä   takasi.
               come-3  DEM3.LOC back
               comes back from there

5   Vera:      nii tulkaa       e illemmalla.
               PRT come-IMP.2PL   evening-COMP-ADE
               yes come later in the evening

6              (0.6)

7→Sepe:        mno [↑soi]t:tele< t (.) tännepäin      sitte_ku<
               PRT  call-FRE-IMP          DEM1.LOC.about then  when
               well give us a call here when

8   Vera:           [(vai)]
                    (or )

9              (.)

10  Vera:      joo:.=
               PRT
               yeah

11⇒Sepe:       =ku se on ö  paikalla ni m: (.) [me tul]laan.
               when DEM3 be place-ADE PRT        1PL come-PAS-4
               when he's back and w- (.) we'll come

12  Vera:                                       [joo:. ]
                                                 PRT
                                                 yeah

13  Sepe:      [↑.jeh   ]
                yeah

14  Vera:      [>selvä<,]
                okay

15  Sepe:      ↑tehään näin.
               let's do it that way.
```

Having heard that Simppa is out, Sepe explains the reason for his call using the past tense *oltiin tulossa* ('were coming', lines 1–2), which marks the original plan as not valid any more. He then presents a somewhat vague alternative plan ('∅ must wait now until Simppa comes back', lines 3–4), which leaves open whether he and his partner will still come over to Simppa and Vera's or not. As a response to this, Vera suggests a solution for the get-together, namely that Sepe and his partner come later in the evening (line 5). She does not, however, specify the time by which Simppa will be home. Instead of straightforwardly agreeing to come (which would require Sepe to call first and check whether Simppa has returned), Sepe first requests Vera to let him know when Simppa is home, and then commits to coming over himself (lines 7 and 11).

Like in (1)–(3), the proposal for a division of labor is accomplished via a combination of clauses, as shown in Table 4:

Table 4. Division of labor in example (4)

Ex.	Clause 1	Combining element	Clause 2
(4)	[↑soi]t:tele< t (.) tännepäin sitte_ku< =ku se on ö paikalla give us a call here when when he's back	ni and	m: (.) [me tul]laan. w- (.) we'll come

Like in the English example (3), the speaker here first issues a directive to his interlocutor to do something, and then links the directive to a commitment to do something himself in order to achieve a common goal: in this example the common goal is getting together for coffee. Like in the previous Finnish example (2), the two clauses that accomplish these two social actions are combined with the particle *ni(in)*.

Although the order of actions being forwarded is different in (3) and (4) from that in (1) and (2), the phenomenon is the same: in both languages proposing to share the workload with one's interlocutor via a combination of two clauses. The agent of the action in one clause is typically first person: *I/we* or *minä/me*; the agent of the action in the other clause is typically second person, *you* or *sinä/te*. However, the order of the actions can be either "I"-"you" or "you"-"I". The combining element, *and* in English or *niin* in Finnish,[3] can be lexically explicit as in (1)–(2) and (4), or it can remain unexpressed as in (3).

Data and methodology

We have assembled a small collection of cases like those in (1)–(4) for both English and Finnish, using a moderately large corpus of everyday British and American English conversation as well as the Finnish Conversation Data Archive (located at the University of Helsinki). Currently there are approximately 54 exemplars in our collection, 27 for each language. The forms used in each exemplar have been tracked in tables like those shown above.

For each division-of-labor case we have carried out a close analysis of the sequential and interactional context in which the structure is found using the methods of Conversation Analysis (see, e.g., Sidnell & Stivers 2013). At the same time we have analyzed the linguistic forms encountered using the methods of Interactional Linguistics (see, e.g., Couper-Kuhlen & Selting

---

3   The combining element *ja* 'and' is also documented in Finnish: see ex. (9) below.

2001). Our aim has been to understand what the division-of-labor structure is doing – why and when it is used – and how it is formed in the two languages, English and Finnish. We also wished to learn what similarities and differences there are between division-of-labor structures in the two languages in order to come to an appreciation of the language-independent and the language-specific dimensions of this phenomenon.

In the following we first explore the activity contexts in which division-of-labor structures occur and propose what we believe is their rationale (section 3). Next, we explore the linguistic forms used to promote a division of labor in the two languages and point out the recurrent features of the division-of-labor patterns documented, analyzing some of the similarities and differences between English and Finnish variants of the practice (section 4). In conclusion, we single out the specific and unique characteristics of the division-of-labor practice as a combination of two clauses and two actions (section 5).

Activity contexts and rationale for dividing the labor in talk-in-interaction

One of our initial observations was that the division-of-labor phenomenon is recurrently found in specific sequential environments. For instance, a good number of the structures in our collection are located in the context of *requests*. In (1) Emma has requested her daughter Barbara to call up Bud and persuade him to come down for Thanksgiving; in (3) Lesley has requested her greengrocer to deliver her groceries another day; and in (4) Vera has requested Sepe and his partner to come later in the evening. In these cases the division-of-labor structures are used by requestees in responding (positively) to a request. They use them to signal commitment to do what has been requested but at the same time to make a complementary request of their own: in (1) Barbara asks Emma to call her early the next morning, in (3) the greengrocer asks Lesley to leave her order with him, and in (4) Sepe asks Vera to let him know when Simppa comes home. These reciprocal requests are understood to be asking for actions that will complement what the requestee is committing to do in the service of a common goal, i.e., as part of a joint venture.

Yet divisions of labor are also sometimes used by a requester who is asking for something but at the same attempting to reduce the workload associated with that request for the requestee. Consider, for instance, the following sequence:

(5) "Avaimet virtalukkoon" 'Keys in the ignition' (Sg94_A5: [00:02:07])
Matti has lent his excavator to Pekka, who needs it to remove some big stones from his yard. Now, however, Matti has phoned Pekka to announce that he needs to get the excavator back by Monday because he has sold it.

```
1  Matti:  no   joka  tapaukses   se   (.)  'te  maanantaina  täytyy
           PRT  any   case-INE    DEM3       PRT monday-ESS   must-3
           well in any case it needs to be picked up on Monday

2           kuitenki hakee    se   pois, ni   saat     toisen
            anyhow   pick up  DEM3 away  PRT  get-2SG  another-GEN
            so you'll get another one to replace it

3           tilalle  jos  tarvi(it [sit),]
            instead  if   need-2SG  (PRT)
            if you need one

4  Pekka:                            [ .nhh]h >tota noin ni  joo.
                                                  well yeah.

5           =katotaan sitä n't öö öh:
            let's see now uhm

6           .hh sä haet sen pois koska.h
            when will you pick it up

7  Matti:  [(-)        ]

8  Pekka:  [>voit sä ha]kee sunnuntainaki jos sä haluut<.h=
           you can pick it up already even on Sunday if you want to

9  Matti:  =ö:e:m minä viitti [py-
           no I won't bother

10 Pekka:                     [hh

11 Matti:  ei si(i)tä pyhänä kato mirk- mitään virkaa
           no use you see on a Sunday

12         sinne t'lee: ö:y k- asiakas (.) maanantaina (sinne.)
           the client will come on Monday
```

((20 seconds omitted, in which Matti explains that he has sold the excavator and participants talk about its price.))

```
13   Matti:  =okei [tota (.)]
             PRT    PRT
             okay well

14   Pekka:        [.mhhh   ]

15 → Matti:  jätä          maanantaiaamuna        avai[met< (.)]
             leave.IMP.2SG monday-morning-ESS     key-PL
             leave the keys on Monday morning
```

183

```
16    Pekka:                                      [mhhh        ]

17 →  Matti:  siihen    virtalukkoo.
              DEM3.ILL  ignition-ILL
              in the ignition

18    Pekka:  [joo:.       ]

19 →  Matti:  [ja   ovi au]ki.
              and  door   open
              and the door open

20    Pekka:  joo:.

21 ⇒  Matti:  ni minä:  (.) tota haen          päivä[n mittaan.        ]
              PRT 1SG       PRT  pick up-1SG   day-GEN   along
              and I will        pick [it] up during the day

22    Pekka:                                         [meneeks    ne    ovet]
                                                     go-3-Q-CLI  DEM3.PL door-PL
                                                     do the doors lock

              lukkoonki.
              lock-CLI

23    Matti:  >ei: tarvii ovia          lukkoon laittaa  ku  jätät
              NEG  need   door-PL-PAR   lock    put-INF  PRT leave-2SG
              no need to lock the doors just leave

24            avaimet virtalukkoon vaa[n<. ]
              key-PL  ignition-ILL  just
              the keys in the ignition
```

This sequence is initiated by an informing that the excavator needs to be picked up on Monday (lines 1–2), and Pekka's question about the pick-up time as well as his offer to give up the excavator already on Sunday (lines 5 and 8) are based on this knowledge. Matti declines the offer to pick up the excavator already on Sunday by referring to his own assessment of the situation: Sunday is a holiday and the excavator is only needed on Monday (lines 9, 11–12). The question about the pick-up time is, however, left open while the participants talk about the price of the excavator. Yet, it is potentially relevant for Pekka, in case he needs to be home when Matti comes on Monday. Matti then returns to the pick-up time first by straightforwardly requesting Pekka to leave the keys in the ignition and the door open (lines 15, 17), and then committing to come and pick up the excavator sometime during the day (line 21).

Since Matti is the owner of the excavator and a professional who deals with landscaping machinery, he has both deontic and epistemic authority over the procedures via which the machine should be returned. He is also displaying this authority by not accepting Pekka's offer to return the excavator already on Sunday, by not giving an exact pick-up time, and by taking command over the procedures. Yet, by asking Pekka to leave the keys in the ignition and the door open, and by committing to pick up the excavator, he also liberates Pekka from staying home and waiting. By using a division-of-labor structure, Matti thus relinquishes part of his deontic authority and that way evens out the situation.

Here a division-of-labor structure is used by the requester in order to achieve a common goal, namely the successful return of the excavator:

Table 5. Division of labor in example (5)

Ex.	Clause 1	Combining element	Clause 2
(5)	jätä maanantaiaamuna avai[met< (.)] siihen virtalukkoo. [ja ovi au]ki. leave the keys on Monday morning in the ignition and the door open	ni and	minä: (.) tota haen päivä[n mittaan. I will pick [it] up during the day

As in our previous examples (3) and (4), the first clause here is a directive to the recipient (Other) to do something, and the second clause functions as a commitment by the speaker (Self) to do something. However, whereas in examples (3) and (4) the division-of-labor structure was used by the requestee, in this example it is used by the requester in order to share the rights and responsibilities connected with a joint project.

In yet other cases, the division-of-labor structure appears in the context of *offers*. For instance, in (2) Irja is offering to buy her daughter a new overcoat. And in the following examples (6) and (7), Milly is offering to take her friend Gina to the Bible group meeting that evening.

(6) "Go ahead Milly" (sbl031-4)
Gina has called Milly and after listening at some length to Milly's problems, has offered to take her to the Bible group meeting that evening. So far Milly has avoided any commitment.

```
1    Gin: hhh we:ll 'ee wil hh I
2         tell you wha:t wu- (.) eh-ihHe (.) you haven't eaten yet?
3    Mil: no we're just[now ]e a t ing.]
4→   Gin:              [well]why don'yo]u go ahead Milly hh
5         (0.2)
6⇒   Gin: en u-I:'ll sto:p o:n my way down en: if you feel like (.)
7         coming with me fi:ne an:d if y'[do:n't w h y     ]
8    Mil:                                [you're still go]↓*ing.
9         (0.3)
10   Gin: hh yeh I think I'll go o:n.=
11   Mil: =ah hah.
```

185

Prior to this episode Milly has been somewhat reluctant to accept Gina's offer of taking her to the Bible group meeting that evening. Rather than force an answer immediately, Gina now proposes a division of labor in the work of reaching a decision. She first suggests that Milly should go ahead and have her evening meal (line 4) and she then commits to stopping by on her way to the Bible group meeting to find out whether Milly will come with her (line 6). The common goal in this joint venture is to facilitate a (positive) decision by Milly about participating in the Bible group meeting that evening.

Table 6. Division of labor in example (6)

Ex.	Clause 1	Combining element	Clause 2
(6)	[well]why don'yo]u go ahead Milly	en	u-I:'ll sto:p o:n my way down

Several seconds later, as Milly initiates closings in the telephone call, the matter comes up again:

(7) "Stop by" (sbl031-6)
(Later in the same telephone call as (6).)

```
1    Mil: [THA:NK]S FER C]AHLLING ME:[a n d u h]=
2    Gin:                             [('t)ALRIGHT]=
3    Gin: =we [ll then ↑w]e:'ll hh
4    Mil:    [I really  ]
5         (.)
6→   Gin: we-:'ll keep it y-y- (.) k you thin[k ↓abou]*it.↓
7    Mil:                                    [y e: s.]
8         (.)
9    Mil: [hh
10⇒  Gin: [end uh
11        (0.2)
12   Mil: well may[b e I can(w)    ]
13   Gin:         [do you want me to] stop by:?
14   Mil: hh we:ll you ↑better no:t may:be: uhm becuz I- I sorta
15        dou:bt I: think Jan has a lotta wo:rk=
16   Gin: =[°Ohh°
17   Mil: =[en I'm sort'v uh t hhh MAYBE I'll ca:ll you if I decide
18        I can go [: would that be] be[tter? ]
19   Gin:          [↑ o k a : y    ]   [↓swel]l.
```

When Milly moves into pre-closing in line 1, Gina returns to her offer: *well then we'll hh* (line 3) and *we'll keep it y-y-* (line 6).[4] She then breaks off and again launches a division of labor, first instructing Milly to think about coming to the Bible group (line 6) and then projecting a second, complementary action of her (Gina's) own (line 10). Although this second

---

4   This turn-constructional unit is projectably launching 'we'll keep it you know... (open/at the back of our mind)'.

action is not fully expressed, it can analyzably be anticipated that it will be a promise by Gina to stop by on her way to the Bible group meeting in case Milly decides to join her. Evidence for this will be seen in line 13: here subsequent to Milly's silence in line 11 and her turn-initial *well* in line 12 – both foreshadowing a dispreferred response – Gina shifts from a projected promise ('I'll stop by') to a deontically weaker *do you want me to stop by?*. That is, rather than present her stopping by as a foregone conclusion, Gina now presents it as a mere possibility, giving Milly the opportunity to evaluate its desirability.

Table 7. Division of labor in example (7)

Ex.	Clause 1	Combining element	Clause 2
(7)	`you thin[k ↓abou]*it.↓`	`end uh`	`([do you want me to] stop by:?)`

The first clause of this structure directs Other to carry out an action, while with the second clause, Self commits to carrying out a complementary action in the service of achieving a common goal, facilitating a (positive) decision by Milly about attending the Bible group meeting that evening.

In cases such as (4), (6), and (7), the division-of-labor structure is used to initiate an offer: the <u>offerer</u> commits to doing something but also directs the offeree to do something complementary, e.g., in (4) to buy the coat, in (6) to finish eating first, and in (7) to think about attending the Bible group meeting. As (4) makes particularly clear, in promoting a division of labor, offerers are in a sense reducing their own workload.

Yet divisions of labor can also be proposed by <u>offerees</u> in responding (positively) to an offer:

(8) "Chairs" (sbl025-30)
Claire and Chloe are making plans for an upcoming bridge party that Chloe will be hosting at her house. On the occasion of Chloe's last bridge party, Claire had provided her with chairs. Towards the close of this conversation, Claire now suddenly asks whether she should bring the chairs again.

```
1   Cla:   hhhh do you want me bring the: chai:[rs?
2   Chl:                                      [hahh
3          plea::: (.) NO*: (0.2) °yah,°
4          (0.3)
5   Chl:   I:'ve got to get ch*airs. bring'em one more t*ime.

(17 lines omitted))

22→ Chl:  [hh we:ll I'll keep sort of lookin
23⇒       but bring 'em one more time
24        maybe by: next time I can get some.
```

This sequence begins when Claire offers to bring chairs along to the bridge party that Chloe is hosting (line 1). Chloe initially rejects this offer (line 3), but then reverses her position in line 5 and asks Claire to bring the chairs *one more time* after all (line 23). But Chloe also commits to continuing the search for chairs herself (line 22).

Table 8. Division of labor in example (8)

Ex.	Clause 1	Combining element	Clause 2
(8)	we:ll I'll keep sort of lookin	but[5]	bring 'em one more time

In (8) then, the speaker is deploying a division-of-labor structure to reduce the workload of her interlocutor: by promising to keep looking for chairs herself, she implies that her interlocutor will not have to bring chairs again to future bridge parties. Together the two actions contribute to a common goal, i.e., hosting bridge parties at which there are enough chairs for everyone. Like in (4) and (6)–(7), the offer is transformed here into a joint venture through a proposal to share the work involved.

To summarize the argument so far: we have found divisions of labor primarily in two sequential contexts: (a) requests, where the structure can be deployed either by requesters or requestees, and (b) offers, where it is deployed either by offerers or offerees. These two sequence types, requests and offers, have in common that they typically involve asymmetric relations between the participants: one participant (Self) lays claim to having the deontic right to determine the future behavior of another (Other) (for more on deontic rights in talk-in-interaction see Stevanovic 2013). When Self *requests* Other to do something, this invites a commitment by Other to comply; when Self *offers* to do something for Other, this invites a commitment by Other to accept the plan. Divisions of labor transform such asymmetric situations into more symmetric ones by proposing that Self and Other share the work involved in the service of pursuing a larger common goal.

Note that the division-of-labor pattern is particularly at home in request and offer sequences whose trajectory has been in some way problematic. The problem or obstacle may be explicit, as in (8), where Chloe first adamantly rejects Claire's offer of bridge-table chairs, only later to request them after all. Also in (2), Irja expresses reluctance to browse the shops with her daughter to look for a coat, and in (3), Mr Bathwick rejects Lesley's request to deliver her green groceries on another day. In other cases, however, the problem or obstacle remains implicit, being indexed, e.g., by a recipient's hesitation

---

5   We attribute the use of *but* in this instantiation of the pattern to the fact that the context implies incompatibility between the two actions mentioned (if Claire looks for chairs and finds some, then Chloe will not need to bring any). Claire is basically denying this incompatibility by implying 'Although I'll do my part, your part is still needed'.

or lack of full commitment to a request or offer. This then prompts the co-participant to propose a second, alternative version of the offer or request, one involving a division of labor. We can observe something like this happening in (9) below:

(9) "Lehmät" 'Cows' (SG 112:B2)
Vikke and Missu are organizing a housewarming gift for a mutual friend of theirs. Here they are arranging how to include their other friends in the financing of the gift.

```
1  Vikke:    voisikkohan   sää   soittaa    Liinalle?,
             can-CON-2SG-Q-CLI 2SG  call       Liina-ALL
             could you call Liina

2  Missu:    .h voim       mää   soittaa,h
             can-1SG       1SG   call-INF
             sure I can call (her)

3            (.)

4  Missu:    .hh ja tota pitäskö    sit  soittaa   vielä >#m#<
                 PRT PRT need-CON.3-QPRT call-INF  still
             and uhm should one also call

5            Miialle ja Ninnulle ja, (.) Marialleki   et
             Miia-ALL and Ninnu-ALL and   Maria-ALL-CLI COMP
             Miia and Ninnu and            Maria (to find out)

6            mitä  ne      om     miältä.
             what  DEM3.PL be.3SG mind-PART
             what they think

7  Vikke:    °mm,° *.nii*

8            (0.3)

9→ Missu:    tai no jos sanos        vaikka       Mar:- tota: .hh
             PRT PRT if  Ø say-CON.3SG for instance Mar-  PRT
             or what if Ø tells for example Mar:- um

10→          Miialle et <soittais?>,
             Miia-ALL COMP call-CON.3
             Miia to call

11           (3.8)

12→ Missu:   soittais vaikka      #m# Marialle ja
             call-CON.3 for instance  Maria-ALL and
             to call for instance Maria and
```

```
13⇒           mää,  (.) sanosin   >Liinalle et   soittais Ninnulle⁶
              1SG       say-CON-1SG Liina-ALL   COMP call-CON.3 Ninnu-ALL
              I    (.)  would tell Liina to call Ninnu

14            ni    ei  tarviit  tässä nii kauheesti;<=
              so    NEG need     PRT   so  terribly
              so (one) needn't here now so terribly [much]

15  Vikke:    =mm, (.) no mää voin    soittaa  kyl  Miialle ja
                       PRT   PRT 1SG can-1SG call-INF PRT   Miia-ALL and
              well I can surely call Miia and

16            Mariall[e ku]  oon     menossa töihin   ni.
              Maria-ALL  when be-1SG go-INE  work-PL-ILL PRT
              Maria when I go to work so.

17  Missu:           [nii;]

18  Missu:    .hhhhhh °no joo. (.) ihan sama,°
              well yes. (.) whatever.

19  Vikke:    mhh otetaan se sitten_näi.
              let's do it like that then.
```

In line 1, Vikke asks Missu to call Liina, who Missu knows better, and to include her in their gift-giving plan. Missu agrees to do this (line 2) and then reciprocates by suggesting that their other friends (Miia, Ninnu, and Maria) should also be called to ask what they think about the housewarming gift (lines 4–6). Vikke only acknowledges this as a possibility with the particles *mm nii* 'mm' (line 7) (see Sorjonen 2001). After a short pause (line 8) Missu proposes an alternative plan, namely to set up a 'round robin' of telephoning (lines 9–14). She does this by using a division-of-labor structure:

Table 9. Division of labor in example (9)

Ex.	Clause 1	Combining element	Clause 2
(9)	tai no jos sanos vaikka Mar:- tota: .hh Miialle et <soittais?>, (3.8) soittais vaikka #m# Marialle or what if Ø would tell for example Mar:- um .hh Miia to call (3.8) to call for instance Maria	ja and	mää,(.) sanosin >Liinalle et soittais Ninnulle I (.) would tell Liina to call Ninnu

---

6 We note that in this case the first part of the division-of-labor pattern (lines 9–12) is a complex clause and involves several self-repairs.

In this formulation, by using the zero-person form *jos Ø sanos* 'if Ø would tell', Missu first suggests that some unnamed person should call Miia to initiate one part of the round robin, and then proposes herself to call Liina and thereby initiate the other part of the round robin. Although Vikke's role is merely implicit, it can nevertheless be inferred that the unnamed person who should execute the other part is Vikke, and Vikke's response reveals an understanding that she was the one meant: she commits to do the calling by saying *no mää voin soittaa kyl Miialle ja Marialle* 'well I can surely call Miia and Maria' (lines 15–16).

In (9) Missu's initial suggestion (lines 4–6) to call around to other friends about the gift-giving is merely treated as one possibility among others by Vikke (lines 7–8). It is arguably Vikke's hesitation that prompts Missu to propose a division of labor as an alternative. Divisions of labor thus provide participants with a way to pursue a successful outcome of request and offer situations that are in danger of miscarrying.

The rationale behind these uses, we submit, is to shape what is inherently an asymmetric situation (request or offer),[7] with one speaker displaying strong deontic rights over another within a specified domain of action, into something more symmetric. Stated somewhat differently, the division of labor transforms a unilaterally motivated request or offer into a joint venture, one in which the work of the project is distributed more equally between the participants.

The symmetry achieved with such a division of labor expresses itself not only through a sharing of the workload, but also through a sharing of deontic rights and responsibilities for deciding on and planning the joint project. For example, reconsider (1), where Emma has requested Barbara to call up Bud and persuade him to come down for Thanksgiving. In replying *I'll call him tonight and you call me at nine tomorrow morning*, Barbara is not only *submitting* to Emma's deontic authority but is also claiming some deontic rights for herself: she is agreeing to do what Emma has asked, but she is also asking in return that Emma call *her* to find out what Bud said. Similarly, e.g., in (5): by using a division-of-labor structure in lines 3–9, Matti is giving up some of his deontic rights over Pekka by volunteering to do part of the work himself, namely to come and pick the excavator up, and simultaneously liberating Pekka from having to sit home and wait. He is thus suggesting that they share responsibility for the success of this joint venture.

---

7   One anonymous reviewer suggested that even within the division-of-labor pattern, clause 1 can be seen as proposing something asymmetrical, which is then balanced out by the action of clause 2. However, this perspective is at odds with our understanding of the division-of-labor pattern as a holistic structure (see below), although we do not deny that the structure emerges incrementally in real time (Linell 2013). Moreover, we are not arguing that all asymmetries need to be balanced out. Instead, it is primarily those asymmetric sequences with problematic trajectories that find resolution through the division-of-labor practice.

Formal means in English and Finnish divisions of labor

So far we have seen that the underlying phenomenon of promoting a division of labor between participants in the service of a common goal is the same in both English and Finnish. And indeed when we look at the linguistic structures through which these divisions of labor are accomplished, there are striking similarities. Abstracting away from the specific forms documented in the tables for each of our examples to more schematic lexico-syntactic formats, we find that for each language there are two abstract constructional schemas involved.[8] What we are calling **Schema 1** in both English and Finnish has a second-person subject or verb form in clause 1 (or a zero-person form in Finnish)[9] and a first-person subject or verb form in clause 2. X and Y represent the actions encoded in clause 1 and clause 2 respectively.

Table 10: Schema 1 in English and Finnish

Clause 1: Other		Combining element	Clause 2: Self	
ENGLISH[10]				
(PRON2) IMPERATIVE	X	*(and)*	PRON1 DECLARATIVE MODAL *will*	Y
why NEGATIVE INTERROGATIVE PRON2		*and*	PRON1 DECLARATIVE MODAL *will*	Y
FINNISH[11]				
IMPERATIVE [2]	X	*niin*	(PRON1) DECLARATIVE INDICATIVE-1[12]	Y
DECLARATIVE INDICATIVE-2	X	*niin*	PRON1 DECLARATIVE INDICATIVE-1	Y
Ø DECLARATIVE INDICATIVE-3	X	*niin*	DECLARATIVE INDICATIVE-1	Y
jos PRON2 DECLARATIVE INDICATIVE-2	X	*niin*	PRON1 DECLARATIVE INDICATIVE-1	Y

(X is an action to be carried out by Other, Y is an action to be carried out by Self)

What we are calling **Schema 2** in both English and Finnish has a first-person subject or verb form in clause 1 and a second-person subject or verb form in clause 2:

---

8   We adopt the term *constructional* schema from Ono & Thompson (1995), who use it to refer to conversational patterns that through recurrent use have conventionalized into more abstract grammatical prototypes that participants attend to.
9   For more on zero-person forms in Finnish, see Laitinen (2006).
10 The description for English is given in terms of sentence type: declarative, interrogative, imperative.
11 The description for Finnish includes sentence type (declarative, interrogative, imperative) as well as grammatical mood (indicative, conditional, etc.).
12 In colloquial Finnish a passive form can be used with 1st person plural meaning (see, e.g., example (4)); an overt 1st person plural pronoun is used as a subject in all of our cases except for one institutional call where there is no ambiguity as to who will be the agent of the action, so we have included these cases under 1st person forms.

Table 11: Schema 2 in English and Finnish

Clause 1: Self		Combining element	Clause 2: Other	
English				
PRON1 DECLARATIVE MODAL *will*	X	*and*	PRON2 IMPERATIVE	Y
PRON1 DECLARATIVE MODAL *will*	X	*and*	PRON2 DECLARATIVE MODAL *can*	Y
why NEGATIVE INTERROGATIVE PRON1	X	*and*	PRON2 DECLARATIVE MODAL *can*	Y
FINNISH				
PRON1 DECLARATIVE INDICATIVE-1	X	*niin*	PRON2 DECLARATIVE INDICATIVE-2 MODAL (*saada* 'get to')	Y

(X is an action to be carried out by Self, Y is an action to be carried out by Other)

What these two schemas in English and Finnish have in common is that they represent **paratactic clause combinations** (Matthiessen & Thompson 1988) with a conjunction or connective particle as an explicit combining element between them.[13] As can be seen in Tables 10 and 11, in English the combining element is a coordinating conjunction *and*. In Finnish, however, the combining element is *niin* ('and/so/then'), which is also used in conditional constructions [*jos* 'if'... *niin* 'then'] (see also Vilkuna 1997). Nevertheless, in our Finnish division-of-labor patterns there is no strong conditionality ('if-and-only-if') between the two parts, not even in cases where clause 1 is initiated with *jos* ('if'). *Jos*-initiations in our division-of-labor structures are more closely related to *jos*-initiated directives (see Hakulinen et al. 2004: 1570; Laury 2012) than to canonical conditional constructions.

Schemas 1 and 2 have a number of characteristics in common. For one, there are (i) both semantic and lexico-syntactic constraints on the composition of the clause combinations involved. Each of the two clauses encodes a future concrete action, one with Self as agent and one with Other as agent. And each of the two clauses has recurrent forms:

Table 12. Recurrent forms in English and Finnish divisions of labor

	RECURRENT FORMS IN ENGLISH	RECURRENT FORMS IN FINNISH
Self	*I will...*	*(minä) teen* 'I (will) V'
	why don't I...	*me tehdään* 'we (will) V'
		minä tekisin 'I would V'
Other	*(you) V-IMP*	*tee* 'V-IMP'
	why don't you...	*(sinä) teet* 'you V'
	you can...	*jos sinä teet* 'if you V'

13 This is not to deny that due to its origin as the plural instructive form of the demonstrative *se*, Finnish *niin* is more diverse in meaning and use than English *and*.

Moreover, the two actions X and Y are ordered chronologically: X in clause 1 precedes Y in clause 2 in time.[14]

In addition, there are predictable relations between Schemas 1 and 2. The choice of one or the other schema is not free but is determined by how Self and Other map onto the chronologically ordered actions X and Y: If Other is the agent of X, then Schema 1 (Other-Self) is appropriate; if Self is the agent of X, then Schema 2 (Self-Other) is appropriate. Schema 2 is thus the counterpart to Schema 1, and vice versa, in terms of the mapping of agency.

Finally, in both schemas the combining element, if explicit, is *and* in English and *niin* or *ja* in Finnish.

On semantic and lexico-syntactic grounds, Schemas 1 and 2 would seem to represent variants of one and the same practice: together they could be said to constitute a *social action format* (Fox 2007; Kärkkäinen & Keisanen 2012) for the division of labor in talk-in-interaction. This hypothesis is further corroborated when we look at the prosodic-phonetic and pragmatic features of the schemas.

(ii) Prosodically, the two parts of the clause-combination structure are routinely produced either as a single intonation phrase or as two intonation phrases that cohere prosodically (see Couper-Kuhlen 2009; 2012 for more on the prosody of clause combining). In (4), for instance, the speaker makes no prosodic break at the joint between the two clauses: *ku se on ö paikalla ni m:* 'when he's back and w-' (line 11). In this case then, the two parts are produced in one intonation phrase. But if each part does form its own intonation phrase, then often (but not invariably) the first has final continuing intonation and the second picks up intonationally from where the first left off. In other words, the two units are produced together on one line of pitch declination (see also Couper-Kuhlen 1996). This is what we find happening in (1), where the speaker uses slightly rising pitch at the end of the first intonation phrase/clause (line 22) and the pitch of the second intonation phrase/clause begins from there. Finally, even if clause 1 is delivered in one or more intonation phrases with final intonation (as in exs. 5 and 7, where the pitch at the end of the first part is low-falling), it nevertheless pragmatically projects a subsequent part, in that it leaves open the question of 'why that now' and thus foreshadows that more will come. Thus, there is reason to believe that the schemas are partially conventionalized conversational routines in the sense of Ono and Thompson (1995).

(iii) Finally, there are pragmatic constraints on the clause combinations documented in our schemas. For instance, the Self part is pitched as a **commitment** that the speaker intends or (more weakly) is prepared to carry out some action in the future. The Other part is pitched as a **directive**, a request or (more weakly) a suggestion that the interlocutor carry out a complementary action in the future. Together the two actions could be said to implement an *action combination* (Kärkkäinen & Keisanen, 2012) – Schema 1: [directive & commitment] and Schema 2: [commitment & directive] – for the achievement of a common goal. In (1) the common goal

---

14 This is assuming that the two actions X and Y have a natural chronological order.

might be said to be bringing off a mutually rewarding Thanksgiving dinner; in (2) managing a daughter's winter wardrobe needs in a mutually agreeable fashion; in (3) achieving a mutually satisfactory sale and delivery of fresh green groceries to Lesley; in (4) coordinating a mutually agreed upon coffee date, and so forth. Together, the combined actions thus contribute to a joint venture in which the work is divided more or less equally between the two participants.

Yet although the two schemas have in common that they build an action combination, each individual schema has alternate forms for the implementation of the actions in question: for instance, in English we find both an imperative form *X!* and an interrogative form *why don't you X?* for the directive part; in Finnish we have an imperative form *tee!* 'X!', a declarative indicative form *teet* 'you X' , and a declarative conditional form *tekisit* 'you would X'(± *jos*) for the directive part. These alternate forms are not interchangeable with one another: they position the speaker as displaying differing degrees of deontic authority (locally claimed or displayed deontic rights) and/or they represent the likelihood or advisability of the future action taking place with varying degrees of certainty. For instance, in English an imperative *X!* construes the speaker as having stronger rights to determine the future course of events than does an interrrogative *why don't you X?*. While imperative *X!* (± *you*) presents the other's compliance as self-evident or a foregone conclusion, *why don't you X?* allows Other to weigh in on the advisability of the action. In Finnish, the IMPERATIVE forms display stronger deontic rights than do, e.g., *jos* + CONDITIONAL and ∅ person forms (see Couper-Kuhlen & Etelämäki, 2015). The latter forms present the desirability of the nominated action and the action itself as not yet certain, in contrast to IMPERATIVE and INDICATIVE, which treat both the desirability of the action and the action itself as more certain.

Moreover, the alternate forms appear in different sequential positions in extended sequences of talk. In English, for instance, a division of labor with an interrogative *why don't you X?* implementing the directive action is more likely to be found at the beginning of extended sequences. By contrast, a division of labor with imperative *X!* (± *you*) is more likely to be found at the end of sequences, once the particulars of each party's contribution have been worked out. Recall that in (6) we found Gina using a [directive & commitment] action combination to promote Milly's decision to come to the Bible group with her. In line 4 she uses *why don't you X?* to suggest that Milly should first finish eating and then she (Gina) will stop by to see if she wants to come along. But in (7), which takes place several seconds later in the same phone call, Gina again uses a [directive & commitment] action combination in pursuit of the same goal; however, this time she chooses an imperative *(you) X!* form: *you think about it* (line 6) to implement the directive part. Thus, in this extended sequence the interrogative *why don't you X?* form is found when the speaker is promoting something for the first time, whereas the imperative *(you) X!* form is found in a similar division of labor when the sequence is about to be closed down. We conclude that the two forms, *why don't you X ?* and *(you) X!* have their own sequential slots, or home environments, in extended sequences.

In Finnish the situation is similar: deontically weaker forms for dividing the labor are found early in extended sequences, stronger deontic forms later. Zero-person forms are used when negotiation is needed as to how the labor will be divided among the participants (see also Couper-Kuhlen & Etelämäki, 2015). For instance, in (9) the division of labor being promoted (lines 9–14) is made only tentatively at an early point in the sequence, with forms that display a weak deontic stance (Stevanovic 2013) by virtue of treating the future actions as hypothetical (*jos*, conditional verbs) and leaving the agent of the future action unclear (zero-person forms).[15] This allows for maximum negotiation over what will be done and how the work will be divided. Once the tasks and the distribution of agency and responsibility between the participants have been determined, more definitive formulations are used, as we see happening in line 20, when Vikke initiates sequence closure by saying *otetaan se sitten_näi* 'let's do it like that then'.

In sum: In both English and Finnish, forms that index less authority and less certainty are used in proposing divisions of labor early in extended sequences, whereas forms that encode more authority and more certainty come later in extended sequences. For these reasons we believe that the alternate forms in the two schemas should be thought of as clustering together for the realization of each variant of the division-of-labor practice (see Figure 1).

Figure 1: Relationship between schemas and alternate forms (AF)

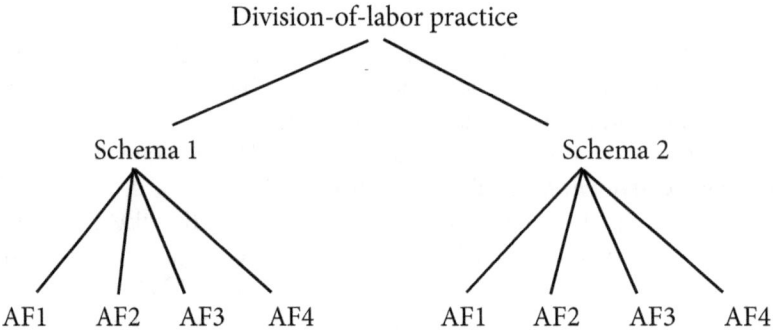

Yet although there are similarities between divisions of labor in English and Finnish, there are also some significant cross-linguistic differences. For one, the languages provide different resources for the division of labor. Finnish, for instance, allows for more formal variation due to the fact that (i) second person singular and plural are morphologically distinct in verb inflections (cf., e.g., *tulkaa* 'come-IMP.2PL' in (4) vs. *jätä* 'leave.IMP.2SG' in (5)), and that (ii) there are morphological inflections for marking conditional mood

---

15 Stevanovic (2013: 23) introduces a notion of *deontic gradient*: deontically weaker forms display a deontically weaker stance, i.e., lay weaker claims to deontic rights, and respectively, deontically stronger forms display a deontically stronger stance, i.e., lay stronger claims to deontic rights.

on verbs (cf. the conditional verb forms *sanos* 'say-CON.3SG' and *sanosin* 'say-CON.1SG' in (9)). Moreover, whereas in English, person expression is always clearly encoded as either 1p or 2p, in Finnish, person may be left unexpressed through the use of zero-person forms (Laitinen 1995; 2006; Couper-Kuhlen & Etelämäki 2015): see, e.g., *jos sanos* 'if ∅ would say' in (9).

But it is not only that the two languages provide different grammatical resources for accomplishing similar tasks: even when they have the same or similar resources, they use them differently. For instance, English speakers make use of *wh*-negative interrogatives in both parts of the construction, i.e., for directing (*why don't you X?*) as well as for committing (*why don't I X?*). Finnish has such a resource but in our data speakers do not use it for this purpose. Finnish has a modal verb *voida* 'can' but unlike the English speakers, the Finnish speakers in our data prefer to use conditional inflections on the verb instead. On the other hand, based on our analysis, Finnish speakers appear to make greater use of *jos* 'if'-clauses and conditionality than do English speakers for this purpose.

All in all, it is our impression that Finnish speakers use more indirect practices in dividing the labor for the pursuit of a common goal. We find Finnish participants more frequently negotiating from the outset questions like: What is the labor, i.e., does this really need to be done? Should the labor be divided at all? If so, how should it be divided? This is different from English, where the speakers in our data appear to propose a division of labor without having negotiated the fundamentals. For more on this see Couper-Kuhlen and Etelämäki (2014). Yet regardless of these differences, the underlying phenomenon is the same: the joining of two clauses for the implementation of an action combination in order to transform a request or offer into a joint venture.

Summary and conclusion

We have argued that in both English and Finnish, speakers in request and offer sequences make use of a combination of two clauses in which one refers to something the speaker (Self) will do and one, to something complementary the recipient (Other) will do in the future. We have dubbed these action combinations [directive & commitment] and [commitment & directive] and argued that they are implemented by recurrent forms, or formats, for promoting a division of labor. We have shown that these formats are deployed in situations that would otherwise involve a steep deontic gradient, with one party displaying stronger rights over the other in bringing about some particular future action. They are often found in request and offer sequences that have had a problematic trajectory. The rationale for using them is to re-construe the situation as more symmetric deontically, with the parties now sharing not only the work but also rights and responsibilities with respect to the success of what has become a joint venture.

There are other possible mappings between conjoined clauses and actions. For instance, two clauses can be combined for the implementation of one action as, e.g., in conditionals such as *if your husband would like their address my husband would gladly give it to him* (Curl 2006:1261), or *jos me tullaan **niin** varmaan tullaan ehkä yheksän maissa* 'if we come so we will probably not come until about nine' (Laury 2012: 218). This situation could be schematized as in Figure 2:

Figure 2: Conjoined clauses for the implementation of a single action

Two clauses can also be conjoined but implement two separate actions, as, e.g., in the case of *and*-prefaced questions invoking a larger agenda-based activity: (from an informal medical encounter between a health visitor and a new mother) HV: *How old's your husband.* (M: *twenty-six in April.)* HV: ***And** does he work?* (Heritage & Sorjonen 1994: 5). In this case the schematization in Figure 3 would be appropriate:

Figure 3: Conjoined clauses for the implementation of separate actions

In the light of this, we believe that our phenomenon is a particularly telling case of combining clauses in order to combine actions, because it establishes an *iconic* relationship between two conjoined clauses (*sinä teet X **nii** minä teen Y* 'you do X **and** I'll do Y') and two conjoined actions ([directive & commitment] or [commitment & directive]) as a division-of-labor practice. This could be schematized as in Figure 4:

Figure 4: Conjoined clauses for the implementation of conjoined actions

The actions being linked are at once immediate social actions implemented through language and future bodily actions to be carried out in the material world.

In terms of combining social actions, the closest relatives to this phenomenon might be [denial (*no*) & account] (Ford 2001), or [affirmation (*yes*) & elaboration] (Steensig & Heinemann 2013). Further kindred action combinations are [referent identification & offer] (Kärkkäinen & Keisanen 2012), and [acceptance & fulfillment of a request] (Rauniomaa & Keisanen 2012). However, the difference between all these and the pattern in focus here is that the action combinations these analysts describe involve only <u>one</u> agent and do not necessarily involve a combination of <u>clauses</u>, whereas the division-of-labor action combination involves <u>two</u> agents and <u>two</u> combined clauses. Our action combination is thus an example *par excellence* of the combining of clauses and actions.

We have seen that the division-of-labor practice is attested in both English and Finnish talk-in-interaction. This gives us reason to believe that it may be a more widespread social phenomenon: promoting a future action involving the other, whether through requesting or offering, can be a delicate matter and social actors can encounter problems in trying to do so. Dividing the labor with the practice we have described offers a way out, namely by transforming an asymmetric situation into a more symmetric one and sharing the burden and cost of the undertaking as a joint venture.

References

Couper-Kuhlen, Elizabeth. 1996. Intonation and clause combining in discourse: The case of 'because'. *Pragmatics* 6(3): 389–426.
Couper-Kuhlen, Elizabeth. 2009. On combining clauses and actions in interaction. *Virittäjä*. Journal of the Society for the Study of Finnish (Kotikielen Seura, vsk. 113), Helsinki. http://www.kotikielenseura.fi/virittaja/verkkolehti/2009_3.html
Couper-Kuhlen, Elizabeth. 2012. Turn continuation and clause combinations. *Discourse Processes* 49(3/4): 273–299.
Couper-Kuhlen, Elizabeth & Marja Etelämäki. 2014. On divisions of labor in request and offer environments. In Paul Drew & Elizabeth Couper-Kuhlen (eds.), *Requesting in social interaction*. 115–144. Amsterdam: Benjamins.
Couper-Kuhlen, Elizabeth & Marja Etelämäki. 2015. On nominated actions and their targeted agents in everyday Finnish conversation. *Journal of Pragmatics* 78: 7–24.
Couper-Kuhlen, Elizabeth & Margret Selting (eds.). 2001. *Studies in interactional linguistics*. Amsterdam: John Benjamins.
Curl, Traci S. 2006. Offers of assistance: Constraints on syntactic design. *Journal of Pragmatics* 38: 1257–1280.
Ford, Cecilia E. 2001. At the intersection of turn and sequence. Negation and what comes next. In Margaret Selting & Elizabeth Couper-Kuhlen (eds.), *Studies in interactional linguistics*. 51–79. Amsterdam: Benjamins.
Fox, Barbara A. 2007. Principles shaping grammatical practices: An exploration. *Discourse Studies* 9(3): 299–318.
Hakulinen, Auli, Maria Vilkuna, Riitta Korhonen, Vesa Koivisto, Tarja Riitta Heinonen & Irja Alho. 2004. *Iso suomen kielioppi*. Helsinki: Finnish Literature Society.
Hakulinen, Auli & Leelo Keevallik. Forthcoming. Epistemically reinforced *kyl(lä)/küll*-responses in Estonian and Finnish: Word order and social action. In Marja-Liisa Helasvuo & Ritva Laury (eds.), *Journal of Pragmatics*, Special issue.

Heritage, John & Marja-Leena Sorjonen. 1994. Constituting and maintaining activities across sequences: *And*-prefacing as a feature of question design. *Language in Society* 23: 1–29.

Kotilainen, Lari 2007. *Kiellon lumo. Kieltoverbitön kieltokonstruktio ja sen kiteytyminen.* Helsinki: Finnish Literature Society.

Kärkkäinen, Elise & Tiina Keisanen. 2012. Linguistic and embodied formats for making (concrete) offers. *Discourse Studies* 14(5): 587–611.

Laitinen, Lea. 1995. Nollapersoona. *Virittäjä* 99: 337–358.

Laitinen, Lea. 2006. Zero person in Finnish. A grammatical resource for construing human reference. In Marja-Liisa Helasvuo & Lyle Campbell (eds.), *Grammar from the human perspective. Case, space and person in Finnish.* 209–232. Amsterdam: Benjamins.

Laury, Ritva. 1997. *Demonstratives in interaction. The emergence of a definite article in Finnish.* Amsterdam: John Benjamins.

Laury, Ritva. 2012. Syntactically non-integrated Finnish 'jos' (*if*)-conditional clauses as directives. *Discourse Processes* 49: 213–242.

Linell, Per. 2013. The dynamics of incrementation in utterance-building: Processes and resources. In Beatrice Szczepek Reed & Geoffrey Raymond (eds.), *Units of talk – Units of actions.* Amsterdam: John Benjamins.

Matthiessen, Christian & Sandra A. Thompson. 1988. The structure of discourse and 'subordination'. In John Haiman & Sandra A. Thompson (eds.), *Clause combining in grammar and discourse.* 275–329. Amsterdam: Benjamins.

Ono, Tsuyoshi & Sandra A. Thompson. 1995. What can conversation tell us about syntax? In Philip W. Davis (ed.), *Alternative linguistics: Descriptive and theoretical modes.* 213–271. Amsterdam: Benjamins.

Quirk, Randolph, et al., eds. 1985. *A comprehensive grammar of the English language.* London: Longman.

Rauniomaa, Mirka & Tiina Keisanen. 2012. Two multimodal formats for responding to requests. *Journal of Pragmatics* 44: 829–842.

Schegloff, Emanuel A. 1988. Goffman and the analysis of conversation. In Paul Drew & Anthony Wootton (eds.), *Erving Goffman. Exploring the interaction order.* 89–135. Cambridge: Polity Press.

Sidnell, Jack & Tanya Stivers (eds.). 2013. *The handbook of conversation analysis.* Chichester: Wiley-Blackwell.

Sorjonen, Marja-Leena. 2001. *Responding in conversation. A study of response particles in Finnish.* Amsterdam: Benjamins.

Steensig, Jakob & Trine Heinemann. 2013. When 'yes' is not enough – as an answer to a yes/no question. In Beatrice Szczepek Reed & Geoffrey Raymond (eds.), *Units of talk – Units of action.* 207–241. Amsterdam: Benjamins.

Stevanovic, Melisa. 2013. *Deontic rights in interaction. A conversation analytic study on authority and cooperation.* PhD thesis. Department of Social Research, University of Helsinki.

Vilkuna, Maria. 1997. Into and out of the standard language: the particle *ni* in Finnish. In Jenny Cheshire & Dieter Stein (eds.), *Taming the vernacular: From dialect to written standard language.* 51–67. London: Longman.

Lauri Haapanen
http://orcid.org/0000-0002-1973-4843

8. Directly from interview to quotations? Quoting practices in written journalism

Introduction

This chapter shifts the perspective from the analysis of the emergence of embodied and spoken interaction to a different channel and temporal dimension of interaction.[1] I will focus on the process of constructing direct quotations in written journalistic articles and offer a unique glance at journalistic work processes. By examining empirical data drawn from Finnish media, we will discover that the ostensibly static text surface connects the spoken interaction between journalists and their interviewees to the pre-planned architecture of the article in the making, and further to the values and purposes of the publication and its publisher.

In general, written quotations are defined as being approximately verbatim repetitions of the original spoken utterances. Theoretically speaking, this is possible: a quotation can be defined in terms of a verbatim representation of the original text, or by faithfulness to it (Short et al. 2002). In other words, a direct quotation would then represent the reported event in a manner that is faithful to the form, content, and speech act value of the original (for example, see Short 1988: 69–71).

This definition also serves as a goal in many practical guidebooks on quoting: "Never alter quotations even to correct minor grammatical errors or word usage" (Goldstein 2009: 232; see also Adams 2001: 80–83; Brooks et al. 2002: 85–86; Kramer & Call 2007: 107–109). However, some guidebooks are not as inflexible in their approach. To paraphrase their general views, utterances could and should be merged, edited, and cleaned up as long as the factual content is maintained (e.g., Blundell 1988: 148; Ruberg 2005: 123; Töyry et al. 2008: 92–93). Perhaps surprisingly, there are also numerous guidebooks that comment hardly at all on the issue of modifying quotations (e.g., Clark 2006; Flaherty 2009; Jacobi 1991; Lundberg 1992, 2001).[2]

---

1   I am grateful especially to Ylva Byrman, Merja Helle, Henna Makkonen-Craig, Maija Töyry, Eero Voutilainen, and the editors of this volume for their valuable comments on the different stages of the manuscript and to Elina Sokka for helping me to convey my arguments precisely and grammatically in English.
2   López Pan (2010) has made a similar review of quoting instructions in the Spanish media. His findings are in line with mine.

Many countries have established some type of ethical code for journalists. For example, in Europe, such a code exists in at least 46 countries.[3] However, only a handful of codes are related to the practice of quoting at all, and even then, they are very vague. In Finland, *Journalistin ohjeet 2014* [Guidelines for Journalists] does not provide guidelines on quoting practices. However, since the year 2000, the self-regulating committee for Finnish journalism practices, Julkisen sanan neuvosto [Council for Mass Media], has reviewed six cases that mainly concern quoting, and one can extract from the resolutions by the committee their position on quoting: The linguistic form of the "direct" quotations can be edited, several utterances can be merged into one quotation, and the quotations can be "written" into a scene that is different from the original one, as long as the meaning is retained.[4]

Regardless of these slightly differing guidelines, it can be stated that the foundation of quotation lies in the more or less verbatim repetition of the original utterance – "by using direct quotes, you [the journalist] are telling the readers that you are putting them directly in touch with the speaker" (Brooks et al. 2002: 73). Furthermore, the illusion of being in touch with the original speaker's voice also serves as the basis for the majority of the functions of quotations in journalistic texts. For example, quotations are thought to enhance the reliability, credibility, and objectivity of an article and to characterize the person quoted (in research literature, see, e.g., Cotter 2010: 145–151; Haapanen 2011; Nylund 2006: 161. In guidebooks, see, e.g., Blundell 1988: 141–152; Clark 2006: 128–132).

Based on my own decade-long experience as a journalist, I challenge the more or less verbatim-oriented perception of direct quotations in journalism by suggesting that they are not as "direct" (in the sense of *verbatim*) as is widely assumed and stated. The research presented below is linguistically oriented and attempts to answer two research questions:

1. What types of modifications are made when transferring discourse (= meaningful semiotic human activity[5]) from a journalistic interview to direct quotation in a written journalistic article?

2. What is the explanation for these modifications?

These questions are essential, as little is known about actual quoting practices (Clayman 1990: 79; Nylund 2006: 151. For an overview of

---

3   The list of ethical codes for journalists: http://ethicnet.uta.fi/codes_by_country (visited 17 March, 2016).
4   http://www.jsn.fi/. The document numbers of the cases referred to are 5719, 4814, 4239, 4022, 3563, and 3249.
5   To me, *discourse* comprises all forms of meaningful semiotic human activity in its context as a part of social action (see Blommaert 2005: 2–3), contrary to another common (especially in social sciences) definition of *a discourse* as 'a consistent use of language in a given field of social practice' (e.g., *political discourse, feminist discourse, medical discourse*, etc.).

research, see Haapanen & Perrin 2017).[6] Although the research on quoting in television news has been studied in the last two decades (e.g., Ekström 2001; Kroon Lundell & Ekström 2010; Nylund 2003), only two published studies have used relevant empirical data to examine the "directness" of *written* journalistic quotations. Johnson Barella (2005) discovered that in examining spoken data from press conferences and speeches, only one out of five quotations was absolutely verbatim. Overall, the variety of modifications ranged from small to substantial. Lehrer (1989) drew her data from public meetings, hearings, and lectures and reported that quotations had often been modified substantially, although these non-verbatim quotations were rarely considered to be incompatible with what was intended (ibid. 120–121).

Without data from the actual spoken event, Méndez García de Paredes (2000) examined the coverage of the same event in different newspapers, while Bruña (1993) focused on the changes made in the phrases that were both in the text body and between quotation marks in the headline. In addition, journalist-researcher Bell (1991) analyzed his own work[7] retrospectively and stated that "de-pronominalization [replacing the pronoun with the noun it is referring to] is one of the few tamperings I would permit with a direct quote: otherwise it should remain verbatim what the source said." Some perceptions of the veracity of quotations without empirical data or with only limited empirical data are also presented by Caldas-Coulthard (1993; 1994), Cotter (2010), Kuo (2007), Satoh (2001), Short (1988), Tuchman (1978), and Waugh (1995).

The rest of this paper consists of three main sections. First, I introduce the subdiscipline of applied linguistics referred to as media linguistics and then establish the theoretical foundations for the practice of quoting and the interplay of *form* and *meaning*. In addition, I present my data and the methods of analysis. Second, the empirical analysis forms the main part of the paper, and it is divided into four subsections. In the final part, I will present a summary of the findings and my conclusion.

Framework, data, and methods

As journalistic media constitute a socially significant area of activity whose language use can differ from the use in other areas, this paper can be situated as part of an emerging subdiscipline of applied linguistics referred to as media linguistics (*Media Linguistics Research Network 2016*; Perrin 2013a; 2013b). When addressing the research questions of media linguistics, it is necessary to utilize concepts and theories from neighboring disciplines

---

6   More generally, the recontextualization of oral discourse into written form has been studied within several domains, such as police interrogation / report (e.g., Jönsson & Linell 1991; van Charldorp 2014), meeting / minutes (e.g., Nissi & Lehtinen 2015) and parliament talk / record (e.g., Voutilainen 2016).
7   It should be mentioned that Bell "recorded" his interviews only by taking notes. See my discussion of recording practices in the subsection entitled 'Monologization of the interview'.

such as journalism studies and sociology. Furthermore, media linguistics programmatically focuses on the production process, because "[m]edia discourse continues to be predominantly investigated from a product-oriented [vs. process-oriented] perspective or even as easily accessible everyday language" (*Media Linguistics Research Network 2016*) and because "lack of attention to the news production process is bound to generate weak hypotheses" (NewsTalk&Text Research Group 2011: 1843–1844).

This section consists of three subsections. First, I will present an overview of quoting from the perspective of a dialogistic theoretical framework. I will then introduce the data and methods. Third, I will discuss the notion of media concept, which will be used to structure and relate my results to the wider picture in the process of producing journalistic articles.

Quoting and recontextualization

Journalistic guidebooks discuss the correspondence between the original utterance and the quotation based on the terms of *form* and *meaning*, but they do not explain form or meaning in any detail. I argue that these two concepts have been used in an overly simplistic way.

First, despite language-related conventions governing how sound waves are presented as ink graphemes on paper, several features of oral communication do not have any absolute equivalence in writing. Thus, in terms of linguistic form the relationship between the original utterance and the quotation is always somewhat deficient. Second, the term of meaning is also loosely defined, as it can be understood either from a semantic or a pragmatic point of view. To analyze the form or the meaning of language in use within a dialogistic theoretical framework, a third component is needed: *contexts*. According to the *theory of contexts* (Linell 1998a; 1998b), utterance (≈ linguistic form), understanding (≈ situated meaning) and contexts (of which Linell prefers to use the plural form[8]) comprise an organic whole; they arise from each other, they will be interpreted against each other, and they renew and modify each other. Linell describes this reciprocal dependence as follows (1998a: 139):

- Understanding is understanding-of-discourse-in-contexts.
- Utterances are expressions-of-understandings-in-contexts.
- Contexts are partly products and projects of sense-making activities, of producing-and-understanding-discourse-in-prior-contexts.

---

8   Linell prefers the plural form *contexts* to the singular form *context* because the given piece of discourse is not embedded within, nor does it activate, only one particular context, but a matrix of different types of contexts. Furthermore, Linell speaks of contextual resources because no context is a context by itself, but it can be made into an actual, relevant context through the activities of the interlocutors. (See Linell 1998a: 128–134.)

Within the production of newspaper and magazine articles, the contexts change drastically when information is drawn from a spoken face-to-face interview and used in a written print or screen-based publication. Thus, if we endeavor to assess whether the form is "direct" (= *verbatim*) or the meaning is "direct" (= *equivalent*), it is necessary to examine and compare the original (interview) and the final (quotation) discourses in their separate contexts. The process of quoting can be analyzed and described by applying the concept of *recontextualization*. Recontextualization is defined by Linell as the "dynamic transfer-and-transformation" of some part or aspect from one discourse to another (Linell 1998a: 154). Linell also observes that, "[w]hen parts of texts or discourses are relocated through recontextualization, they are often subject to textual change, such as simplification, condensation, elaboration and refocusing" (ibid. 155). As a consequence, the process of quoting requires reconciling the contradictions that are necessarily created by the changes in contexts.[9]

When recontextualizing journalistic interview discourse, the most obvious contextual change will occur between the oral and the written modality of language. Whereas oral language is auditory, evanescent, and primarily temporally structured, written language is visual, enduring, and spatially organized (for example, see Wold 1992: 176–180). However, the significant variable in transferring discourse from an interview to quotation is not this modal dichotomy *per se*. Instead, the dichotomy results from the spoken and written language being used in different communicative situations, and further, that each of these particular situations affects the textual features of the discourse. As a consequence, no linguistic or situational characterization of speech and writing can be generalized for all spoken and written genres (Biber 1988).

For these reasons, the relation within and among journalistic interviews and articles in written media is complex and associated with a variety of different situational, functional, and processing considerations. Formulating direct quotations therefore involves addressing not only the disparity between spoken and written language, but also the contexts involved. Thus, recontextualizing a form and/or meaning from one context (= oral face-to-face interview) to another (= particular part in a particular article in a particular written medium) is not a mechanical and systematic operation. Instead, recontextualization is a dynamic and highly situation-dependent operation, involving numerous aspects that need to be taken into account. For these reasons, the recontextualized discourse is, at best, an *illusion* of spoken discourse, rather than the true and concrete equivalence of it. This illusion is often created with only a selection of vernacular cues instead of fully mimicking an original discourse (Makkonen-Craig 1999), and these particular vernacular cues and other aspects of oral discourse are selected for a quotation to meet the rhetorical purpose of the person who is making

---

9 On recontextualization, see also Sarangi 2008, cf. entextualisation Bauman & Briggs 1990; Blommaert 2005. See also Rock 2007: 22–23 for an exhaustive list of complementary concepts for such a repetition-related phenomenon.

that quotation (Haapanen in press 2017; Clark & Gerrig 1990; Wade & Clark 1993).[10]

Thus, it can be concluded that even those journalists who do aim for identical representation of form and/or meaning in their quoting – and think that it is achievable – are bound to fail due to the difference in context. This conclusion is contrary to the guidance and perceptions offered in guidebooks, but it will be supported by the data analyzed in this paper.

Data and methods

To address my research questions, I have collected three types of empirical data: The recordings of authentic interviews conducted by journalists; the published articles based on these interviews; and stimulated recall sessions with some of the above-mentioned journalists. Stimulated recall is a method used here to retrospectively explore and explain the journalists' motivations and strategies for making[11] quotations. Let us now introduce the data and the analytical methods.

The *first data set* consists of 20 recordings of authentic journalistic interviews and press conferences from 16 experienced journalists (henceforth *informant-journalists*) who worked for various established publications as full-time employees or as freelancers. I asked the journalists to record one or two interviews, but I did not disclose the exact objective of this study. I also received permission to copy the notebooks of the journalists who took notes by hand. The length of the interviews varied tremendously, ranging from 1 minute 48 seconds to 1 hour 45 minutes.

For my *second data set*, I collected the articles that were based on the interviews and press conferences of the first data set. To facilitate analyzing the visual elements of the collected articles, they remained in their published layout. The total number of the articles[12] was 21, and they were from newspapers, magazines, customer magazines ("B-to-C magazines") and web-publications. Each of the data examples presented in this paper originates from a different medium.

Data sets 1 and 2 were both collected from Finnish media and they are originally in the Finnish language. My transcriptions of the interviews are simplified versions of conventional conversation analysis transcription.[13] The precision of transcriptions is guided by appropriateness in my analysis. The English translations are not verbatim, but strive for idiomaticity and intelligibility. When referring to either data set 1 or 2, the number of the

---

10 The Finnish language is ideal for using vernacular cues to create this illusion. This is because Finnish has a direct one-to-one relationship between the spelling and the sound and hence one can mimic special pronunciation in detail (e.g., *minä, mä, mää, mnää, mie* are dialectal variations for the pronoun 'I').
11 I prefer the verb *making* over *writing* when dealing with the production-process of an article. This term emphasizes that the inscription is merely a minor stage in the work process compared to activities such as planning and information-gathering.
12 The inconsistency between the number of recordings and the number of articles comes from the fact that there are two journalists in my data set who wrote an article on the same press conference.
13 For transcription symbols, see pp. 7–8.

example is followed by letter "a" (=interview) or "b" (=published article), respectively. Letter "c" refers to a notebook source. In the transcripts I made, unless otherwise mentioned, the abbreviation "IN" refers to "interviewee" and "JO" to "journalist [interviewer]."

Data sets 1 and 2 are analyzed according to *comparative linguistic text analysis* (cf. Arffman 2007: 112–113 and *version analysis*, Perrin 2013b: 62). In this context, *text analysis* refers to the description and interpretation of both the form and content of the discourses. *Linguistic* refers to the fact that the focus of investigation is not only on the discourse as a textual whole, but also more specifically on its linguistic level, on the words and clauses in their co-text. The term *comparative* emphasizes that the analysis examines neither the original discourse (data set 1) nor the final discourse (data set 2) *per se*, but instead compares the two with each other in order to detect any discrepancies between them.

The *third data set* consists of so-called *stimulated recall* sessions (SR) (DiPardo 1994).[14] Traditionally, an SR begins with videotaping a selected informant at work, after which s/he is asked to view and comment on the video. The method reconstructs the informants' thought processes while they worked. For example, compared to semi-structured interviews, SR extends beyond a recitation of socially valorized practices (Haapanen in press 2017) and encourages the "informants [to] discuss actions that they actually engaged in during ongoing interactions, not idealized actions they might or should take, or actions that they imperfectly remembered taking" (Dempsey 2010: 351).

When applying this method, I first localized and transcribed a section or sections from an interview that the specific quotation was based on. Then, in the SR, the informant-journalist and I read her/his article (data set 2) along with the transcript made of the original interview (data set 1). My main objective was to account for her/his writing strategies and conscious writing practices when formulating quotations, and to demonstrate how institutional framing affects quoting activities.[15] Some of the questions presented in the SRs were as follows: How do you describe your process of quoting in this particular case? Why did you do it this way? Why did you select this particular segment to be quoted? Why did you position the quotation in this particular place? Why did you edit the quoted material in this way? What influenced the process?

I conducted an SR with 11 of the 16 informant-journalists from data set 1. In this paper, I quote explicitly 7 of these SRs (11 excerpts, numbered I–XI in order of appearance). The quoted excerpts are included in the appendix in

---

14 The SR has been most frequently used in the analysis of learning processes, interpersonal skills, and decision-making in the field of educational, medical/clinical, and second-language research (for an overview, see Lyle 2003: 862–863), but it has also been applied to media research (for example, see Rautkorpi 2011). For a discussion of the selection of methodology and the course of my SR sessions in detail, see Haapanen (in press 2017).
15 For a similar approach, *cue-based retrospective verbal protocol* for studying the process of newswriting, see Perrin 2013b: 63–64.

their entirety. The SRs were conducted in Finnish; the English translations are my own.

To explain the modifications revealed by the text analysis of data sets 1 and 2 and justified by informant-journalists in SR sessions, I exploit the notion of *media concept*, which is a theoretical modeling of the process of creating a media product (for further detail, see the next subsection). By connecting the results from the analysis of all three data sets to this modeling, I can explain the observable activities of the quoting process as parts in the broader contexts of production (cf. Layder 1993: 51).

All data sets were collected during 2012–2014. All the data examples in this analysis (from data sets 1–3) are anonymized, and I will consistently use the feminine pronoun regardless of the gender of the person in question.

The notion of media concept

The notion of *media concept* was formulated by the Finnish journalism scholars Merja Helle and Maija Töyry. This concept is based on cultural-historical activity theory and developmental work research (Cole 1996; Engeström 1987; Virkkunen 2006). It looks at any human activity as an activity system that includes the subject, object of activity, tools, rules, community, and division of labor. Thus, also journalistic work is not merely an individual or independent craft but is heavily influenced by the external and internal contexts of the work process. The media concept is an extension of an activity system adapted to media research (Helle 2010; Helle & Töyry 2009). It can be used as a tool for analyzing and developing media products, and for understanding their use. In linguistic research the media concept has been used to compare the relationship between the intended aims of journalists and the journalistic texts produced (Jaakola et al. 2014).

The media concept introduces and organizes relevant extra-linguistic contexts and contextual resources that affect the process of creating any specific media product. The three components of the media concept are mutually constitutive and closely intertwined:

Figure 1. Components of a media concept (Helle & Töyry 2009: 502).

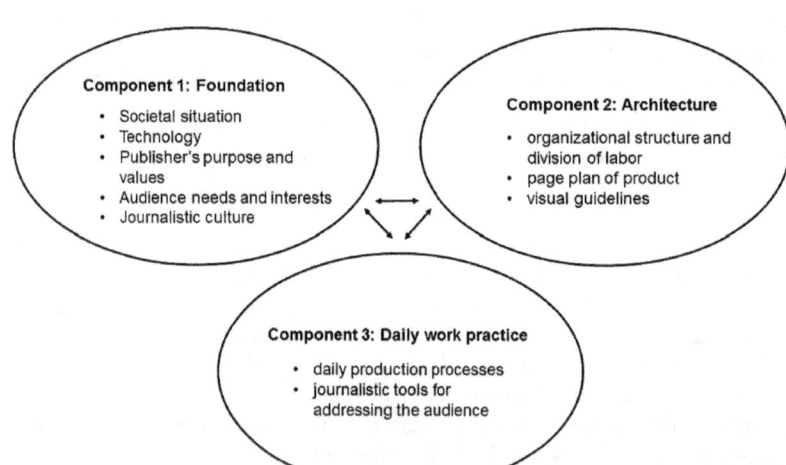

Component 1 of the media concept consists of the publisher's values and purpose and the financial basis of the publication. Values can be financial or ideological, whereas the purpose could refer to maximal profit, dissemination of ideology, or wide circulation versus a precise target group. The financial basis could consist of subscription fees, advertising revenue, and/or subsidies from some interest group. In addition, Component 1 includes the needs and interests of the desired audience, the journalistic culture, as well as the societal context. Journalistic culture refers to the close socio-cultural context in which all the persons involved in this particular activity (that is, creating a media product) operate. Societal context refers to the rules and regulations as to what kinds of media can exist and be consumed.

Component 2 consists of what is referred to as the *architecture of the whole*. This architecture is usually rather stable and formalized from issue-to-issue. This component can be described as a "template" to achieve the values and purpose of Component 1, and it can be considered from the perspectives of both the organization and content. The organizational architecture includes management and production principles and the division of labor (for example, a regular employee versus a freelancer, or an individual versus co-operational work process). The architecture of the content refers to the fact that each media product usually has more or less standardized structure for presenting content (for example, the specific combination of article types in a certain order, fixed visual guidelines) and explicitly determined targets and instructions for each article type[16] for the editorial office.

Component 3 comprises the daily production processes and practices through which the "template" is implemented. This is the "hands-on" level, where the concrete decisions, such as considering how the communicative means (entertaining, informative, persuasive and/or commenting) are achieved to meet the purpose of the publisher, probable contradictory aims (of editorial, advertising and circulation departments, etc.) are negotiated, and the interviews, writing, editing, and layout design are created. Contrary to the stable and formalized Component 2, the daily practices of the editorial staff may vary in terms of which journalist is assigned to write a particular article, and how the gathering of information is conducted and also should vary (for instance, with respect to topics, viewpoints, and interviewees) to sustain the readers' interest and thus ensure their loyalty to the particular media product.

---

16 Helle & Töyry (2009) employ the term *story type* (in Finnish *juttutyyppi*). They use it as a broad tool for analyzing and developing journalistic content and editorial processes. It is determined not only by a designated *article type* (news, profile, investigative reporting, etc.), but also the visual design both within the scope of a single article and the structure of a publication as a whole. (see also Töyry et al 2008.) However, because the term is not yet firmly established outside the Finnish mediascape, in this paper I employ the term *article type* in its traditional meaning, as it serves my needs better.

From verbatim quoting to substantial modifications

The first subsection examines cases that contain a quotation that is the closest to verbatim quoting in my collection. Subsequently, cases will be presented that contain discrepancies between the original and final discourses on two levels, one linguistic and the other textual. The third subsection will focus on one particular strategy for making quotations: when the journalist's words in the interview have been quoted as the interviewee's own words in the article. Finally, I will analyze the manner in which the interactional nature of an interview is "monologized" into written quotation. I will also analyze the way in which the manner of documenting an interview (for example, note-taking by hand versus tape-recording) influences the formulation of quotes.

In every subsection I will present either one or two data examples. These have been selected to be not only representative examples of the phenomenon under examination, but also to be representative examples of the data. At the beginning of every subsection, I will analyze the (possible) modifications that have been made when the discourse has been transferred from an original context to the final one. I will then propose reasons for these modifications drawn on stimulated recall sessions and relate these reasons to the notion of media concept.

Verbatim quoting

This subsection focuses on the occurrence of verbatim quoting in my data. Example (1) is from a prominent Finnish newspaper, and the interviewee in this article is the President of Finland, Sauli Niinistö.[17] This interview was conducted on a one-on-one basis and the topic referred to as the *child issue* with Russia was a current topic at that time.[18] The original interview consisted of three questions that were asked and answered one-by-one. Before posing her questions, the journalist summarized the situation: that Russia would impose an embargo against Finland if the country did not agree to make a bilateral child agreement with Russia. The first question-answer sequence (ex. 1a) concerned the president's response to the Russian government on the issue.

Example (1a) [Child Agreement, transcript, IN = President of Finland Sauli Niinistö]

01   JO: ((...)) miten vakavana asiana pidätte tätä ja
           ((...)) how serious do you consider this matter to be and

02   miten aiotte vastata tähän asiaan
           how are you going to respond to this matter

---

17 In this example I mention the identity of the interviewee as an exception, because it is essential for my analysis. However, this does not put the anonymity of the journalist at risk.

18 The "child issue" was an accusation made by Russia against Finland in the autumn of 2012 regarding the treatment of Russian citizens in Finland.

03 IN: no minun tehtäväni ei ole vastata
          well it is not my role to answer

04   vaan päinvastoin (2.0) öö me olemme öö
          but on the contrary (2.0) um we have um

05   ulkoministeri Lavrovin vierailun yhteydessä (.)
          during the visit of Foreign Minister Lavrov (.)

06   keskustelleet (.) siitä (.) Venäjän ehdotuksesta ja
          discussed (.) this (.) Russia's proposal and

07   ne olisivat tällaisen komission kannalla (.)
          they would be in favor of this kind of commission (.)

08   <meidän> ehdotuksemme on ollut että (.) viranomaiset harrastavat
          our proposal has been that (.) the authorities engage in

09   mahdollisimman pitkälle menevää yhteistyötä (.)
          as extensive cooperation as possible (.)

10   <ja muuten> (.) juuri viime viikolla
          and by the way (.) just last week

11   ennen tähän- tämän kohun nousua (.) Suomesta (.)
          before there- this issue came up (.) Finland (.)

12   lähetettiinkin (.) tällainen yhteyshenkilö (.)
          sent (.) this type of contact person (.)

13   tiedosto Venäjän viranomaisille (.)
          file to the Russian authorities (.)

14 JO: selvä
          right

Example (1b) [Child Agreement, published]

(…). Miten vakavana asiaa pidätte ja mitä siihen vastaatte Astahoville?
"Minun tehtäväni ei ole vastata. Päinvastoin, olemme ulkoministeri (Sergei) Lavrovin vierailun yhteydessä keskustelleet Venäjän ehdotuksesta, jossa he olisivat tällaisen komission kannalla. Meidän ehdotuksemme on ollut, että viranomaiset harrastavat mahdollisimman pitkälle menevää yhteistyötä. Muuten viime viikolla juuri ennen tämän kohun nousua Suomesta lähetettiin tällainen yhteyshenkilötiedosto Venäjän viranomaisille."

(…). How serious do you consider the matter to be and what are you going to answer to Astahov?
"It is not my role to answer. On the contrary, during the visit of Foreign Minister (Sergei) Lavrov, we have discussed Russia's proposal in which they would be in favor

of this kind of commission. Our proposal has been that the authorities engage in as extensive cooperation as possible. By the way, last week, just before this issue came up, Finland sent this type of contact person file to the Russian authorities."

The entire interview proceeded smoothly and lasted less than two minutes. The questions had been carefully planned in advance, and the published article retains the same question-answer-structure. In addition, both the questions and the answers are presented in the article.[19]

At first glance, the published quotation seems highly faithful to the original utterance. The linguistic form is predominantly verbatim, and the uniformity of the situational meaning is also preserved, with the discourse being an answer to (nearly) the same question both in the interview and in the article. A facile explanation for the "directness" is the status of the speaker – who would dare to alter the speech of the president (see, e.g., Davis 1985: 47; Bell 1991: 205; Satoh 2001: 189). I will argue, however, that this is not the primary reason for the directness of this quotation. Let us now focus on this quotation in more detail.

Perhaps the most conspicuous differences pertain to the rhythm of the discourses. The Finnish president had pauses and twice a quiet *öö* 'um' sound (line 4) that occurred between his words, but these features have not been preserved in the quotation. This solution is predictable and obvious because language features of this type are almost always ignored in published texts. Moreover, there are few established marking conventions for these language features in journalistic publications. Some other alterations have also been made in the quoted passage, as demonstrated in the following extracts i–iv (taken from example 1):

Table 1. Comparative analysis of interview and published quotations in example (1).

	Interview	Published quotations
(i)	…yhteistyötä (.) <ja muuten> (.) juuri viime viikolla… cooperation (.) <and by the way> (.) just last week	…yhteistyötä. Muuten viime viikolla juuri… cooperation as possible. By the way, last week, just
(ii)	…vastata vaan päinvastoin… to answer but on the contrary	…vastata. Päinvastoin… to answer. On the contrary

[19] However, the questions do not have quotation marks around them, which is a common convention in the written media field. Additionally, it is worth mentioning that the question sequences in the interview actually consisted of three turns: The journalist's question, the interviewee's answer, and the journalist's feedback [line 14: *selvä* 'right']. This three-part exchange is very typical in my first data set (= the recordings of journalistic interviews). However, in journalistic articles, this turn-taking system is simplified by frequently omitting the follow-up, as in example (1), and often the question is likewise left out (Caldas-Coulthard 1993: 199–202; Makkonen-Craig 2014: section 4). Similarly in television news productions, "[a]nswers are routinely divorced from the questions that elicited them" (Ekström 2001: 570).

| (iii) | ... (.) Venäjän ehdotuksesta ja ne olisivat... *Russia's proposal and they would be* | ...Venäjän ehdotuksesta, jossa he olisivat... *Russia's proposal in which they would be* |
| (iv) | ...ennen tähän- tämän kohun... *before there- this issue* | ...ennen tämän kohun... *before this issue* |

In (i), a change occurs in the word order (the place of *juuri*, 'just,'). Additionally, the connectives *ja* 'and' in (i) and *vaan* 'but' in (ii) have been omitted from the published quotations, and instead, a sentence boundary has been inserted. The syntax of spoken language differs from the syntax of written language, and the connectives and other similar features are also used differently in speech than in writing: For example, spoken language frequently uses connectives to join utterances solely to create a link between utterances on a pragmatic basis (e.g., Laury 2008). By deleting these speech-like features in the published quotations, the utterances resemble the standard written language more closely, and this reaffirms the formal register pursued in the article. Similarly, in (iii), the connective *ja* 'and' has been replaced by a more explicitly subordinating connective *jossa*, 'in which.' The writing here needs to be more linearly explicit, because the information structure of written discourse must be marked by grammatical means, whereas spoken discourse can also utilize prosody and paralinguistic means (Biber 1988: 38).

Another alteration in (iii) worth mentioning is the replacing of the personal pronoun *ne* 'they' with *he* 'they' in the quotation. According to the norms of Standard Finnish, the third-person pronouns *hän* 's/he' and *he* 'they' are the only accepted pronouns to refer to humans. However, in colloquial Finnish, the demonstrative pronouns *se* 'it' and *ne* 'they' are typically used for third-person human reference. In this light, the president's choice of pronoun would have created a strong impression of informality in the written quotation. Especially in this type of "fact-based" news article, the pronoun *ne* would be startling and draw attention to irrelevant associations, whereas in some other article type, such as *a profile article*, these types of word choices could serve a characterizing function (see Haapanen 2011: 78–79). In a similar manner, the president's self-correction in (iv) has been "cleaned up." Although self-repairs are common and inconspicuous in spoken interaction, they are eye-catching and very distinctive in written formats.

I propose that the main reason for the almost verbatim representation of the discourse in example (1) is not the respectful attitude towards the person quoted (although naturally, the premise of journalists is to respect their interviewees), but that the president was well prepared to respond to questions on a current topic, something I also observed while working as a press officer in the Office of the President at the time of this interview. In other words, the president had already generally formulated his answers prior to the interview. Due to this, his utterances – even though not written down – sound rather formal and thus meet the intended linguistic formality of quotations in this type of news article. [20]

In terms of the media concept, the planning and conducting of the interview as well as the writing of the article in example (1) belong to Component 3 (= the daily production processes and practices). However, the simple and straightforward course of the concrete production process was due to the fact that the interview and the intended linguistic formality of the article – the "template" of Component 2 (= the architecture of the whole) – happened to correspond to each other. However, the spoken-like linkage between clauses in extract (iii), the choice of a pronoun in (iii), and the self-correction in (iv) do not fit that frame, and thus they have been "amended."

In this particular case, the quotations were extremely verbatim apart from some minor modifications. In other words, example (1b) is a *direct quotation* in the manner prescribed by the journalistic field. In this light, it is interesting that only few quotations in my data are as close to the spoken utterance in the interview as this example. Additionally, it is important to note that in many cases, the modifications made to one quotation vary extensively. In other words, some part of the quotation can be verbatim, whereas another part can be substantially modified.

Discrepancies in linguistic composition

This subsection addresses the differences in the data between the original and the final discourses in terms of linguistic features. I illustrate this variation with example (2) from an interview and a broad profile article based on it, published in a culture-oriented magazine. The interviewee is a Finnish actress who describes her first impressions of a large film studio.

Example (2a) [Film Studio, transcript] (IN=Interviewee / JO=Journalist.)

```
01   IN:  (.) kiehtoo et on ne samat (.)
          (.) it's fascinating that there are the same (.)

02        jättimäiset studiorakennukset mihin rakennetaan [sit sisälle
          gigantic studio buildings where they build       [then inside

03   JO:                                                  [mm mm
                                                          [mm mm

04   IN:  kokonaiset metsät  [ja
          whole forests      [and

05   JO:                     [joo
                             [yeah
```

[20] I also have a second interview with President Niinistö in my data. For this interview, he did not have the opportunity to prepare for the topic and questions, and the "unscriptedness" results in some complexity in his utterances. As a consequence, the linguistic form of the quotations was modified more on this occasion.

06 IN: ja (.) kylät
        and (.) villages

07 JO: ((naurua))
        ((laughter))

08 IN: jotka £sit   [poltetaan
        that are £then [burned down

09 JO: [((naurua))
                      [((laughter))

10 IN: nii oli ihan sellai£ pyörryttävää et yhtäkkii menee (.)
        so that it was kinda like£ too much that all of a sudden ((you)) go ((there)) (.)

11   kun siel oli se kyläkin joka oli semmonen? (.)
        because there's this village, which was like (.)

12   <mitä mä sanoisin (.) minkä torin kokone se ois>
        well, how would I put it (.) what size of market place it would be

13   >varmaan tommonen< (.) ää (.) Hietsun kirppiksen [kokonen alue (.)
        probably like maybe (.) um (.) an area the size of the Hietsu flea market

14 JO: [joo joo
                                                        yeah yeah

15 IN: se oltiin niinku (.) öö (.) ulkopuolelta se nätti
        it had been like (.) um (.) from the outside it looked

16   vaan sellaselt laudotetulta alueelta? (.) ja sit kun sinne astuu sisään (.)
        only like a boarded up area (.) and then when you go in (.)

17   niin siellä oli kokonainen semmone
        then there was like a whole

18 JO: joo
        yeah

19 IN: kylä (.) ties miltä luvulta
        a village (.) who knows from what period

20 JO: ((naurua))
        ((laughter))

21 IN: koska se oli vähän niinku luvuton
        because it was a little like out of no period

22 JO: joo
        yeah

23   IN: toi (.) aikakausi (.) nii sitä et (.) et (.) et (.)
            that (.) era (.) so that (.) that (.) that (.)

24   joo et on se noin kivaa kun on rahaa ((nauraen puhuttu))
            yeah so it's real nice when you have money ((spoken with laughter))

25   JO: ((naurua))
            ((laughter))

26   IN: tehä (.) niinku ihan mitä vaan että (.)
            to do (.) like whatever that (.)

Based on the interview above, the journalist produced the following quotation.

Example (2b) [Film Studio, published]

Ensimmäiset päivät studiolla olivat huikeita.
"Kun näki ne jättimäiset rakennukset ja niiden sisällä kulisseiksi rakennetut kokonaiset kylät ja metsät, jotka lopuksi poltetaan, siinä mietti, että kiva kun on niin paljon rahaa, että voi tehdä mitä vaan. Siellä oli Hietsun kirppiksen kokoinen kylä."

The first days at the studio were fantastic.
"When you saw those gigantic buildings and inside of them entire villages and forests built as sets, which are in the end burned down, you were thinking that it's great to have so much money that you can do whatever you want. There was a village the size of the Hietsu flea market."

The interview and the quotation display substantial discrepancies, as I will explain later in this subsection. In other words, the original discourse has been modified extensively during the quotation-making process. In terms of the media concept, these concrete acts belong to Component 3, the daily production process comprising the planning and conducting of the interview and the writing of the article. Nonetheless, it is evident that there are also other factors governing these concrete processes.

As I suggested when analyzing example (1) [Child Agreement], the need to modify the quotation depends on the difference between the original discourse and the intended final discourse. In example (1), these two discourses mainly coincided, but in example (2), it is obvious that these two "poles" are rather far apart. Next, I will present some findings concerning the linguistic differences between spoken utterances and written quotations and discuss further what causes this difference.

The interview in example (2) was not conducted in a formal style. According to the SR, the journalist had not prepared for the interview by formulating specific questions beforehand, but had only written down some general themes to cover. As a result, the interview became very "interactional", in that the journalist and the interviewee cooperated in organizing the flow and structure of the interview. The text analysis and the SR also confirmed that the interviewee's speech was exceedingly spontaneous and impromptu and therefore it was replete with repetitions, run-on sentences, hesitations, self-repairs, and other features of talk-in-interaction. Furthermore, during the interview, the interviewee's pronunciation of the words was truncated, which is typical of spoken language. All this resulted in a need for the journalist to make major alterations to the linguistic form of the quoted text. A few examples from the differences in the interview and published quotations are the following:

Table 2. Comparative analysis of interview and published quotations in example (2).

	Interview	Published quotations
(i)	...(.) kiehtoo et on ne samat (.) jättimäiset studiorakennukset mihin rakennetaan sit sisälle kokonaiset metsät ja ja (.) kylät... *(.) it's fascinating that there are the same (.) gigantic studio buildings where they build then inside whole forests and and (.) villages*	Kun näki ne jättimäiset rakennukset ja niiden sisällä kulisseiksi rakennetut kokonaiset kylät ja metsät,... *When you saw those gigantic buildings and inside of them entire villages and forests built as sets*
(ii)	...kokone... *the size of*	...kokoinen...
(iii)	...siel... *there*	...siellä...
(iv)	...(.) kun siel oli se kyläkin joka oli semmonen? (.) <mitä mä sanoisin (.) minkä torin kokone se ois> >varmaan tommonen< (.) ää (.) Hietsun kirppiksen kokonen alue (.)... *because there's this village, which was like (.) <well, how would I put it (.) what size of market place it would be> >probably like maybe< (.) um (.) an area the size of the Hietsu flea market*	...Siellä oli Hietsun kirppiksen kokoinen kylä. *There was a village the size of the Hietsu flea market.*

The syntax in (i) has been reconstructed substantially, and the phonetic form of the words in (ii) and (iii), was supplemented in the text even though this is a relatively informal article type.

In addition to the requirements of the intended register, the SRs I conducted serve as evidence that the article must function as an independent, dramaturgically consistent story, not as an account of the course of the journalistic interview. As a consequence, the original discourse requires reorganizing and editing in order to be shaped as coherent and concise quotations that can be positioned in a logical relationship with their surrounding text. One obvious example of this process is presented in (iv), where the lengthy speculation about an appropriate comparison to illustrate the size of the set is represented in the quotation by one clause only. In addition to being a content-driven summary of the interviewee's talk, the clause is also placed at the end of the quotation. This transfer could be explained by observing that the core of the utterance has been formulated in a simpler form in order for the quotation to serve the objectives that were established for the overarching plot of the article (cf. Haapanen in press 2017).

When quoting, one needs to intentionally extract the selected information from the conversation and then edit it into a quotation. In this particular case, the quoted discourse needed to be shaped into a forward-oriented response to the prior text. This prior text presented an assertion, and the quotation offered an illustration for it. When examining this quotation, an additional influence on the "planting" of the quotation is the abbreviation of *studiorakennukset*, 'studio buildings', into *rakennukset*, 'buildings'; since the text prior to the quotation has already established the context for the quotation – *Ensimmäiset päivät studiolla olivat huikeita*, 'The first days at the studio were fantastic' –, it would be, according to the SR, a waste of space, and would also be tautological to repeat the word *studio*, '(film) studio.'

Thus far, taking into consideration the media concept, the immediate motives for the modifications I have presented above can be explained in terms of Components 2 and 3. These pertain to the article's formal requirements and the concrete composition process (planning, interviewing, and writing), respectively. Nevertheless, the data clearly suggest that extensive modification of the text is not solely related, on the one hand, to the differences between spoken and written discourse and the original and intended register (for example, standard / colloquial language), and on the other hand, to dramaturgy. Let us now turn to the analysis of some linguistic features that support the existence of Component 1.

Despite the extensive standardization of the quoted discourse described above, the intended article type may evidently contain – or even require – some spoken-like features. For example, apart from the last clause, the whole quotation consists of one long clause complex.[21] In addition, there is the speech-like spelling *mitä vaan*, 'whatever,' (*mitä vain*, in standard language), a lexical colloquialism *kirppis*, 'flea market,' (*kirpputori*, in standard language), a casual word *kiva*, 'nice,' and a colloquial nickname, *Hietsu* (more formally the name would be *Hietalahti*). The SR revealed that the journalist was utilizing these spoken-like features to create an illusion of spoken language in the text, although the text is still far removed from the original spoken discourse behind the quotation. My position is that this illusion-making works because readers have "learned," for example, from fiction, an inaccurate conception of what spoken discourse looks like in its written representation (cf. Haviland 1996: 49). This conception makes it difficult for the average reader to decipher informal face-to-face

---

21 Although the clause chains that occur in spoken language may indeed be rather lengthy (see Auer 1992), recursion (successive embedding) – as in the quotation in question (ex. 2b) – appears to be strictly limited (Laury & Ono 2010). Thus, the quotation is not to present a *realistic* representation of spoken language, but to create an *illusion* of it.

interaction as described in detail by linguists. This needs to be taken into consideration as a part of the societal context in which all newspapers and magazines are produced. In the modelling of the media concept, the societal context belongs to Component 1. In practical terms, if a journalist intends to create an illusion of spoken language, she would paradoxically achieve better results by not quoting verbatim, but rather by selecting only some particular vernacular features to achieve the desired impression (for similar observations about fiction, see Koivisto & Nykänen 2013; Tiittula & Nuolijärvi 2013; Leech & Short 2007). One illustration of this is that in one of my data interviews, the interviewee stated *nätti ja söötti*, 'pretty and cute,' words which also appeared in a journalist's notebook. However, the published story read *kaunis ja söötti*, 'beautiful and cute'. In the SR, the journalist explained that in her opinion, replicating both vernacular words would have created "a too strong impression of spoken language."

I will discuss one additional linguistic feature in terms of Component 1 of the media concept. Let us return to the words *Hietsun kirppis*, 'the Hietsu [Hietalahti] flea market,'[22] in example (2). The use of the nickname indicates the colloquial register of the article. Furthermore, using the proper name, and especially the nickname, of a specific district in downtown Helsinki, is a decision that may reflect the values and ideologies of this particular publication. The majority of people living in the Helsinki metropolitan area undoubtedly recognize the nickname, whereas it is probably less familiar to people who live in other areas of Finland. Moreover, out of those people who are familiar with the nickname, only some have actually visited the square where *Hietsun kirppis* is located. The usage of this specific word can therefore be interpreted as reflecting a type of arrogance, or at least a metropolitan-centric outlook. This word choice is likely to be intentional, because the magazine in which the article was published is known for its thorough editing culture. Owing to these circumstances, the linguistic composition of the original discourse has been so substantially modified that this particular word could also have been changed if so desired. As demonstrated above, the analysis of the linguistic choices in quotations (Component 3) can lead to the more foundational factors that affect the process of creating quotations (Component 1). Next, I will present some further findings that belong to Component 1 of the media concept.

Most of the informant-journalists claimed in their SRs that the values and purpose of the target publication affect not only the choice of the article type, the topic, and the interviewee but also whether or not the article includes quotations, what the target tone (such as fact-oriented/lively/striking) and the target register (standard / colloquial language) are, and the degree to which quotations are modified (the number of spoken-like syntactic structures, words, or spellings) (for example, see [I] and [II] in the appendix). Additionally, acknowledging the audience arose several times as a justification for modifications: "You know that people talk in a way that

---

22 *Hietsun kirppis*, 'the Hietsu flea market' is rather well-known among people living in the Helsinki metropolitan area.

you understand when you speak with them, but then if you write that down, it can no longer be understood by anyone who wasn't present at the time; so you have to write it so that the reader can understand what's being said. And that's the main starting point, to ensure that the reader understands." ([III] in the appendix.)

Overall, the aspects belonging to Component 1 were rarely mentioned in the SRs. My assumption regarding this is that the publisher's values and purpose as well as the journalistic culture are learned through actual work on the one hand, and as tacit information on the other. In other words, they are institutionalized into the activities one normally performs unconsciously as a member of a social group such as an editorial staff (Perrin 2013b: 55). Therefore, the matters belonging to Component 1 are difficult for the journalist to verbalize for the researcher. As one informant-journalist described in the SR: "Every publication or magazine has its own nature ((…)). You know it and you tune into it, but it's hard to conceptualize it, or to break it down to something like five bullet points." ([IV] in the appendix). (See also Helle & Töyry 2009: 503.) In addition, some factors[23] may be so obvious that the informant-journalists did not even mention them, especially because they were aware of my own background as a journalist.

To summarize my findings thus far, Component 1, which encompasses the values and purpose of the publisher, the needs of the audience, as well as the journalistic and societal context, creates the basis for Component 2 by first setting the goals for a particular article (ex. 1: informative *news article* versus ex. 2: entertaining *profile article*), and then by allowing these goals to affect the article's determined length, structure, and style (ex. 1: compact, question-answer organization, standard language, versus ex. 2: broad, dramaturgically independent, colloquial features). Component 2 functions as a motive for the modifications that are performed during the daily production processes that comprise Component 3. In other words, these motives steer the planning of the interview (ex. 1: fixed questions, versus ex. 2: general themes), its conduct (ex. 1: journalist-driven, versus ex. 2: interactional), and the concrete writing-process (the functions, length, frequency, tone, and register of quotations) (cf. Kroon Lundell & Ekström 2010).

Discrepancies in textual composition

As mentioned in the previous subsection, some words, phrases, and clauses can be omitted from quoted discourse. Even so, it is sometimes not sensible to speak of omission because a quotation can be composed of two or more separate segments of discourse clearly lifted from different parts of an interview. In this subsection, I will first analyze the relationship between the original and final discourse from the textual point of view. I will then proceed to highlight a particular aspect in creating quotations, how a journalist's utterances are transferred to an interviewee's quote.

---

23 For instance, the basic structure of the journalistic text: headline + standfirst / subhead + text body.

The next data excerpt, example (3), is from the news section of a prominent Finnish newspaper. This article concerns a criticism that was expressed towards the social services of a Finnish municipality. The focus of the criticism is the expense caused by the temporary lodging that was purchased from a certain private company.

Example (3b) [Housing, published]

Jatkuvat asumisjärjestelyt eivät kuuluisi sosiaalityöntekijöille, HAASTATELTAVA huomauttaa.
"Se on muusta ihmisten tukemisesta pois. Virastoa on syyllistetty, mutta olemme toimineet lakiin perustuen ja ihmisiä heitteille jättämättä."

Constantly spending time on arranging housing isn't really part of the social worker's work, THE INTERVIEWEE points out.
"It is time away from other kinds of support for people. The office is being blamed, but we have acted according to the law and without abandoning people."

The published quotation comprises two segments of discourse. These segments are from different parts of the interview.

Example (3a) [Housing, transcript]

01   JO: tarkoittaako se sitä että kun te joudutte hoitamaan (.)
         does this mean that when you have to take care of (.)

02   tämmöstä määrää niinku asumisongelmia
         so many of these, like, housing problems

03   niin se on sitten <resursseista> sitten pois jostain muualta?
         so it is then taken from other resources, from somewhere else

04   IN: on (.)
         yes (.)

[17 minutes omitted. At the end of the omitted sequence, immediately before line 5, the journalist and the interviewee have concluded that the problems in emergency housing should be solved by politicians, not by the social work sector. The journalist and the interviewee agree that this problem is difficult, but they look forward to the public discussion that might arise after this news article is published. At this point, there is a prolonged pause.]

05   (3.0)

06   IN: .hh niin sen mä niinku tiedän että et-
         .hh the thing I sort of know is that

07   meitä on syyllistetty tässä (1.5) mutta
         we have been blamed for (1.5) but

08 JO: mm
       mm

09 IN: haluan nyt puolustautua että (.)
       I now want point out in our defense that (.)

10   olemme tehneet sen niinkun (.)
        we have done it like (.)

11   lakiin perustuen ja ihmisiä heitteille jättämättä.
        according to the law and without abandoning people

12 JO: mm
       mm

The two segments of discourse (lines 1–4 and 5–12) that were used to construct the quotation were actually stated seventeen minutes apart. The SR indicated that the reasons for this integration originated from Component 2 of the media concept, which relates to the required length, compactness, and storyline of the article (see [V] in the appendix). Many informant-journalists raised the same point regarding the integration of extended or multiple segments of discourse into a single quotation. They supported this practice if it did not alter meaning. Strictly speaking, it is impossible to achieve an equivalence of the meanings. As stated by Linell (1998a), when the context changes, the meaning will change as well. Nevertheless, it is rational to adopt a more practical position on the issue – this practical orientation is also the mindset of journalists in their everyday work.

To illustrate the journalists' practices, let us compare the meanings of examples (3a) and (3b). The published quotation begins with *Se on muusta ihmisten tukemisesta pois* 'It is time away from other kinds of support for people.' The first word of the quotation, the pronoun *se* 'it,' has the same referent as *jatkuvat asumisjärjestelyt* 'constantly spending time on arranging housing,' which is placed in the text before the quotation. During the interview, the interlocutors have discussed "the resources" (line 3) and "taking care of housing problems" (lines 1–2). Although the interview and the article do not have the same wording, the meaning can be assessed to be moderately equivalent. Let us move then to the second sentence of the quotation: Whereas it is rather verbatim from the linguistic point of view, the perception changes when we focus on the meaning. The second sentence begins with the clause *Virastoa on syyllistetty* 'The office has been blamed.' The cause for this blame has not been exposed, but due to the adjacency of the two sentences comprising the quotation, the primary reading is that the cause would be *jatkuvat asumisjärjestelyt* 'constantly spending time on arranging housing'. However, the quoted discourse is decontextualized from the end of the interview and the actual referent is (more or less) *hätämajoituksen ostaminen yksityiseltä palveluntarjoajalta* 'the purchase of emergency housing from the private service provider' (for a longer version of example 3, see Haapanen 2016a: 231–234). Although the difference between the meaning of the original and the final discourse is rather minor and subtle, it nonetheless exists. In my data, the same observation often applies to cases where the quotation is constructed from several different parts of the interview.

However, if we shift the orientation so that we perceive the term *meaning* from the perspective of social actions, the relation between the original and the final discourse is direct: During lines 5–12 and immediately before them at the end of the omitted sequence in example (3a), several lingering turns and pauses have occurred as well as "reinvocations of the reason for initiating the conversation," which indicate that the interlocutors are preparing to close the conversation (Schegloff & Sacks 1973: 90–91). The sequence occurred during the last minutes of the 35-minute interview. Respectively, the quotation based on this sequence finished the article.

Next I will highlight one particularity of making quotations: the manner in which discourse produced by the journalist in the interview is attributed to the interviewee through quoting. The first clause of the quotation in example (3) (*Se on muusta ihmisten tukemisesta pois* 'It is time away from other kinds of support for people') is attributed to the interviewee, although the linguistic form and content is mainly based on the utterance produced by the journalist herself. In other words, in the published article, the journalist's question (lines 1–3) is edited into a declarative sentence and planted into the mouth of the interviewee.

An analysis of the original and the final discourse does not lead us further than that, but utilizing the SR allows us entry to behind the scenes.

The journalist explained in the SR that she had not prepared all of the questions in advance, but formulated them – especially the exact wording – during the interview (see [VI] in the appendix). This is related to Component 2 of the media concept. First, the article type and the topic of the article in the making on the one hand, and the journalist's workload on the other, steer the need for sufficient preparedness. Second, the SR data indicate that when a journalist writes an article for the written media, it is possible and – at least tacitly – acceptable to attribute the journalist's discourse to that of the interviewee.[24]

Example (4) is further evidence of the same phenomenon and it originates from an interview for an article in a customer magazine (4a). The interviewee is the director of a company that manufactures high technology devices.

Example (4a) [Market, transcript]

01 JO: teidän asiakkaat ni siis ne on sairaaloita ja (.) vastaavia
         your customers then they are like hospitals (.) and such

02 IN: ne on sairaaloit joo
         they are hospitals, yeah

[24] The data in this paper contain three similar cases. This case was from a newspaper, while the other two were published in a magazine and in a business-to-customer-magazine. The last instance will be analyzed as example (4) below.

03 JO: joo (.) mut alust asti on siis ollu niinku selkeet et (.)
         yeah (.) but from the beginning it has been kinda clear that (.)

04   se on ulkomaille myös suuntautuvaa
         it's also directed abroad

05 IN: joo
         yeah

06 JO: tai siis että (.) markkinana on koko maailma (.) eiks näin
         I mean (.) the whole world is the market (.) isn't it

07 IN: kyllä joo joo (.)
         yes, yes that's right (.)

Based on the conversation above, the journalist composed the following quotation (ex. 4b), which is attributed entirely to the interviewee:

Example (4b) [Market, published]

"Olemme tähdänneet kansainvälisille markkinoille alusta alkaen, ja asiakkaitamme ovat sairaalat eri puolilla maailmaa. Tähän mennessä olemme toimittaneet noin pari sataa laitetta, joista kotimaahan on mennyt vain puolenkymmentä", HAASTATELTAVA kertoo.

"We have targeted international markets from the beginning, and have hospitals from around the world as our customers. So far, we have delivered about two hundred devices, of which only half a dozen have been sold in this country," THE INTERVIEWEE says.

As in example (3), the quotation in example (4) is based predominantly on what the journalist herself said (lines 1, 3–4, 6). The interviewee confirmed the information (*ne on sairaaloit joo*, 'they are hospitals, yeah' [line 2]; *joo*, 'yeah' [line 5]; *kyllä joo joo*, 'yes, yes that's right' [line 7]). Once again, the SR provides further evidence for this analysis.

The SR disclosed that the journalist's original article assignment defined "internationalization" as the main topic of the article. In other words, the company and its director were selected because the magazine wanted to highlight the international markets of the company. When the journalist called the interviewee for the first time, the journalist told her that the central point of the article would be the international markets of the company. In the actual interview, the journalist wanted to introduce this main topic to the discussion to verify that her information was correct and to elicit more information on it. Nevertheless, as they had already discussed that specific topic – internationalization – over the phone, there was no need to ask any explicit questions related to it during the interview. Finally, when the journalist was writing her article, she wanted to "let the interviewee say the main point" ([VII] in the appendix), even though the quoted utterance was never actually uttered during the interview. To summarize, the purpose and needs of the publication prompted the journalist to use the quote as a text-linguistic device so as to formulate the interviewee's standpoint, rather than quoting it per se. Regarding the media concept, the intended content and outline of the article (Component 2) govern the journalist's quoting processes (Component 3).

In the stimulated recall sessions, both journalists (of ex. 3 and ex. 4) remarked on the questionable nature of the work practice discussed: "When you haven't prepped all the questions beforehand, your own phrasing might be bad, and you'll get a sort of yes-or-no answer. Well, that probably kinda should be written down word for word." "Well, strictly speaking, you probably shouldn't put that as a quote" (see [VI] and [VIII] in the appendix). This is natural, because guidebooks and ethic codes are strictly against this phenomenon, as well as against all types of fabrication of quotations:

Never intentionally misquote (Stein 1995: 241).

Fabricating a direct quote, even from general things that a source has said or from what the source might say if given the chance, is never a good idea (Brooks et al. 2002: 85).

Don't "invent" quotations. Your job is to put your sources on record – not put words into their mouths. If a source refuses or is unable to give you the quote you need, go back for another interview or go to another source. (Ruberg 2005: 122.)

Yet, despite the guidelines and ethic codes, this phenomenon is rather common. This is understandable from the perspective of work practices: If a journalist has prepared sufficiently well, she probably already knows in advance the main points of the interview discussion and introduces them to the discussion herself. The role of the interviewee then becomes affirmative, leading to confirmations such as "yes," or "that's right." However, these short utterances would not make the article sufficiently vital and impressive in their verbatim form (quotations have multiple functions in the narration of an article, see Haapanen 2011). Thus, the apparent contradiction between 'etic' guidance and 'emic' practice clearly necessitates further ethical consideration.

From the perspective of the media concept, this peculiar yet common practice is caused by the predetermined viewpoint of the article (Component 2), which is then reflected in the concrete work processes used in producing the planned article (Component 3). Considering the current journalistic culture (Component 1), this is a somewhat "naturalized" and economic strategy to produce an article for print media.

MONOLOGIZATION OF THE INTERVIEW
This section discuss one special aspect of recontextualization through which the frequent and robust interaction between two (or more) participants in the journalistic interview is eliminated in the articles. In other words, the journalist not only asks the questions, but she also keeps the interview

conversation going and structures it by using frequent response particles and other responsive elements, including gestures and laughing. All this is obscured from the readers through a procedure which I have labeled *monologization*.[25] (On *monologization* in more detail, see Haapanen 2016b.) In this connection, I also focus on the work practices of documenting an interview, because these practices reflect on the process of monologization of the interview.

First, due to "monologization," the sequential positioning of the quoted text in the final discourse does not match its positioning in the original discourse. For example, from the typical three-part structure of an interview (the journalist's question, the interviewee's answer, the journalist's feedback), only the answer is typically exposed in the article. This results in the fact that quoted discourse which originally was a response to a question often appears to be expressed as if it had been stated on the interviewee's own initiative (similarly in television news production, see Ekström 2001: 571). Yet, this type of *sequential repositioning* is often far more extensive than merely a concealment of the responsiveness of a quoted discourse, as shown in my data.

Example (5a) [Restriction] is an excerpt from an interview for a business magazine that deals with the interviewee's career and the company. The interviewee was a non-native Finnish speaker and consequently she not only had a foreign accent (not indicated in the transcript), but she also made frequent errors in inflection and word choice. These features were cleaned up in the quotations, and the SR confirmed that the journalist did not even consider quoting the non-native-like Finnish verbatim in the article. According to the media concept, it is not common in the current journalistic culture (Component 1) to replicate defective language skills; this can be done only with a firm justification from the viewpoint of the article (Component 2), as stated in the SR (see [IX] in the appendix). In addition to influencing linguistic modifications discussed in the previous subsections, the non-native delivery likewise highly influences the structure of the interview and, thus, the practice of quoting.

Prior to the transcribed excerpt in example (5a) below, the journalist and the interviewee discussed the financial turnover of the company. The interviewee stated that the turnover has not been large yet.

Example (5a) [Restriction, transcript] [26]

01   IN: mutta mä halusin niinkun (.) ensi vuonna mä piti (.)
           but I kinda wanted that like (.) next year I was going to (.)

---

25 The everyday perception of the words *dialogue* and *monologue* well reflects the contrast between a journalistic interview as a discourse with relatively frequent turn-taking by two (or more) participants, and a quotation as a discourse by a single language user.
26 Erroneous inflections occur throughout the interviewee's utterances. Yet these inflections have not been replicated in the translation.

```
02          lopetta tämä rajoitus (.) oma        [rajoitus
            end this restriction (.) my own      [restriction

03   JO:                                         [nii (.) et (.)
                                                 [yeah (.) that (.)

04          ett sä voisit kasvaaki vai                       [sitäksä tarkotat joo
            that you could also grow ((your business)) or    [is that what you mean yes

05   IN:                                                     [joo joo
                                                             [yes yes

06   IN:    ja nimen[omaan nyt-
            and right now-

07   JO:            [nii et se on ollut sun päässä  [oleva rajoitus
                    [so that it has been in your head [the restriction

08   IN:                                            [joo
                                                    [yes

09          se on mun päässä (.) mä tiedän mä tiedän (.)
            it's in my head (.) I know I know (.)
```

The SR established that in this particular excerpt, it was difficult for the journalist to understand what the interviewee meant. But as is characteristic of a face-to-face conversation, the journalist could immediately check whether or not she had understood correctly. She wanted to affirm that *tämä rajoitus* 'this restriction' referred to some aspect that prevented the interviewee from expanding her business (line 4). The interviewee confirmed this assumption (line 5). The journalist then posed another question concerning whether she had inferred correctly that the obstacle for expansion was of a mental nature (line 7), and received another affirmative answer (lines 8–9). To summarize, the structure of the interview is highly interactional.

Based on these negotiations over meanings, the journalist wrote the following excerpt:

Example (5b) [Restriction, published]

Ensi vuonna HAASTATELTAVAN tavoite on kasvattaa yritystä. Tähän asti hän on tyytynyt elättämään itsensä. "Mielessäni on ollut este kasvulle, mutta nyt on aika poistaa se."

Next year the goal of THE INTERVIEWEE is to grow her business. Until now, she has been content to be able to provide for herself. "There has been an obstacle to growing in my mind, but now is the time to remove it."

The interactive negotiation is concealed from the reader of the published quotation. Rather than repeat the turn-taking verbatim, the journalist corrects the interviewee's language and presents *her own* formulation of the jointly produced understanding. Yet according to the informant-journalist in the SR, the interviewee did not object to the use of quotation on reading the article prior to its publication.

Next, I will analyze how the manner of documenting an interview influences monologization. The notebook of the journalist (ex. 5c) reveals that the interaction was already filtered out during the interviewing situation in real time. Picture 1 is an image from the notebook.

Picture 1. [Example (5c), Restriction, notebook]

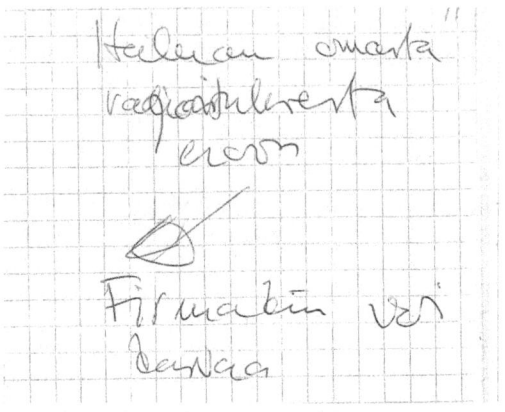

Haluan omasta rajoituksesta eroon
↓
Firmakin voi kasvaa

I want to end my own restriction
↓
The company can also grow

As picture 1 indicates, the interactional nature of the interview is no longer visible in the notebook. In other words, from those few words (and one arrow) written in the notebook, it is unclear which of the words were originally uttered by the journalist and how the turn-taking unfolded.

Because the method of documenting an interview (such as tape-recording, note-taking, and memory) is one of the essential variables in journalistic work practices, I will discuss these methods in detail from the perspective of quoting. I will focus on two somewhat opposite documentation practices that were used by the journalists in example (2) [Film Studio] and example (5) [Restriction]. As we have seen, extensive editing of the quoted discourse was required in both cases.

In example (2) the journalist tape-recorded the interview and then roughly transcribed it from beginning to end. With this method, the most extensive modifying process took place when the journalist sketched and wrote the article based on her transcription. In example (5), however, the journalist documented the interview only by taking notes.[27] In this, as in other cases in my data, *taking notes* seems to necessitate that, first, a journalist demarcates a segment from a longer, conceptually and intentionally continuous and coherent stretch of discourse – fairly forcefully in the case of a talkative interviewee. Then, she writes it down, eliminating, abbreviating, and/or summarizing the original discourse. Thus, a substantial part of the modifying process has already been completed during the interview situation itself and almost in real time, because it is difficult to assume that when the journalist writes her article afterwards based on these few key clauses in her notebook, she cannot – and is not required to – recall the exact turn-taking anymore. To summarize, when documenting an interview by taking notes, the notes – rather than the original discourses – become the basis for the quotations. (See also Haapanen 2016a: 241–244.)

My data also show that journalists base their quotations and articles not only on tape recordings and/or notes, but also on their own memory. This is demonstrated by the following brief example (6) from a newspaper. The interview (ex. 6a) is one of the cases where I have access to the tape-recording that the journalist herself, however, did not use when writing the article (ex. 6b). During this interview, the interviewee stated *eihän se nyt voi sillä lailla loppua että siinä niinkun paha ei saa palkkaansa*, 'it really cannot end in such a way that the evil won't get its pay.'[28] The utterance using this proverb was not written down in the journalist's notebook. Nevertheless, the quotation included the clause *Ja että paha saa palkkansa*, 'And the evil will get its pay.' Thus it would appear that the journalist based the inscription on her memory rather than her notes.

In general, it would appear that while it is relatively easy to recall content, keywords, or proverbs, human memory is an unreliable source for replicating exact wordings (for example, see Clark & Gerrig 1990: 796–797). Additionally, by examining my data from the perspective of work practices, it is evident that the most verbatim quotations in the data (especially when the quotation is longer than only a few words) are based on tape-recordings (on the practice of taking notes, see [X] in the appendix).

The examples above indicate that work practices – such as tape-recording versus note-taking – clearly influence the recontextualization of the interviews in quotation. As a rule, however, the method of documentation

27 I asked the informant-journalists to create articles (both interview and the writing-process) as they would normally do. Some of the informant-journalists were used to taking notes by hand, and did not ordinarily tape-record the interview, but at my request, these informant-journalists made tape-recordings for my use only.
28 The underlined section is an adaption of the Finnish proverb *paha saa palkkansa*. The proverb means that one gets due punishment (lit. *palkka*, 'a pay') for his or her misdeeds. In the quotation based on this utterance, the proverb is in its traditional form. An approximate English gloss of this proverb would be *the chickens come home to roost*.

and the verbatim character of the quotations do not correlate. If the original discourse is radically different from the intended final discourse, substantial modifications are needed, regardless of the method and precision in the documentation of the interview (see also Haapanen 2016a).

In terms of the media concept, the choice of the documentation method is a journalistic tool to perform the journalist's daily production duties (Component 3). On the other hand, the choice of documentation practices also seems to be affected by the workload and time resources of journalists (see [XI] in the appendix), which can be categorized under the division of labor (Component 2), and by the journalistic culture, which represents Component 1 of the media concept. In other words, why would a journalist tape-record and perform the time-consuming and laborious procedure of transcribing, if it is not necessary to produce quotations that follow every detail of the interviewee's speech?

Summary and conclusions

The analysis of published articles, original interviews, and stimulated recalls in my data demonstrates that the relation between an interview and a quotation is highly case-dependent. As a result, it is impossible to predict the form of a quotation merely by reviewing what is stated in the original interview. Conversely, determining what was actually expressed in an interview cannot be inferred from a written quotation.

In some rare instances, the linguistic and textual form of the original discourse remains unchanged in the final discourse. But even then, due to the nature of the oral and written modalities, many aspects of spoken delivery cannot be reproduced in writing. Yet it is far more common that the discourse is modified in one way or another, resulting in deletions, insertions, revisions, and changes in word order. The modifications vary in quantity and quality, and range from word-level changes to substantial alterations of the discourse. Furthermore, journalists can merge texts from different parts of an original discourse into one quotation.

Another common practice is for quotations to be "monologized," where the co-construction (in terms of both form and meaning) of the original discourse between the journalist and the interviewee is reduced to a monologue by the interviewee. In light of journalistic professional guidance, this procedure seems controversial. However, if we disentangle ourselves from the verbatim-oriented position and rethink the phenomenon in a dialogistic theoretical framework (e.g., Linell 2009), the discourse segment in question is a social action. In this social action, a question being responded to by a "yes" makes the constructed meaning a collaborative enterprise. In other words, the "yes" makes the content of the journalist's question something that the interviewee is co-responsible for, and hence it can be attributed to the interviewee in the quoted representation.

In terms of meaning, the same heterogeneity applies to the relation between the original and the final discourses. Thus, it is not unusual for quotations, in their contexts, to be interpreted somewhat differently than the original discourse they were based on.

It is important to note that not only is there extensive variation in the modification of quotations within one article, but there is also a wide range of variation in modifications within one quotation. In other words, some part of the quotation may be verbatim, whereas another part may be a complete rewording.[29] In addition, no single factor (for instance, an article type, a work practice, the topic of the article, or a target medium) seems to determine how a quotation is modified in my data. However, my data set is clearly too small to make any broader conclusions.

The heterogeneity and unpredictability of the quotation-making process raises the question of what accounts for the modifications in quotation-making. First, the main actors who create the article are the journalist and the interviewee. The journalist (and the editorial staff the journalist works with) determines the topic and whom to interview. She then produces the interview situation jointly with the interviewee(s), and exploits the original discourse as source material when writing the article. In the threefold modelling of the media concept, the journalistic work process comprises Component 3, that is, the daily production processes.

Nevertheless, my analysis suggests that a journalist by no means creates an article solely according to her own free will. Instead, she produces the intended article type, which is a predetermined part of the structure of a media product. Additionally, she is unavoidably influenced by her employer's division of labor and the work load caused by it. The article type and the work load constitute what is referred to as the architecture of the whole, which comprises Component 2 of the media concept.

The architecture of the whole does not come into existence spontaneously, but it is a result of the well-thought-out objective of the publisher. When running their businesses, publishers have informative, ideological, financial, and perhaps other goals as well. To attain these goals successfully, the publisher must define the target audience, and determine how to create a permanent relationship with it. For example, they accomplish this by understanding and satisfying the audience's needs and interests. This is the core of Component 1 of the media concept. But in addition to the publisher and the audience, any specific media is influenced by the prevalent journalistic culture. Within the parameters of this paper, that culture creates the foundation for the general conception of how spoken discourse is transferred into written form, and how the interactional nature of the interview is reduced to monologuous quotations.

The main conclusion of my paper is that these factors, grouped into the three components of the media concept, create the complex relation between the original discourse (= the interview) and the final discourse (= the published quotation); they also govern the work practices in journalism. Furthermore, all things considered, quoting is not a mechanical and

---

29 These results challenge the practice of grouping quotations according to any one type of modification, as Johnson Barella (2005) has done.

systematic process, but it is carefully self-monitored by the journalist. In addition, no single unambiguous definition for "directness" seems to exist that would apply to all direct quotations in my data. Instead, direct quotations are text elements in an article that combine the discourse of an interview and the multifaceted purposes and aims of a journalist, publication, and publisher. (Similarly in television news production: see Nylund 2003; Kroon Lundell & Ekström 2010. For more detail on quoting practices, see Haapanen in press 2017.)

As demonstrated in this study, the reality of making quotations is not in line with the perceptions in the guidebooks nor with those shared by the audience.[30] I would argue that this means that the rare references to quoting offered in guidebooks resemble noble declarations more than serious guidelines for daily work. The SRs I conducted showed that the journalists themselves recognize the actual daily work practices presented in this paper – although several informant-journalists were rather surprised during the SR to discover the extent of the modifications they had actually made. Nevertheless, the informant-journalists did not express concern regarding the prevalent perceptions on quoting.

As for the underlying reasons for the phenomenon in the previous paragraph, I have two educated guesses. First, to uncover all the modifications and pure fabrications that occur in quoting practices might cause the audience to be perplexed and would result in accusations, even if these modifications were done out of necessity and were created to serve the readers. The second point is that the majority of the rhetorical and narrative functions of quotations[31] (see Haapanen 2011) are based on the idea of verbatimness. As Stimson (1995: 69) has stated, "readers apparently assume they are hearing a person's actual words within quote marks, and journalism is happy to let them think so."

To conclude, rather than stirring up a hornet's nest in the profession, perhaps for journalists and media publishers, it is both useful and safe to sustain this illusion.

---

30 As a matter of fact, the audience's viewpoint needs to be researched more (see, however, Culbertson & Somerick 1976).
31 Quotations enhance such factors as the plausibility that the quoted person's speech has been reproduced in an authentic verbatim way, they reflect a speaker's unique manner of using language and his or her first-hand experiences, and they characterize the quoted speaker (Haapanen 2011).

References

Adams, Sally. 2001. *Interviewing for journalists.* Abingdon: Routledge.
Arffman, Inga. 2007. *The problem of equivalence in translating texts in international reading literacy studies.* Jyväskylä: Institute for Educational Research, University of Jyväskylä.
Auer, Peter. 1992. The neverending sentence: Rightward expansion in spoken language. In Miklós Kontra & Tamás Váradi (eds.), *Studies in spoken languages: English, German, Finno-Ugric.* 41–59. Budapest: Linguistics Institute at the Hungarian Academy of Sciences.
Auer, Peter. 2009. Thoughts on the temporality of spoken language. *Language Sciences* 31(1): 1–13.
Bauman, Richard & Charles Briggs. 1990. Poetics and performance as critical perspectives on language and social life. *Annual Review of Anthropology* 19: 59–88.
Bell, Allan. 1991. *The language of news media.* Oxford: Blackwell.
Biber, Douglas. 1988. *Variation across speech and writing.* Cambridge: Cambridge University Press.
Blommaert, Jan. 2005. *Discourse – A critical introduction.* Cambridge: Cambridge University Press.
Blundell, William E. 1988. *The art and craft of feature writing.* New York: Plume.
Brooks, Brian S., George Kennedy, Daryl R. Moen & Don Ranly (The Missouri Group). 2002. *News reporting and writing*, 7th edn. Boston: Bedford.
Bruña, Manuel. 1993. El discurso indirecto en periódicos franceses y españoles. In Grupo Andaluz de Pragmática, *Estudios pragmáticos. Lenguaje y medios de comunicación.* 37–79. Sevilla: Departamento de Filología Francesa, Universidad de Sevilla.
Caldas-Coulthard, Carmen Rosa. 1993. From discourse analysis to critical discourse analysis: The differential re-presentation of women and men speaking in written news. In John M. Sinclair, Michael Hoey & Gwyneth Fox (eds.), *Techniques of description: Spoken and written discourse.* 196–208. London: Routledge.
Caldas-Coulthard, Carmen Rosa. 1994. On reporting reporting: The representation of speech in factual and factional narratives. In Coulthard Malcolm (ed.), *Advances in written text analysis.* 295–320. London: Routledge.
Clark, Herbert & Richard Gerrig. 1990. Quotations as demonstrations. *Language* 66(4): 764–805.
Clark, Roy Peter. 2006. *Writing tools – 50 essential strategies for every writer.* New York: Little, Brown and Company.
Clayman, Steven E. 1990. From talk to text: Newspaper accounts of reporter-source interactions. *Media, Culture and Society* 12: 79–103.
Cole, Michael. 1996. *Cultural psychology. A once and future discipline.* Cambridge, MA, London: Belknap Press.
Cotter, Colleen. 2010. *News talk. Investigating the language of journalism.* Cambridge: Cambridge University Press.
Culbertson, Hugh M. & Nancy Somerick. 1976. Quotation marks and bylines – What do they mean to readers. *Journalism Quarterly* 53: 463–469.
Davis, Howard H. 1985. Discourse and media influence. In Teun A. Van Dijk (ed.), *Discourse and communication: New approaches to the analysis of mass media discourse and communication.* 44–59. Berlin: De Gruyter.
Dempsey, Nicholas P. 2010. Stimulated recall interviews in ethnography. *Qual Sociol* 33: 349–367.
DiPardo, Anne. 1994. Stimulated recall in research on writing: An antidote to "I don't know, it was fine". In Peter Smagorinsky (ed.), *Speaking about writing – Reflections on research methodology.* 163–181. Thousand Oaks: Sage Publications.

Ekström, Mats. 2001. Politicians interviewed on television news. *Discourse & Society* 12(5): 563–584.

Engeström, Yrjö. 1987. *Learning by expanding: An activity-theoretical approach to developmental work research.* Helsinki: Orienta-Konsultit.

Flaherty, Francis. 2009. *The elements of story – Field notes on nonfiction writing.* New York: HarpenCollins.

Goldstein, Norm. 2009. *The associated press stylebook and briefing on media law 2009.* New York: Basic Books.

Haapanen, Lauri. 2011. Sitaattien tehtävät ja tekeminen kaunokirjallis-journalistisissa lehtijutuissa. *Media & viestintä* 34(3): 64–89.

Haapanen, Lauri. 2016a. Haastattelupuheen rekontekstualisointi sitaateiksi lehtijuttuun [Recontextualizing interview discourse into quotations for written media]. *Virittäjä* 120(2): 218–254.

Haapanen, Lauri. 2016b. Monologisation as a quoting practise. Obscuring the journalist's involvement in written journalism. *Journalism Practice.* Published online July 27th.

Haapanen, Lauri & Daniel Perrin. 2017. Media and quoting. In Daniel Perrin & Colleen Cotter (eds.), *The Routledge handbook of language and media.* New York: Routledge.

Haapanen, Lauri. In press 2017. Rethinking quoting in written journalism: An intertextual chain from an interview into quotations. *Cahier de l'Institut de Linguistique et des Sciences du Langage.* Lausanne: Université de Lausanne.

Haviland, John B. 1996. Text from talk in Tzotzil. In Michael Silverstein & Greg Urban (eds.), *Natural histories of discourse.* 45–78. Chicago: University of Chicago Press.

Helle, Merja. 2010. Toimitustyö muutoksessa. Toiminnan teoria ja mediakonseptin käsite tutkimuksen ja kehittämisen kehyksenä [Changing journalism: Activity theory and media concepts as frames for research and development]. Tampere: University of Tampere. http://urn.fi/urn:isbn:978-951-44-8313-4 (visited 17 March, 2016.)

Helle, Merja & Maija Töyry. 2009. Media concept as a tool for analyzing change in media. In Pirkko Oittinen & Hannu Saarelma (eds.), *Print media. Principles, processes and quality.* 497–530. Helsinki: Paper Engineers' Association/Paperi ja Puu Oy.

Jaakola, Minna, Maija Töyry, Merja Helle & Tiina Onikki-Rantajääskö. 2014. Construing the reader: Multidisciplinary approach to journalistic texts. *Discourse & Society* 25(4): 640–655.

Jacobi, Peter P. 1991. *The magazine article.* Bloomington: Indiana University Press.

Johnson Barella, Doris. 2005. La literalidad en el uso de las citas directas en las noticias de la prensa regional Navarra. Dos casos: Diario de Noticias y Diario de Navarra. *Comunicación y Sociedad* 2: 109–140.

Journalistin ohjeet 2014 [Guidelines for Jounalists]. Julkisen sanan neuvosto [Council for Mass Media in Finland]. http://www.jsn.fi/en/guidelines_for_journalists/ (visited 17 March, 2016.)

Jönsson, Linda & Per Linell. 1991. Story generations. From dialogical Interviews to written reports in police interrogations. *Text* 11(3): 419–440.

Koivisto, Aino & Elise Nykänen (eds.). 2013. *Puhe ja dialogi kaunokirjallisuudessa.* Helsinki: Suomalaisen Kirjallisuuden Seura.

Kramer, Mark & Wendy Call (eds.). 2007. *Telling true stories – A nonfiction writers' guide from the Nieman Foundation at Harvard University.* London: Plume Books.

Kroon Lundell, Åsa & Mats Ekström. 2010. "Interview bites" in television news production and presentation. *Journalism Practice* 4(4): 476–491.

Kuo, Sai-hua. 2007. Language as ideology – Analyzing quotations in Taiwanese news discourse. *Journal of Asian Pacific Communication* 17(2): 281–301.

Laury, Ritva (ed.). 2008. *Crosslinguistic studies of clause combining: The multifunctionality of conjunctions.* Amsterdam: John Benjamins.

Laury, Ritva & Tsuyoshi Ono. 2010. Recursion in conversation: What speakers of Finnish and Japanese know how to do. In Harry van der Hulst (ed.), *Recursion and human language*. 69–92. Berlin: Mouton de Gruyter.
Layder, Derek. 1993. *New strategies in social research*. Cambridge: Policy Press.
Leech, Geoffrey & Mick Short. 2007. *Style in fiction: A linguistic introduction to English fictional prose*. Harlow: Pearson Longman.
Lehrer, Adrienne. 1989. Remembering and representing prose: Quoted speech as a data source. *Discourse Processes* 12: 105–125.
Linell, Per. 1998a. *Approaching dialogue – Talk, interaction and contexts in dialogical perspectives*. Amsterdam: John Benjamins.
Linell, Per. 1998b. Discourse across boundaries: On recontextualisation and the blending of voices in professional discourse. *Text* 18(2): 143–157.
Linell, Per. 2009. *Rethinking language, mind, and world dialogically*. Charlotte, NC: Information Age Publishing.
López Pan, Fernando. 2010. Direct quotes in Spanish newspapers. Literality according to stylebooks, journalism textbooks and linguistic research. *Journalism Practice* 4(2): 192–207.
Lundberg, Tom. 1992. *Tuhannen taalan juttu*. Jyväskylä: Weilin-Göös.
Lundberg, Tom. 2001. *Kirjoita, vaikuta, menesty!* Helsinki: WSOY.
Makkonen-Craig, Henna. 1999. Speech quotations in newspapers as a form of language use. In Timo Haukioja, Ilona Herlin & Matti Miesvaara (eds.), *SKY Journal of Linguistics* 12. 111–144. Helsinki: The Linguistics Association of Finland.
Makkonen-Craig, Henna. 2014. Aspects of dialogicity: Exploring dynamic interrelations in written discourse. In Anna-Malin Karlsson & Henna Makkonen-Craig (eds.), *Analysing text AND talk / Att analysera texter OCH samtal*. FUMS Rapport 233. Uppsala: Institutionen för nordiska språk, Uppsala universitet. http://uu.diva-portal.org/smash/get/diva2:757298/FULLTEXT02.pdf (visited 17 March, 2016.)
Media linguistics research network 2016. http://www.aila.info/en/research/list-of-rens/media-linguistics.html (visited 17 March, 2016.)
Méndez García de Paredes, Elena. 2000. La literalidad de las citas en los textos periodísticos. *Revista Española de Lingüística* 30(1): 147–167.
NewsTalk&Text Research Group. 2011. Towards a linguistics of news production. *Journal of Pragmatics* 43(7): 1843–1852.
Nissi, Riikka & Esa Lehtinen. 2015. Conducting a task while reconstructing its meaning: Interaction, professional identities and recontextualization of a written task assignment. *Pragmatics* 25(3): 393–423.
Nylund, Mats. 2003. Asking questions, making sound-bites: Research reports, interviews and television news stories. *Discourse Studies* 5(4): 517–533.
Nylund, Mats. 2006. Journalism's vitality. On the narrative functions of quotes. In Mats Ekström, Åsa Kroon & Mats Nylund (eds.), *News from the interview society*. 147–164. Göteborg: Nordicom.
Perrin, Daniel. 2013a. Investigating language and the media: The case of newswriting. *AILA Review* 26(1): 57–78.
Perrin, Daniel. 2013b. *The linguistics of newswriting*. Amsterdam: John Benjamins.
Rock, Frances. 2007. *Communicating rights: The language of arrest and detention*. Basingstoke: Palgrave Macmillan.
Ruberg, Michelle (ed.). 2005. *Handbook of magazine article writing*, All New 2nd Edition. Ohio: Writer's Digest Books.
Sarangi, Srikant. 1998. Rethinking recontextualisation in professional discourse studies. *Text* 18(2): 301–318.
Satoh, Akira. 2001. Constructing imperial identity: How to quote the imperial family and those who address them in the Japanese press. *Discourse Society* 12: 169–194.

Schegloff, Emanuel A. & Harvey Sacks. 1973. Opening up closings. *Semiotica* VIII(4): 289–327.

Short, Michael. 1988. Speech presentation, the novel and the press. In Willie Van Peer (ed.), *The taming of the text: Explorations in language, literature, and culture.* 61–79. London: Routledge.

Short, Mick, Elena Semino & Martin Wynne. 2002. Revisiting the notion of faithfulness in discourse presentation using a corpus approach. *Language and Literature* 11(4): 325–355.

Stein, Sol. 1995. *Stein on writing.* New York: St. Martin's Griffin.

Stimson, William. 1995. Two schools on quoting confuse the reader. *The Journalism Educator* 49(4): 69–73.

Tiittula, Liisa & Pirkko Nuolijärvi 2013. *Puheen illuusio suomenkielisessä kaunokirjallisuudessa.* Helsinki: Suomalaisen Kirjallisuuden Seura.

Tuchman, Gaye. 1978. *Making news – A study in the construction of reality.* New York: Free Press.

Töyry, Maija, Panu Räty & Kristiina Kuisma. 2008. *Editointi aikakauslehdessä.* Helsinki: Taideteollinen korkeakoulu.

Van Charldorp, Tessa. 2014. "What happened?" From talk to text in police interrogations. *Language & Communication* 36: 7–24.

Virkkunen, Jaakko. 2006. Dilemmas in building shared transformative agency. *Activités* 3(1): 44–66.

Voutilainen, Eero. 2016. Tekstilajitietoista kielenhuoltoa: puheen esittäminen kirjoitettuna eduskunnan täysistuntopöytäkirjoissa. In Liisa Tiittula & Pirkko Nuolijärvi (eds.), *Puheesta tekstiksi. Puheen kirjallisen esittämisen alueita, keinoja ja rajoja.* 162-191 Helsinki: Suomalaisen Kirjallisuuden Seura.

Wade, Elizabeth & Herbert H. Clark. 1993. Reproduction and demonstration in quotations. *Journal of Memory and Language* 32: 805–819.

Waugh, Linda R. 1995. Reported speech in journalistic discourse: The relation of function and text. *Text* 15(1): 129–173.

Wold, Astri Heen. 1992. Oral and written language: Arguments against a simple dichotomy. In Astri Heen Wold (ed.), *The dialogical alternative towards a theory of language and mind.* 175–193. Oslo: Scandinavian University Press.

Appendix

Original excerpts and their English translations from stimulated recall sessions (I–XI)

(I)

RESEARCHER: Jos ajattelet eri lehtiä, mihin teet, niin ajatteletko muokkaamista eri tavoin?

INFORMANT-JOURNALIST: Joo. Ehkä niin päin että kun tunnen [Lehden 1]:n niin hyvin ja tiedän että siellä ollaan avoimia kaikelle uudelle, niin uskallan kokeilla rohkeammin. Sitten varmaan johonkin [lehti 2]:aan en edes uskaltaisi kokeilla, että siellä pysyisin hyvin yleisellä ja neutraalilla tasolla.

RESEARCHER: When you think of the different publications you're working for, do you regard modification differently?

INFORMANT-JOURNALIST: Yeah. Maybe because I know [Magazine 1] so well and I know that they are open to new things, so I dare to experiment more boldly. Then again, for some [Magazine 2] I wouldn't even dare to try anything and would keep things at a very general and neutral level.

(II)

INFORMANT-JOURNALIST: On sovittu, että sitaateista tehdään oikeakielisiä. Eli jos joku sanoo jotain kieliopin vastaisesti, niin sitten se korjataan, koska sen ((= sitaatin)) pitää olla luettavaa tekstiä, ja jos se ((= epäkieliopillisuus)) vaikeuttaa sitä ymmärtämistä, niin silloin sitä muutetaan. Täytesanat otetaan pois.

INFORMANT-JOURNALIST: It's been agreed that quotations are to be made (so they are) grammatically correct. So if someone says something that's grammatically incorrect, it will be corrected, because the text ((= the quotation)) must be readable and if it ((= the ungrammaticality)) makes it harder to understand, then it will be altered. Fillers (and some hesitations) are taken out.

(III)

INFORMANT-JOURNALIST: Ihmisethän puhuu sillä tavalla että sen ymmärtää kun sen kanssa puhuu, mutta sitten jos semmosen kirjoittaa ulos, niin sitä ei ymmärrä enää kukaan tilanteen ulkopuolella ollut, eli se täytyy kirjoittaa niin että se lukija ymmärtää mistä siinä puhutaan. Että se on se päälähtökohta, että lukija ymmärtää.

INFORMANT-JOURNALIST: You know that people talk in a way that you understand when you speak with them, but then if you write that down, it can no longer be understood by anyone who wasn't present at the time; so you have to write it so that the reader can understand what's being said. And that's the main starting point, to ensure that the reader understands.

(IV)

RESEARCHER: Osaatko sitä arvioida, että miten se ((= lehti)) vaikuttaa muokkaamiseen – eli ei juttutyyppi vaan se lehti?

INFORMANT-JOURNALIST: Kyllä se jutun julkaisualusta vaikuttaa ((…)) jokaisella julkaisulla tai lehdellä on oma henki ((…)) sen tietää ja siihen asettuu mutta sitä on vaikea käsitteellistää, tai purkaa vaikka viideksi ranskalaiseksi viivaksi.

RESEARCHER: Could you assess how it ((= the publication)) affects modification – *it* meaning not the article type, but the magazine.

INFORMANT-JOURNALIST: For sure, the publication platform has an effect ((…)) every publication or magazine has its own nature ((…)). You know it and you tune into it, but it's hard to conceptualize it, or to break it down to something like five bullet points.

(V)

INFORMANT-JOURNALIST: Meillä on tosi tiiviit tilat ((= juttupaikkojen merkkimäärät)) ja siinä pitää pystyä usein kertomaan monipuolisesti isoja asioita. Sen takia on mun mielestä perusteltua tehdä tuontyyppisiä [muutoksia], jotka ei muuta sitä merkitystä millään tavalla.

INFORMANT-JOURNALIST: We have really tight space restrictions and at the same time, we have to cover major issues from multiple angles. So that's why I think it's justifiable to make those kinds of changes, since they don't alter the meaning in any way.

(VI)

INFORMANT-JOURNALIST: Jos olisin tv-toimittaja, niin mun ois varmaan pitänyt miettiä nää kysymykset tarkemmin ennakkoon. Mutta kun ((…)) ei ole kaikkia kysymyksiä miettinyt etukäteen, niin oma muotoilu saattaa olla huono, jolloin sä saat sellaisen kyllä–ei vastauksen. Varmaanhan se niinku pitäis kirjoittaa auki ((= sanatarkasti, muuntelematta)).

INFORMANT-JOURNALIST: If I were a TV journalist, I probably would have had to prepare these questions more carefully in advance. But when you haven't prepped all the questions beforehand, your own phrasing might be bad, and you'll get a sort of yes-or-no answer. Well, that probably kinda should be written down word for word ((= verbatim, without modifications)).

(VII)

INFORMANT-JOURNALIST: Tää ((=asia)), mitä tässä nyt tarkastellaan, oli sen jutun pääpointti. Niin siksi halusin antaa haastateltavan sanoa [lehdessä] sen jutun pääpointin.

INFORMANT-JOURNALIST: This ((=matter)), what we're looking at now, was the main point in that article. So that's why I wanted to let the interviewee say the main point [in the article].

(VIII)

INFORMANT-JOURNALIST: Jos oikein tiukkoja ollaan, niin totahan ei välttämättä vois laittaa sitaatiks. Mutta mä luulen, että tää on hyvin tyypillinen tapaus mihin sä tuut törmäämään, tai mä voisin kuvitella, että aika moni toimittaja tekee tällasta.

INFORMANT-JOURNALIST: Well, strictly speaking, you probably shouldn't put that as a quote. But I think that this is a really typical case that you will run into, I mean, I can imagine that quite many journalists do something like this.

(IX)

RESEARCHER: Sitaattien tarkoitus ei siis ollut kuvailla puhujaa?

INFORMANT-JOURNALIST: Ei. Jos puhekielisyyksiä on valittu niin niillä pitää olla joku pointti sen jutun kannalta, mutta tässä ((= jutussa)) niillä ei ollut. Ja tässä ei myöskään ollut tarkoitus korostaa sitä, että nyt ne puhuu huonosti suomea. ((…))

RESEARCHER: Eli jos puhekielisyyden valitsee niin se on ennemmin leimanomainen juttu kuin suora lainaus?

INFORMANT-JOURNALIST: joo, se on niinku tarkoituksella silloin. Että meidän lehdessä sitaatit on yleiskirjakieltä, ja sit jos sinne ((= sitaattiin)) on laitettu puhekielisyys, niin se on sen takia että on haluttu sillä korostaa esim jotain siinä tyypissä tai jotain muuta, et niin se on.

RESEARCHER: So the purpose of the quotes was not to describe the speaker?

INFORMANT-JOURNALIST: No. If colloquialisms have been selected then they have to have some point in the story, but in this one ((= story)) they didn't have any idea. But the idea here wasn't to emphasize the fact that they speak broken Finnish either. (...)

RESEARCHER: So if you choose a colloquialism, it's more about characterization of the quotation than making a direct quotation?

INFORMANT-JOURNALIST: Yeah, it's on purpose in that case. In our magazine the quotes occur in standard language, and if any colloquialisms are used ((= in the quotation), they're used to emphasize things like something in that person or something else like that, that's the way it is.

(X)

RESEARCHER: Miten muuten kun nyt teit nauhurin kanssa mutta joskus teet [vain] käsimuistiinpanoilla, niin osaatko arvioida että jos olisit tehnyt tämän jutun vain muistiinpanoja tehden, niin...

INFORMANT-JOURNALIST: En ois pystynyt näin tarkkaan, en missään nimessä. ((...)) En mä mitenkään ehdi kirjoittaa näin paljon. ja sit mä en muista, jos mulla on lyhennettyjä sanoja, niin en välttämättä muista mikä se loppuosa oli koska ei se mun tekniikka oo mitenkään niin tarkka. (Similarly, see Lehrer 1989: 122.)

RESEARCHER: By the way, since you used a tape-recorder but sometimes only take notes, can you assess if you had made this article just by taking notes, you would have been able to....

INFORMANT-JOURNALIST: I wouldn't have been able to be this precise, no way. ((...)) I really don't have time to write down this much. And then if I've used abbreviations, I don't necessarily remember what the word actually was because the technique I use isn't that exact at all. (Similarly, see Lehrer 1989: 122)

(XI)

INFORMANT-JOURNALIST: Äänitän harvoin, en tykkää siitä, enemmän käsimuistiinpanoja suosin. Ja yksi syy on se, että jos kaiken äänittäis ja kaiken purkais, niin työaikahan ei riittäis, kun ei se riitä muutenkaan. Niin tuossa säästää sitten aikaa kun ei äänitä kaikkea.

INFORMANT-JOURNALIST: I rarely record on tape, I don't like it, I prefer taking notes. And one reason is that if you record everything and transcribe everything, your working hours won't be enough, because they aren't enough as it is. So you save time when you don't record everything.

List of Authors

Elizabeth Couper-Kuhlen
ⓘ http://orcid.org/0000-0003-2030-6018

Elizabeth Couper-Kuhlen, Dr. habil, Dr. h.c. professorships in English linguistics at the Universities of Konstanz and Potsdam and was Distinguished Professor for Interactional Linguistics at the University of Helsinki from 2009–2103. She is currently associated with the Helsinki Center of Excellence for Research on Intersubjectivity. She has published widely on prosody and grammar in interaction.

Marja Etelämäki
ⓘ http://orcid.org/0000-0002-3896-7159

Marja Etelämäki, FT (Doctor of Philosophy), is Associate Professor at the Department of Linguistics and Scandinavian Studies at the University of Oslo. Her research concerns the relation of grammar to social interaction. In particular, she has worked on indexical elements such as pronouns and particles, and on particular forms of requests. Lately, her interests have also included the ways in which agency and experience are construed in the course of interaction.

Maria Frick
ⓘ http://orcid.org/0000-0001-5089-5752

Maria Frick, FT (Doctor of Philosophy), works as a University Lecturer of Estonian and Finnish language at the University of Oulu. Her research interests fall in the field of interactional linguistics and especially multilingual and multimodal resources in interaction. In her doctoral dissertation (2013), she proposed a model for describing bilingual usage of bipartite constructions, and studied the on-line emergence and conversational outcomes of Finnish-Estonian codeswitching. She has continued research on multilingual conversations, focusing in bilingual punning among peer groups, and is currently starting a study on deontic stance-taking in family settings. She has also examined two different aspects of the multimodality of mundane face-to-face conversations: Firstly, turns that are produced by singing, and, secondly, combinations of a verbal announcement and physical action.

Lauri Haapanen
http://orcid.org/0000-0002-1973-4843

Lauri Haapanen holds the degree of Doctor of Philosophy (FT, 2017) from the University of Helsinki. His article-based dissertation examined quoting practices in written journalism. Currently he is working as a postdoctoral researcher at the Swedish School of Social Science (University of Helsinki) in a project dealing with news automation. Furthermore, he is interested in how journalists participate in, take into account, and are influenced by social media when writing their media items.

Katariina Harjunpää
http://orcid.org/0000-0002-4586-1563

Katariina Harjunpää, FT, received the degree of Doctor of Philosophy from the University of Helsinki in June 2017. In her dissertation she examines bilingual mediating and practices of oral translation in multilingual everyday conversations. Harjunpää currently works as a researcher in the Finland Distinguished Professor project Multimodality: Reconsidering language and action through embodiment. Her research interests include grammar in interaction, dynamics of participation, and embodied interaction.

Leelo Keevallik
http://orcid.org/0000-0003-2175-8710

Leelo Keevallik, Fil.dr. (Doctor of Philosophy), works as a professor in language and culture at Linköping University. She has studied multiple aspects of grammar and interaction, including the function of pragmatic particles and the emergence of multimodal units. Her particular area of interest is the interface between language and the body, currently channelled into the consolidation grant project *Vocal Coordination of Human Action*. She has published in *Research on Language and Social Interaction, Journal of Pragmatics, Discourse Processes*, and in several volumes by John Benjamins, Cambridge University Press, and DeGryuter.

Aino Koivisto
http://orcid.org/0000-0002-9380-5953

Aino Koivisto, FT (Doctor of Philosophy) and Docent, is post-doctoral researcher in the Centre of Excellence in Intersubjectivity in Interaction, University of Helsinki. Her publications deal with interaction and grammar, response particles in conversation and fictional dialogue.

Ritva Laury
ⓘ http://orcid.org/0000-0003-2808-6523

Ritva Laury, PhD, is professor emerita of Finnish at the University of Helsinki and professor emerita of Linguistics at the California State University. Her research has focused on the emergence of grammar from interaction, and has dealt with issues of reference, indexicality, grammaticalization and clause combining, and, most recently, embodied activities in conversation. She is a team leader in the Helsinki Center of Excellence for Research on Intersubjectivity in Interaction.

Saija Merke
ⓘ http://orcid.org/0000-0002-7860-0212

Saija Merke, FT (Doctor of Philosophy), holds the position of University Teacher in Finnish Language and Culture (suomen kielen ja kulttuurin yliopisto-opettaja) at the University of Tampere, Faculty of Communication Sciences (Viestintätieteiden tiedekunta). Her main research interests are Finnish-as-a-foreign-language acquisition and classroom interaction, conversation analysis in second language acquisition (CA-for-SLA), and the expression of feelings and morality in language-learning encounters. Merke has recently published an article on explanation sequences in Finnish-as-a-foreign-language lessons.

Anna Vatanen
ⓘ http://orcid.org/0000-0002-8236-657X

Anna Vatanen, FT (Doctor of Philosophy), is a postdoctoral researcher at the Finnish Centre of Excellence in Research on Intersubjectivity in Interaction and at the Department of Finnish, Finno-Ugrian and Scandinavian Studies, University of Helsinki. She specializes in interactional linguistics and conversation analysis and works on both Finnish and Estonian data. Her research focuses on social actions and the grammatical, prosodic, and other structural features of interaction, the topics including overlapping talk, conversational lapses, affiliation, alignment, and epistemics. She has also published on conversation-analytic methodology.

Abstract

Linking Clauses and Actions in Social Interaction

Edited by Ritva Laury, Marja Etelämäki, Elizabeth Couper-Kuhlen

This volume concerns the ways in which verbal and non-verbal actions are combined and linked in a range of contexts in everyday conversation, in institutional interaction, and in written journalism. The volume includes an introduction which, besides presenting the content of the articles, discusses terminological fundamentals such as the understanding of the terms "clause", "action", "linkage", and "combining" in different grammatical traditions and the ways they are conceived of here. In addition, it deals with open questions collectively formulated by the contributors in planning for the volume concerning the recognition, emergence, and distance of linkage, and the ways these questions are addressed in the contributions to the volume.

Topics treated in the articles include combining physical actions and verbal announcements in everyday conversation, linking of verbal and nonverbal actions, as well as verbal linkages between nonverbal actions by dance teachers when engaging in pedagogical activities. Other topics concern the mediation of questions through informal translating in multilingual conversation in order to organize participation, and the ways in which student requests for clarification and confirmation create learning occasions in a foreign language classroom. Still other articles concern the on-line emergence of alternative questions with the Finnish particle *vai* 'or', delayed completions of unfinished turns, the transforming of requests and offers into joint ventures, and the ways in which direct quotations are created in written journalism from the original talk in the spoken interview.

Most of the papers employ Conversation Analysis and Interactional Linguistics as a theoretical framework. The languages used as data are Finnish, English, Estonian, French, Brazilian Portuguese, and Swedish.

Studia Fennica Ethnologica

Memories of My Town
The Identities of Town Dwellers and Their Places in Three Finnish Towns
Edited by Anna-Maria Åström, Pirjo Korkiakangas & Pia Olsson
Studia Fennica Ethnologica 8
2004

Passages Westward
Edited by Maria Lähteenmäki & Hanna Snellman
Studia Fennica Ethnologica 9
2006

Defining Self
Essays on emergent identities in Russia Seventeenth to Nineteenth Centuries
Edited by Michael Branch
Studia Fennica Ethnologica 10
2009

Touching Things
Ethnological Aspects of Modern Material Culture
Edited by Pirjo Korkiakangas, Tiina-Riitta Lappi & Heli Niskanen
Studia Fennica Ethnologica 11
2008

Gendered Rural Spaces
Edited by Pia Olsson & Helena Ruotsala
Studia Fennica Ethnologica 12
2009

LAURA STARK
The Limits of Patriarchy
How Female Networks of Pilfering and Gossip Sparked the First Debates on Rural Gender Rights in the 19th-century Finnish-Language Press
Studia Fennica Ethnologica 13
2011

Where is the Field?
The Experience of Migration Viewed through the Prism of Ethnographic Fieldwork
Edited by Laura Hirvi & Hanna Snellman
Studia Fennica Ethnologica 14
2012

LAURA HIRVI
Identities in Practice
A Trans-Atlantic Ethnography of Sikh Immigrants in Finland and in California
Studia Fennica Ethnologica 15
2013

EERIKA KOSKINEN-KOIVISTO
Her Own Worth
Negotiations of Subjectivity in the Life Narrative of a Female Labourer
Studia Fennica Ethnologica 16
2014

Studia Fennica Folkloristica

Narrating, Doing, Experiencing
Nordic Folkloristic Perspectives
Edited by Annikki Kaivola-Bregenhøj, Barbro Klein & Ulf Palmenfelt
Studia Fennica Folkloristica 16
2006

MÍCHEÁL BRIODY
The Irish Folklore Commission 1935–1970
History, ideology, methodology
Studia Fennica Folkloristica 17
2008

VENLA SYKÄRI
Words as Events
Cretan Mantinádes in Performance and Composition
Studia Fennica Folkloristica 18
2011

Hidden Rituals and Public Performances
Traditions and Belonging among the Post-Soviet Khanty, Komi and Udmurts
Edited by Anna-Leena Siikala & Oleg Ulyashev
Studia Fennica Folkloristica 19
2011

Mythic Discourses
Studies in Uralic Traditions
Edited by Frog, Anna-Leena Siikala & Eila Stepanova
Studia Fennica Folkloristica 20
2012

CORNELIUS HASSELBLATT
Kalevipoeg Studies
The Creation and Reception of an Epic
Studia Fennica Folkloristica 21
2016

Genre – Text – Interpretation
Multidisciplinary Perspectives on Folklore and Beyond
Edited by Kaarina Koski, Frog & Ulla Savolainen
Studia Fennica Folkloristica 22
2016

Studia Fennica Historica

Moving in the USSR
Western anomalies and Northern wilderness
Edited by Pekka Hakamies
Studia Fennica Historica 10
2005

DEREK FEWSTER
Visions of Past Glory
Nationalism and the Construction of Early Finnish History
Studia Fennica Historica 11
2006

Modernisation in Russia since 1900
Edited by Markku Kangaspuro & Jeremy Smith
Studia Fennica Historica 12
2006

SEIJA-RIITTA LAAKSO
Across the Oceans
Development of Overseas Business Information Transmission 1815–1875
Studia Fennica Historica 13
2007

Industry and Modernism
Companies, Architecture and Identity in the Nordic and Baltic Countries during the High-Industrial Period
Edited by Anja Kervanto Nevanlinna
Studia Fennica Historica 14
2007

CHARLOTTA WOLFF
Noble conceptions of politics in eighteenth-century Sweden (ca 1740–1790)
Studia Fennica Historica 15
2008

Sport, Recreation and Green Space in the European City
Edited by Peter Clark, Marjaana Niemi & Jari Niemelä
Studia Fennica Historica 16
2009

Rhetorics of Nordic Democracy
Edited by Jussi Kurunmäki & Johan Strang
Studia Fennica Historica 17
2010

Fibula, Fabula, Fact
The Viking Age in Finland
Edited by Joonas Ahola & Frog with Clive Tolley
Studia Fennica Historica 18
2014

Novels, Histories, Novel Nations
Historical Fiction and Cultural Memory in Finland and Estonia
Edited by Linda Kaljundi, Eneken Laanes & Ilona Pikkanen
Studia Fennica Historica 19
2015

JUKKA GRONOW & SERGEY ZHURAVLEV
Fashion Meets Socialism
Fashion industry in the Soviet Union after the Second World War
Studia Fennica Historica 20
2015

SOFIA KOTILAINEN
Literacy Skills as Local Intangible Capital
The History of a Rural Lending Library c. 1860–1920
Studia Fennica Historica 21
2016

Continued Violence and Troublesome Pasts
Post-war Europe between the Victors after the Second World War
Edited by Ville Kivimäki and Petri Karonen
Studia Fennica Historica 22
2017

Studia Fennica Anthropologica

On Foreign Ground
Moving between Countries and Categories
Edited by Marie-Louise Karttunen & Minna Ruckenstein
Studia Fennica Anthropologica 1
2007

Beyond the Horizon
Essays on Myth, History, Travel and Society
Edited by Clifford Sather & Timo Kaartinen
Studia Fennica Anthropologica 2
2008

TIMO KALLINEN
Divine Rulers in a Secular State
Studia Fennica Anthropologica 3
2016

Studia Fennica Linguistica

Minimal reference
The use of pronouns in Finnish and Estonian discourse
Edited by Ritva Laury
Studia Fennica Linguistica 12
2005

Antti Leino
On Toponymic Constructions as an Alternative to Naming Patterns in Describing Finnish Lake Names
Studia Fennica Linguistica 13
2007

Talk in interaction
Comparative dimensions
Edited by Markku Haakana, Minna Laakso & Jan Lindström
Studia Fennica Linguistica 14
2009

Planning a new standard language
Finnic minority languages meet the new millennium
Edited by Helena Sulkala & Harri Mantila
Studia Fennica Linguistica 15
2010

Lotta Weckström
Representations of Finnishness in Sweden
Studia Fennica Linguistica 16
2011

Terhi Ainiala, Minna Saarelma & Paula Sjöblom
Names in Focus
An Introduction to Finnish Onomastics
Studia Fennica Linguistica 17
2012

Registers of Communication
Edited by Asif Agha & Frog
Studia Fennica Linguistica 18
2015

Kaisa Häkkinen
Spreading the Written Word
Mikael Agricola and the Birth of Literary Finnish
Studia Fennica Linguistica 19
2015

Linking Clauses and Actions in Social Interaction
Edited by Ritva Laury, Marja Etelämäki, Elizabeth Couper-Kuhlen
Studia Fennica Linquistica 20
2017

Studia Fennica Litteraria

Metaliterary Layers in Finnish Literature
Edited by Samuli Hägg, Erkki Sevänen & Risto Turunen
Studia Fennica Litteraria 3
2008

Aino Kallas
Negotiations with Modernity
Edited by Leena Kurvet-Käosaar & Lea Rojola
Studia Fennica Litteraria 4
2011

The Emergence of Finnish Book and Reading Culture in the 1700s
Edited by Cecilia af Forselles & Tuija Laine
Studia Fennica Litteraria 5
2011

Nodes of Contemporary Finnish Literature
Edited by Leena Kirstinä
Studia Fennica Litteraria 6
2012

White Field, Black Seeds
Nordic Literacy Practices in the Long Nineteenth Century
Edited by Anna Kuismin & M. J. Driscoll
Studia Fennica Litteraria 7
2013

Lieven Ameel
Helsinki in Early Twentieth-Century Literature
Urban Experiences in Finnish Prose Fiction 1890–1940
Studia Fennica Litteraria 8
2014

Novel Districts
Critical Readings of Monika Fagerholm
Edited by Kristina Malmio & Mia Österlund
Studia Fennica Litteraria 9
2016

www.ingramcontent.com/pod-product-compliance
Lightning Source LLC
Chambersburg PA
CBHW080803300426
44114CB00020B/2811